ANATOLIA

ADVENTURES IN TURKISH EATING
ANATOLIA

SOMER SIVRIOĞLU
& DAVID DALE

murdoch books

Sydney | London

View of Galata Tower and the Old City from the rooftop bar at the Hotel Marmara, Istanbul.

CONTENTS

DEDICATION

This book has two inspirations: Musa Dağdeviren, who introduced regional Anatolian food to the world long before it was trendy; and Janni Kyritsis, great chef and great friend, who embodies the notion that generosity of spirit crosses all national boundaries.

One of the few surviving Istanbul street markets, in Kadıköy.

ABOUT THE AUTHORS

Somer Sivrioğlu grew up in Istanbul and moved to Australia when he was 25. He is the chef/owner of Efendy and Anason restaurants in Sydney, where he draws on a multitude of cultural influences to recreate the traditions of his homeland. He is also one of the three judges on *Masterchef Turkey*.

Writer, broadcaster and editor David Dale teaches Media at the University of New South Wales. His earlier books include *The Obsessive Traveller or Why I don't steal towels from great hotels any more*; *The Little Book of Australia*; and (with Lucio Galletto) *The Art of Pasta* and *Coastline: The shared food of Mediterranean France, Italy and Spain*.

Fishing from Istanbul's Galata Bridge, which spans the part of the Bosphorus called The Golden Horn, with beer houses serving seafood on the lower deck. Locals have been fishing and eating in this area for 4000 years, even before Istanbul was called Constantinople, even before Constantinople was called Byzantium. Fishing became a lot easier when the first Galata Bridge was built in 1845.

DAVID'S PREFACE

For a while I was keen to call this book *The Garden of Eden*, but my sensible co-author talked me out of it.

The idea came up when we were flying east from Istanbul and I was studying a map of our destination—the town of Gaziantep near the Syrian border. I said to Somer: 'This river that's labelled Firat—is that the Euphrates?' He replied: 'Yes, that's the old name for it.'

In growing excitement, I asked: 'Is the Tigris also on this map?'

Somer: 'Yes, just down there, it's called the Dicle [dizh-leh] nowadays.'

Me: 'So actually we are headed for the Garden of Eden, where all the fruits and vegetables in the world originated, and where the forbidden apple was probably a fig?'

Somer (eyes narrowed): 'Well, I suppose you could say that.'

One of the first things I learned about Somer Sivrioğlu (pronounced 'Sivriolu', with the 'g' silent, as in tagliatelle) is that he prefers science to superstition, and he's inclined to regard references to Adam and Eve with caution. I share his scepticism, but I love a good story, particularly when it's about food. I was charmed by the notion that Anatolian was the world's oldest cuisine.

We'd met three months earlier when a Greek friend took me to lunch at Somer's restaurant—Efendy, in the Sydney suburb of Balmain. The meal we ate shattered my stereotypes about Turkish food, and our conversation demonstrated that Somer was not only a great cook but also a great scholar.

Our Greek friend, Janni Kyritsis, was happy to concede that while Greek cooking had stagnated, Turkish cooking seemed still to be evolving. With a mischievous smile, Somer told us: 'Turkish is one of the three great cuisines of the world, but only Turks know this. The other two are French and Chinese, but the French got their cream sauces from our *yoğurt*, and the Chinese got their dumplings from our *manti*.'

It became apparent that Somer likes to make fun of his countrymen's tendency to claim ownership of every great cooking technique in the Western world, and to cling to absurd food myths that promote Turkish nationalism. He prefers to use the more ancient word Anatolia when talking about the geographical area that is now called Turkey, and to give credit to the many cultures that contributed to the region's food repertoire.

I asked Somer if he'd be interested in doing a book that would challenge old theories about Turkish cooking and create a few new ones; that would give readers a way to recreate classic dishes at home and also help them understand what they're eating when they visit Turkey.

We worked up a pitch to Sue Hines at Murdoch Books, and three months later were flying towards the Garden of Eden. The town of Gaziantep turned out to be very strange. For breakfast, they eat liver *kebaps* or chilli soup. They make the best baklava in the world, using the best pistachios. They proudly preserve a cooking style that has never needed to make compromises with tourism. Whether or not it was once paradise, it was the best possible place for me to begin my lessons in Anatolian culture.

Gaziantep has a tradition that inspired the way we approached this book. Whenever a family has to spend the day rolling the hundreds of tiny meatballs that go into a festive soup called *yuvalama*, they bring in a professional storyteller to keep the rollers from getting bored.

We decided to tell a tale with every recipe. Sometimes we would talk about the mythical origins of the dish or its ingredients, sometimes we would talk about Somer's first experience of the dish, and sometimes we would talk about its place in the rituals and fashions of ancient and modern Anatolia.

Working with Somer, I learned that Anatolian cooks take a pretty relaxed approach to their creations. They rarely use written recipes and, when they do, the instructions tend to be vague, as in 'measure with your eyes', 'add whatever it needs'; or else poetic, as in 'cut into bird's heads' (cubed), 'small as a rat's tooth' (finely chopped) or 'till the dough has the texture of an earlobe'. We've tried to avoid the vagueness but retain the relaxation. While breads and pastries need precise measures, most other recipes can be varied according to your taste—more chilli, less onion, more vegetables, less meat, as you fancy.

The stories and the recipes are told in Somer's voice. I hope you enjoy your conversation with him and share the joy I experienced in learning about an approach to life's greatest pleasure that is still evolving after 5000 years.

DAVID DALE

SOMER'S PREFACE

The 1970s was an eventful decade in Turkey, and not only because I was born then. In 1971, the military staged a coup for the second time (the first one being in 1960); left-wing students and right-wing militants supported by the government were at war with each other; and day and night curfews were in place.

I grew up knowing the difference in sound between a gunshot in the next street and a bomb in the next suburb. Even in the midst of civil war, my *babaanne* (grandma) retained her sense of hospitality. 'Do not close the door, Somer—our neighbours might think we want to keep them away', she would tell me every time I shut the door to the family apartment in Istanbul.

My grandad had bought the apartment building in the Kadıköy neighbourhood after selling his hotel and *hamam* (Turkish bath) in the rural town of Eskişehir. He'd moved the whole family to the multicultural suburb on the Anatolian side of the city, giving one flat to each of his children so the whole family could live near each other. The block felt like a village, with the hallways full of cooking smells floating from open doorways.

I was lucky to be a kid during that time. People still shared food with their neighbours; every store in your suburb knew your name; the butcher would keep all the high-protein offal for families with growing children; and kids from different ethnic backgrounds not only played together but also ate together in whatever house they happened to find themselves at supper time. We had neighbours with Greek, Armenian and Sephardic Jewish backgrounds, and I was blessed to taste their everyday meals. In an era of curfews, suppression and terror, I felt strangely safe in the company of family, friends and neighbours.

In 1980, Turkey, moving towards a free-market economy, suffered another military coup. My parents separated and I was living in another suburb in another kind of apartment, with double locks on the door. I had more toys and fewer friends, and a lot less diversity in my diet. My friends and I queued for two hours in front of the first McDonald's when it opened in Turkey, so that we could have burgers and Coke.

My priorities began to change after I landed in Australia in 1995. I'd graduated in hospitality from a college in Turkey, and now I was doing my MBA in Sydney, discussing Organisational Behaviour during the day and washing dishes at night. Living close to Sydney's Chinatown, and eating every cuisine but

my own, I re-learned the value of a multicultural society and its contribution to national happiness.

Fast forward to 2007 and I've opened my first restaurant, Efendy, in the Sydney suburb of Balmain. At the time I was trying to persuade Australians to think beyond *kebaps* and serving what I imagined to be 'modern Turkish cuisine'. My first menu at Efendy included okra in truffle oil, crab *mantı* and Turkish coffee crème brûlée.

Looking back, I think I was silly. I was trying to impress by using the trendy ingredients of the time. I wasn't being true to myself or my culture. My excuse was that I thought I didn't have access to the kind of produce I could have found in Turkey, so it would be impossible to cook at the same quality.

My mind was opened by a visit from my culinary hero, Musa Dağdeviren, from the world-famous Çiya restaurant in Kadıköy. When I picked him up at the airport, I apologised that Australian ingredients would be limiting. He asked if there was a Chinatown in Sydney and soon he was showing me all the wild weeds, fruits, vegetables and greens he could use. I'd worked just next door to those markets and I'd never noticed. During that visit, Musa made the best 'Sumac salad' I'd ever eaten using a native Australian fruit called Davidson plum instead of sumac. He showed me Turkish cooking is less about particular ingredients and more about philosophy. It's about sitting at a table in a Black Sea village, sharing a plate of Armenian *topik*, Kurdish *kebap*, Jewish *boyoz* and Greek *tarama*, and washing it down with a glass of *rakı* or *ayran*. It's about the ways different cultures have taken advantage of the abundance of produce in the area now called Anatolia.

The first edition of this book was published in Australia and Britain, and translated into Dutch, German and Turkish. Now I am delighted to introduce this revised edition. Since it first appeared, I have opened a second Sydney restaurant—Anason, in the waterfront quarter called Barangaroo—but my philosophy remains the same: to get the best out of seasonal local produce with techniques tested and proven by my ancestors.

My family and friends are a diverse bunch. We support different football teams, different religions, different politicians, different sexual orientations. We come from different ethnicities. So we are just like Turkey. We argue a lot—as the peoples of Anatolia have done for millennia. But when we sit together around a table, we are united by one idea: we want to enjoy our food. My hope is that this book will do that for you, too.

SOMER SIVRIOĞLU

The Kadıköy apartment block where
Somer grew up: 'We had Greek, Armenian
and Sephardic Jewish neighbours, and
I was blessed to taste their meals'

ESSENTIALS

HISTORY, INGREDIENTS & TECHNIQUES

ESSENTIALS

In this book we'll use the word 'Anatolia' more often than 'Turkey', because that ancient name best conveys the history and diversity of a land that only started calling itself 'Türkiye' (Land of the Turks) in the eleventh century, and only became the Turkish Republic in 1923. We think the term Anatolia suggests the delicious Arab, Armenian, Assyrian, Balkan, Greek, Jewish, Kurdish and Romany contributions to the way modern Turks like to eat.

Turkish people have a passion for eating well. While they're enjoying breakfast, they're planning dinner. They cook a lot at home, but everyone has a favourite *kebap* shop, a favourite lunch *lokanta*, a favourite source of baklava, and a favourite street stall for sobering up with stuffed intestines after a long night drinking *rakı* in a *meyhane*. There is no time of day when you can't get interesting food, so instead of dividing this book into conventional chapters such as starters, mains, desserts and party food, we've arranged the chapters in the form of a typical Turkish eating day.

A LITTLE HISTORY

The first use of the term 'Anatolia' was in clay tablets written 4300 years ago in the cuneiform letters of Mesopotamia, so that suggested a timespan for this book. (We could have taken you back 11,000 years, because the world's first human settlement has been discovered at Göbekli Tepe, near the town of Şanlıurfa in southeastern Anatolia, but information on the cuisine of that period is scarce.)

The Hittites may not have been the first organised civilisation on earth (that title should probably go to the Sumerians), but they do seem to have been the first to use iron weapons; the first to make wine and cultivate olives, almonds and apricots; and were the speakers of a language that turned into most of the dialects of modern Europe.

The Hittite Empire was at its peak 3500 years ago, and Troy was a west-coast branch. The defeat of Troy about 3200 years ago (as reported by Homer) was part of a Greek conquest of Anatolia that was confirmed by Alexander the Great about 2300 years ago. About 2600 years ago, a Greek demigod named Byzas founded the city that came to be called Byzantion (Byzantium), then New Rome, then Constantinople, and finally Istanbul (which literally translates as 'into the city').

The Greek Empire was replaced by the Roman Empire around 2000 years ago and Constantinople became the imperial capital when Rome fell to barbarians in the fourth century.

The last vestiges of Roman-Christian rule were eliminated in the eleventh century by the invading Seljuks (an extended family of Muslims from the northeast, whose empire also included Persia). The Seljuks spoke a language called Turkic.

Western Anatolia got involved in various disputes with European crusaders passing through on their way to Jerusalem, but stayed in Seljuk control until the arrival, around 1300, of an army under the command of a military strategist named Osman in Turkish and known to English speakers as Ottoman. This commander gave his name to an empire that proceeded to invade lands we now call Greece, Hungary, Bulgaria, Iraq, Iran, Syria, Egypt, Libya, Tunisia and Algeria.

One of the obsessions of the Ottoman Turks was the art of food, and at the peak of their power (under Sultan Süleyman the Magnificent in the sixteenth century), the Topkapı Palace in Istanbul had 400 cooks using ingredients and techniques from all over the empire.

In the sixteenth century, Anatolia welcomed Jews and Muslims who were expelled from Spain and Portugal by Christian fundamentalists. They brought new approaches to the way ingredients could be combined.

Then, in the seventeenth century, Anatolia welcomed Spanish and Portuguese traders who brought strange and exciting ingredients from the New World—pumpkins (squash), tomatoes, peppers and potatoes.

Ottoman rule collapsed during the First World War, and in 1923 a bunch of modernisers took over. The first president of the Turkish republic was Mustafa Kemal Atatürk, a soldier who had defeated the Allied invaders at Gelibolu (Gallipoli) in 1915. He abolished the dominance of the Islamic clergy (known as 'the caliphate'), gave women the vote and created a secular democracy. As part of a treaty between the new nation and the Allies, Anatolians of Greek background were told to move to Greece, while Muslims of Turkish background moved from Greece to Turkey.

So you can see why Anatolian food is likely to have a fair bit in common with the cooking of Greece, Syria, Egypt, Armenia, Italy, Spain, Iran and even Hungary, and why so much culinary mythology has developed over the past four millennia.

An Istanbul ferry crosses the Bosphorus from the Asian side of the city to the European shore.

Myths make good stories, so in this book we're going to recount the myths and then try to analyse where they deviate from reality. We are not going to waste time with disputes about which ethnic, religious or national group 'owns' a particular dish. The cooking in a particular area is dictated by the climate, the soil, the range of ingredients available, the survival techniques developed over the millennia, and the cultural assumptions passed on by successive waves of settlers. It's perfectly possible for a dish to be simultaneously Turkish,

Greek, Italian and Syrian, or to be none of the above if it appeared long before those names were on any map. When in doubt, our default position is to describe a dish as 'adapted from the Hittite'.

So how is a non-Turkish-speaking visitor going to tap into this historical, geographical and cultural abundance? In Istanbul most waiters speak enough English to respond to your enthusiastic request to try a range of local specialities and avoid the tourist clichés. Outside Istanbul and the coastal resort towns, two phrases might come in handy in a lunch *lokanta* or *meze* bar: '*Herşey* [hershay] *den az az ortaya lütfen*', which means 'Can I have a variety of small servings, please' (literally, 'Little little in the middle') and '*Ben de şundan* [shundan] *alabilir miyim, lütfen*' ('Could I have those, please'), with which you should point to a dish on another table or on display on the counter.

After the recipes, we provide a list of recommendations on eating places worth visiting in Istanbul and around the countryside. In the unlikely event you don't find great food in Turkey, cook from this book and discover how it should have tasted.

THE REGIONS

The geographers divide modern Turkey into seven regions, which vary greatly in their approach to cooking …

The Marmara region (main cities Bursa, Edirne and Istanbul) contained all the palaces from which the Ottoman sultans controlled their empire, so Turkey's wealth, industry and gourmet faddism are concentrated here. Istanbul, with its 20 million residents, is the heart of the nation (although the political capital is Ankara, 400 km/250 miles away). You can find excellent examples of every region's specialities without leaving Istanbul, because every successful regional restaurant dreams of opening a branch there (even at the risk of losing authenticity). In Istanbul, go for seafood, because the Marmara Sea supplies tasty fish. Edirne is known for its sautéed liver. Bursa is known for *Iskender kebap*.

The Mediterranean coast (main cities Antalya and Adana) grows most of Turkey's fruits and greens. Hatay is the most multicultural city in Turkey, with large communities of Arabs, Christians and Jews—which makes its cuisine fascinating. Antalya is nicknamed 'Antalsky' in the summer months, because of the invasion of Russian tourists. That's when serious foodies leave the coast and head for the mountains.

In the wild and windy Black Sea region (main cities Trabzon and Samsun) the obsessions are hazelnuts, corn, salad greens, and a fish called *hamsi* (somewhere between a sardine and an anchovy). There are alleged to be more than 200 recipes for it, including a *hamsi* jam.

Not surprisingly, the Aegean coast (main cities Izmir and Bodrum) is Greek-influenced. The Greek islands are so close that at night Turks in the Aegean region can see the headlights of cars driving around Kos, Lesbos, Chios and Samos. No wonder it was so easy for the Greeks to invade Troy. It's a wine-making area, more liberal than the rest of Turkey

---

HOW TO TALK TURKEY

After the republic was formed in 1923, Turks moved from the confusing Arabic alphabet to the much simpler Latin alphabet. In this book, we've used the Turkish spellings of dishes and locations.

The names might seem difficult at first, especially since the alphabet has twenty-nine letters, but the spelling is logical and phonetically consistent, once you get the hang of it.

All letters are read as they are written, and they always have the same sound.

A/a B/b C/c Ç/ç D/d E/e F/f G/g Ğ/ğ H/h I/ı İ/i J/j K/k L/l M/m N/n O/o Ö/ö P/p R/r S/s Ş/ş T/t U/u Ü/ü V/v Y/y Z/z

A few letters are pronounced differently from the English alphabet:

A/a = as in far
C/c = as in joke
Ç/ç = as in chair
E/e = as in set
G/g = as in goat
Ğ/ğ = silent g, not pronounced but it extends the preceding vowel
I/ı = (without a dot) pronounced as the last syllable in button
İ/i = (with a dot) as in sit
J/j = as in measure
Ö/ö = as in bird
Ş/ş = as in shut
Ü/ü = as in cube
V/v = like w, as in water

So, for example, *köfte* (meatball) is pronounced 'kirf-teh'; *sütlaç* (rice pudding) is 'soot-latch'; *mantı* (dumpling) is 'mantuh'; *gözleme* (pancake) is 'gers-lemeh'; *yoğurt* is 'yoh-ourt'; *keşkül* (almond pudding) is 'kesh-kool'; kahvaltı (breakfast) is 'kah-waltuh'; and baklava is 'bah-klawa'.

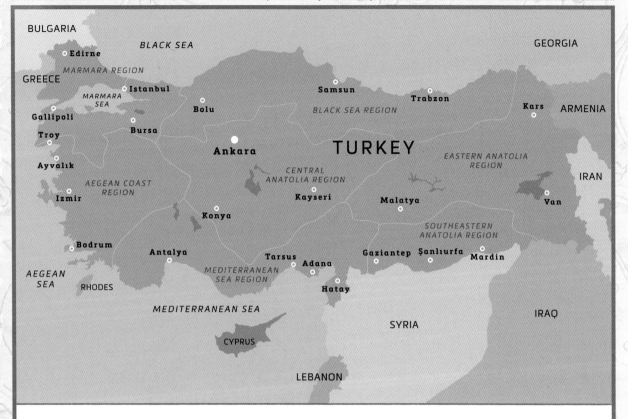

BULGARIA
BLACK SEA
GEORGIA
Edirne
MARMARA REGION
GREECE
Istanbul
MARMARA SEA
Samsun
Trabzon
Kars
ARMENIA
Bolu
BLACK SEA REGION
Gallipoli
Troy
Bursa
Ankara
TURKEY
EASTERN ANATOLIA REGION
IRAN
Ayvalık
AEGEAN COAST REGION
CENTRAL ANATOLIA REGION
Izmir
Kayseri
Malatya
Van
Konya
SOUTHEASTERN ANATOLIA REGION
Bodrum
Antalya
Tarsus
Adana
Gaziantep
Şanlıurfa
Mardin
AEGEAN SEA
RHODES
MEDITERRANEAN SEA REGION
Hatay
IRAQ
MEDITERRANEAN SEA
SYRIA
CYPRUS
LEBANON

THE FOOD REGIONS OF TURKEY

AEGEAN SEA Olives, wines, salads, herbs, wild weeds and seafood
BLACK SEA *Hamsi*, tea, corn, hazelnuts and pide bread
CENTRAL ANATOLIA *Börek* pastries, beef *pastırma*, lamb casseroles and fruit molasses
EASTERN ANATOLIA Cheeses, dried fruits, grains and lamb
MARMARA *Mezes*, white wine, *rakı*, small fish and puddings
MEDITERRANEAN SEA Large fish, salads, oranges, lemons and figs
SOUTHEASTERN ANATOLIA *Kebaps*, bulgur wheat, baklava and peppers

in its attitude to alcohol. The best food is found in its *meyhanes*, which do seafood specialities, and olive oil-braised greens and other vegetables.

Central Anatolia (main cities Ankara, Konya and Kayseri) is the agricultural heartland, growing most of the vegetables and grains. The restaurants tend to specialise in lamb, *börek* pastries and casseroles with bulgur. Konya was one of the first places settled by the nomadic Turkic people when they arrived in the eleventh century, and has become a culinary and cultural centre. The Armenian community in Kayseri made the region famous for beef *pastırma* and *sucuk* sausage. Butter is the main cooking medium here, not olive oil.

Eastern Anatolia (main cities Van, Kars and Malatya) borders Iran, Armenia, Azerbaijan and Georgia, and has a large Kurdish population. On its western side, the climate is ideal for growing apricots, figs, and grapes that turn into powerful red wines. On the east, the cattle, sheep and goats produce wonderful cheeses.

Southeastern Anatolia (main cities Gaziantep, Şanlıurfa and Mardin) has a cuisine influenced by neighbouring Syria and Iraq. It produces the world's best pistachios, and thus the world's best baklava. The climate is harsh in winter and hot and dry in summer, so they've perfected drying, preserving and pickling techniques to keep their eaters happy all year. The famous *isot* chilli pepper and *çiğ köfte* (raw veal and bulgur wheat) come from Şanlıurfa.

THE FIFTEEN FAVOURITE INGREDIENTS

BREAD

Growing up in Istanbul, the only bread I knew was *ekmek*— a torpedo-shaped roll that was made every morning in a wood-fired stone oven by a bakery a few doors from my apartment. No Turks bake their own bread at home because the price of bread has been subsidised by the government since Ottoman times (when the sultans followed the Roman emperors' practice of pacifying the populace with 'bread and circuses').

Bread is subject to a multitude of laws specifying minimum size of loaf (250 g/9 oz), minimum flour type, maximum salt content (1.5 per cent) and hygiene for shops and delivery trucks (delivery truck needs to be washable), and can only use flour, yeast, salt and water.

Although my family was not religious, the holy month of Ramadan was an exciting time for me, because a new kind of bread appeared—a round and fluffy creation called *pide*, designed to be consumed hot as soon as the faithful break their fast at sunset. The cooks elaborated on the basic *ekmek* by putting *yoğurt* or molasses on top. I later discovered that if I visited southeastern Anatolia I could eat pide all year round because it's their standard form of bread. (Pide is not to be confused with pita, which is not a word used much in Turkey. The flatbread called pita by other cultures is called *lavaş* in Turkey.)

So if you go to the southeast of Turkey and ask for *ekmek*, you will get pide. If you ask for pide on the west coast, they will tell you 'It's not Ramadan yet'. In the Black Sea, if you ask for pide, they will ask you 'with cheese or lamb?' In Istanbul tourist restaurants they will serve you pide in the form of a balloon, made by throwing cardboard into the stone oven in the last few seconds of the baking process to create a sudden blast of heat that will make the bread puff up. Do not try this at home.

YOĞURT AND OTHER DAIRY

Being nomadic people, the Turkic groups who reached Anatolia in the eleventh century first drank horse milk. When they settled in one spot, they domesticated cows, sheep and goats, and found new flavour sensations.

Although I am sceptical about the Turkish habit of taking credit for all sorts of culinary creations, I think we are safe in saying those invaders gave *yoğurt* to the world (which is why I've used the Turkish spelling throughout this book). Turks are now the biggest consumers of plain *yoğurt* on the planet—our average consumption is 24 kg (over 50 lb) per person per year. We use it in or with just about everything.

For my grandma, *yoğurt* was as much a medicine as a food. A burnt hand got a *yoğurt* wrapping, a sunburn meant your whole back, neck and face were covered with it. If you got food poisoning, it settled your stomach. My grandma bought her *yoğurt* from a man who walked down her street at the same time every day carrying two pots suspended from a pole that went across his shoulders.

I like to say that I can offer four recipes in which the only ingredients are *yoğurt* and time—in its basic form as a sauce; thickened to become a dip (by hanging in muslin or cheesecloth for three hours over a pot to catch the drips); thickened and sun-dried to become a cheese (hanging for twelve hours); and diluted to become a drink (which we call *ayran*—and okay, I must admit water is another ingredient, unless you got it from the pot under the bag in which you made the cheese).

To make your own yoğurt:
First buy a full-fat natural *yoğurt* (ideally pot-set). Boil 1 litre (35 fl oz/4 cups) of milk for 5 minutes and let it cool until you can keep your finger in it for 10 seconds. Stir 1 tablespoon of the commercial *yoğurt* through it and whisk with a fork to aerate. Cover the pot and leave it overnight in a warm place (in winter, wrap it in a blanket and keep it in the warmest part of the house). It should have turned to *yoğurt* within 8 hours, and then you can keep it in the fridge. You should eat it within 5 days, which won't be difficult if you're cooking Turkish recipes.

Butter is the main cooking medium in eastern Anatolia; on the west coast they follow the Greeks in preferring olive oil. Some of my recipes involve the use of clarified butter (ghee).

To make your own ghee:
Melt butter over very low heat and when it starts to sizzle, pour it into a bowl and put it in the fridge. Next day, scrape the layer of fat off the top. The liquid at the bottom is ghee.

Gözleme are a kind of pancake made popular by Yörük people who bring their food stalls from the mountains to coastal villages.

Somer and his father Güngör checking the daily catch at an Aegean village fish shop.

FETA AND OTHER CHEESES

A text published by the University of Kars (on Turkey's eastern border) identifies 193 types of cheese commonly used in Anatolia—23 of them made in Kars. The favourite type is 'white', a variation on the Greek feta. Mostly it's made from cow's milk, but sometimes from sheep or goat's or a mixture. It's an essential component of breakfast, while other cheeses start to appear later in the day.

Sheep were first domesticated in Anatolia around 10,000 years ago and, soon after that, the habit of storing milk in the stomachs of sheep produced the first cheese (because the milk reacted with stomach enzymes, known as rennet). The first written reference to cheese is in *The Iliad*, where Homer describes a wounded soldier being treated with a mixture of wine, barley and goat's cheese.

Next comes *kaşar*, a semi-hard yellow cheese often melted on toast. For the recipes in this book I've tried to suggest alternatives that might be available in English-speaking countries, but when you're in Turkey, please try every regional artisanal cheese you can, because the more unusual types are at risk of disappearing.

LAMB AND LESSER MEATS

Yes, we do eat chicken and beef (never pork), but I must admit that 80 per cent of the meat consumed in Turkey is lamb. We see it as a main meal, an ingredient in *kebaps*, and a flavouring for rice. We use every part of it, and in this book you'll find recipes for its head, liver and testicles. In 2012, somebody did a census and found that Turkey contained 8 million goats, 14 million cows and 28 million sheep.

Lamb was easily bred in the Anatolian climate, and became hallowed by religious ritual very early in our history. A common prayer goes: 'If you give me this, I will kill a sheep in your name and give it to the needy.' Around 3000 years ago, so the holy texts tell us, the prophet Abraham sacrificed a sheep instead of his son after passing a test imposed by an angel sent from God. Many villages celebrate this in a religious holiday during which a lamb is tethered outside your house all day, then slaughtered, sliced and distributed to your neediest neighbours (you can only keep a third for yourself).

During the four-day religious festival called Kurban Bayramı, it's traditional for rich families to sacrifice a sheep and distribute it to the needy. In the past you'd go and select the animal yourself and watch it being slaughtered with appropriate prayer readings. Nowadays, busy people organise the whole thing online, and never see the sheep or its parts.

There are two varieties of lamb: those with a fatty tail and those with a thin tail. The fat-tailed sheep are highly prized by eastern Turks, who love the flavour of the tail fat, which melts at low temperatures. Some areas use tail fat the way the French use butter—to enrich a casserole. *Kebaps* are healthier because the fat drips off into the embers.

SEAFOOD

Turkey is girt by sea on three sides—the Black Sea at the top, the Aegean on the left and the Mediterranean on the bottom. The seafood varies hugely between regions, getting bigger the further south you go.

Turks don't feel the need for complex recipes for fish, and they don't bother much with fillets. The rule is grill the fish whole if large, and fry the fish whole if small, then serve with lemon and rocket (arugula). They get more imaginative with mussels, calamari, octopus, scallops and shrimps.

Everyone agrees the best fish come from Istanbul's Marmara Sea, which connects the Aegean with the Black, and the best month to eat it is September.

I grew up fishing in the Marmara with my father, who had his own boat and knew how the currents and the seasons affected the availability of the fish. Nowadays, fishing in that area is banned between April and early September, but once the ban is lifted, you will be astounded by the variety at the Kumkapı fish market, and you can eat wonderfully in restaurants along the Bosphorus (I've named a few of my favourites in the recommendations at the end of this book). The fish you should ask for is *lüfer*, which is usually translated as bluefish.

In this book I've tried to replace varieties unique to Turkey with similar fish available in English-speaking countries.

EGGPLANT AND OTHER VEGETABLES

Eggplants (aubergines) are even more common than lamb in Turkish recipes (usually disguised under poetic titles rather than their own name, *patlıcan*), so you might imagine we grew them first. But they seem to have been brought into Anatolia from India by Arab traders at least 3000 years ago. Per capita, Turks are the greatest consumers of eggplants in the world.

The best way to cook eggplant is to pierce the skin with a fork and put it directly over fire—either the embers of a barbecue or the gas flame of your stove. Be careful, though. Historians writing about Istanbul in the seventeenth century record frequent destruction of property due to 'eggplant fires', because householders would put them over flames and walk away, letting them drop onto the wooden floor. You should stay nearby, turning the eggplant with tongs until the skin is blackened. Let it cool and drip in a colander for 10 minutes, then scrape out the flesh. If you're not going to eat it straight away, keep it in water into which you have squeezed half a lemon.

Our next most beloved ingredient is the tomato (*domates*)—which you're going to tell me should not be in this section because it is actually a fruit (but you'll never convince a Turk of this botanical detail). Its omnipresence is surprising since it only entered the Anatolian repertoire in the eighteenth century (imported from the Americas). Turkey is the fourth-biggest producer in the world, eating 11 million tonnes of tomatoes a year.

Every village has a day of the week devoted to a fresh food market where local farmers' wives offer their produce.

The handwritten sign says:
'Very juicy, wonderfully
fragrant, 5 Turkish lira.'

Every market across the land has tubs piled high with mounds of bright-red tomato paste (usually next to a tub overflowing with even brighter peppers). We use it to boost the flavour of everything but fish (which works better with fresh tomato).

To make your own tomato paste:
Slice 1 kg (2 lb 4 oz) of over-ripe tomatoes into quarters and let them rest for a day under a cloth. Then push them through a coarse sieve to get rid of the skins and most of the seeds. Wrap the pulp in a muslin cloth (cheesecloth) and put a weight on the parcel to squeeze the water out overnight.

Stir 1 tablespoon of olive oil and 1 teaspoon of rock salt through the pulp, and simmer for 1 hour, stirring regularly. Put the paste in clean jars, with some more olive oil at the top, and tightly seal the lids. You can keep the paste in the fridge, topping up with more olive oil each time you dig into it.

POMEGRANATE AND OTHER FRUITS

The pomegranate has been a symbol of opulent eating around the Mediterranean for thousands of years. A tradition going back to the Greek occupation of Anatolia is throwing a pomegranate into the doorway of your house on New Year's Eve to ensure abundance for the following year.

Turkey is the third-biggest pomegranate producer in the world, after Iran and India. Turks call it a 'superfruit', believing it to contain an antioxidant that lowers cholesterol.

Every Turkish supermarket sells special-purpose pomegranate seeders and pomegranate juicers, but if you can't find these devices, don't despair. Cut the pomegranate in half, horizontally. Put one half face down over a bowl and tap gently all over the back. The seeds should pop out. Then you can crush them to make juice or use them to decorate dishes, savoury or sweet.

Turkish supermarkets also sell pomegranate molasses.

To make your own pomegranate molasses:
Simmer pomegranate juice in a heavy-based saucepan until reduced to a quarter of its original volume. No need to add sugar.

You can use it in any dish where you might use balsamic vinegar or lemon. In my restaurant, I serve my bread with a saucer containing two tablespoons of olive oil and a teaspoon of pomegranate molasses. I also like to baste lamb in it, because it caramelises the exterior.

When I arrived in Sydney, I was delighted to learn that the Australian term for English people is 'pommie', supposedly because their faces quickly go the colour of my favourite fruit under the hot Australian sun.

The next most popular fruit in Turkey is the fig, which is at its best in autumn. It was apparently the first crop to be cultivated in the world—in southeastern Anatolia, of course, about 10,000 years ago. We use unripened figs in jams, fresh figs in salads, and dried figs in desserts and *dolma* stuffings.

Turkey supplies 80 per cent of the world's dried fruits, particularly apricots, dates and raisins. The Ottoman sultans embraced the Persian passion for combining dried fruits with stewed or roasted meats, as you'll see in our Dinner chapter.

PEPPERS

Before the appearance of chillies and peppers in the seventeenth century, cooks in the Ottoman kitchens used huge quantities of ground black pepper to satisfy the jaded sultans' need for culinary kicks. In the sixteenth century, peppercorns were a major trading commodity, with 1 kg (2 lb 4 oz) costing as much as 35 kg (over 75 lb) of bulgur. Then the long red and green peppers and chillies arrived from the Americas, and the bottom dropped out of the black pepper market, because chilli proved to be a useful preservative us well as a flavour booster.

Heat preference varies hugely around Anatolia. In the southeastern culinary triangle of Şanlıurfa, Gaziantep and Maraş, spice is everything. They give chillies to children to chew on as an appetite stimulant. In villages near Şanlıurfa in late summer, you can see chillies laid out all over the flat roofs, then covered with sheets at night to 'sweat' them. The famous Maraş and *isot* chilli flakes are exported around the world, including to my restaurant in Sydney. Maraş is stronger, with an intense 'mouthburning' flavour. *Isot* (also known as Urfa pepper) is milder but longer lasting.

When I arrived in Australia, I was disappointed to find the peppers were much bigger, with thicker skins, than the ones I knew in Turkey. I have shifted to bullhorn peppers in some of my recipes, because they're closer to the taste and texture I knew in Turkey. Feel free to use whatever form you can find near you, but remember that smaller is better, especially if you are stuffing them.

BULGUR AND OTHER GRAINS

Wheat was first cultivated in eastern Anatolia about 10,000 years ago, and it's likely that before the grains were turned into flour for bread, they were stripped of their skins and boiled, to become a belly filler and a base for roasted meat or vegetables. Much later in history rice arrived from China, and the principle became: rice for the rich, bulgur for the poor. So the poor were better nourished.

In Turkey, bulgur is now sold in four grind classifications: extra fine (for kneading with raw meat in *çiğ köfte*); fine (for lentil *köfte*); coarse (for mixing into salads); and extra coarse (for pilav, served with stews).

To make an interesting bulgur pilav:
Sauté 1 finely chopped onion in butter for 5 minutes, then add 500 g (1 lb 2 oz) of bulgur and sauté for another 10 minutes.

Drying red peppers for winter in Oğuzeli in southeastern Anatolia.

Pistachios and other nuts and pulses for sale at a village shop.

Add 750 ml (26 fl oz/3 cups) of water or chicken stock and simmer, covered, for another 10 minutes. Add a chopped tomato and/or a chopped capsicum (pepper) if you like. Decorate it with chopped flat-leaf (Italian) parsley, and serve with a stew or kebaps, or just with yoğurt as a dish in itself.

Another form of wheat, called freekeh, became trendy in Anatolia 4000 years ago and is now becoming trendy again in the English-speaking world. It is a green wheat that has been roasted; in southeastern Turkey they set fire to the wheat field to burn off the chaff and give the grains a smoky taste.

The name literally means 'rubbed', and of course it comes with a story: around 4000 years ago a bunch of Hittites harvested their wheat when it was unripe and stored it away in a wooden shed, which caught fire. When they recovered the stalks and rubbed off the blackened husks, they found the grains smelled and tasted delicious, and a fad was born.

Freekeh is easier to digest than bulgur, which can bloat you if you eat too much. A bowl of freekeh brings a beautiful aroma to the table, and makes an ideal base for a chicken stew or a healthy dose of fibre mixed into a salad.

RICE

In Ottoman times, rice (pirinç), initially imported from China, was a treat for the aristocrats. If you visited Istanbul's Topkapı Palace 500 years ago, you'd be offered three beautiful dishes: dane-i-sarı (yellow rice, made with saffron), dane-i-yeşil (green rice, made with spinach or fresh herbs), and dane-i-kızıl (red rice made with pomegranate or barberries). Nowadays, every class eats it, but more in Turkey's west than east.

There is much debate about how to get the best out of rice, but below is my preferred way to make an interesting rice pilav, learned from my mother-in-law.

To make an interesting rice pilav:
Soak 200 g (7 oz/1 cup) of rice in 500 ml (17 fl oz/2 cups) of warm water and 1 tablespoon of salt for 1 hour. Rinse the rice and toss with 1 tablespoon of melted butter over medium heat for 2 minutes, then add 250 ml (9 fl oz/1 cup) of water (or chicken stock) and 1 grated tomato, and simmer, covered, for 15 minutes.

PASTRIES—YUFKA, FILO AND BÖREKS

Stuffing and baking pastries is a huge fad in Turkey, but it's rare for Turks to make the basic pastry at home, because so many shops sell sheets of yufka (for böreks) and filo (for baklava). The word yufka meant 'thin' in the old dialect, and that's exactly why you risk frustration if you try it at home. But if you're game, a yufka recipe follows...

To make your own yufka pastry sheets:
Mix 1 kg (2 lb 4 oz) of strong flour with 2 tablespoons of salt and 250 ml (9 fl oz/1 cup) of water. Knead for about 10 minutes until a flexible dough is formed. Divide the dough into ping-pong-ball-sized lumps. Covering your work surface, hands and a thin rolling pin with lots of flour to prevent sticking, roll and pull each ball out into a sheet about 50 cm (20 in) across. If you have a pasta machine, you could use that to start the rolling process, but you'll have to finish it by hand.

Now you need to partly cook the pastry. You'll need a large wok, which will become a device the Turks call a saç.

Scrub the wok clean, inside and out, and put the wok upside down over a lit burner on your stove. Drape a sheet of dough over the wok, and as soon as you see it start to bubble, put another sheet of pastry over it, and flip the pair over. Cook the bottom side of the second sheet for 1 minute or so, then remove the pair (put them on a board next to you) and start again with another sheet. You're cooking every sheet on one side only, then adding its partner and flipping.

You can keep the partly cooked yufka sheets in the fridge for 3 days. When making böreks, always put the stuffing on the uncooked side.

The process for making filo is similar, except that the dough sometimes contains eggs, and must be rolled out even thinner than yufka—as thin as a page of this book, in fact.

In the recipes you're about to read, we'll show you how to make other forms of pastry (gözleme, katmer, mille-feuille), but we'll suggest buying commercial filo, as Turkish families do.

PISTACHIOS AND OTHER NUTS

Almonds and pistachios are the only two nuts mentioned in the ancient religious text that is accepted by Muslims, Jews and Christians (known as the Tevrat, the Torah or the Old Testament of the Bible). Both were first cultivated in Anatolia. Ground almonds became the basis for the favourite sauce of the early Ottoman sultans, and crushed pistachios became the basis for their favourite dessert—baklava.

The world's best pistachios come from Gaziantep in southeastern Anatolia. That's been the case since at least the year 100, when the Roman emperor Trajan organised regular deliveries of pistachios from the village of Zeugma to Rome. They are expensive, but versatile; the wild form makes an interesting form of coffee. Turkey is the third-largest producer in the world, but Iranian and Californian varieties are arguably of lesser quality. Gaziantep pistachios are harvested in midsummer, when they are small enough to be best for baklava.

Turkey produces 75 per cent of the world's hazelnuts, mostly in the Black Sea region. They are roasted for snacking, or turned into oil for frying, paste as a breakfast spread, and meal for cakes.

CHICKPEAS AND OTHER PULSES

When you go out drinking of an evening anywhere in Turkey, you're likely to be given a bowl of what you think are salty nuts. They are more likely to be *leblebi* (toasted chickpeas), bought from nut shops that cook them all day in giant *leblebi* roasters. Chickpeas, now used to bulk out countless casseroles, were first cultivated in Anatolia more than 8000 years ago. In the fifteenth century, a vizier working for the sultan in the Topkapı Palace became famous for surprising his guests by hiding a golden chickpea in one of the dishes in every banquet.

The next most popular pulse is lentils. The green variety is from central Anatolia and used whole in sautés; it's known as poor man's beef, because of its high iron content. The softer red variety from the southeast is used in soups or as a paste in *köfte*.

Turks also use dried beans a lot—in particular the small white ones the Italians call cannellini—and in this book so do we. It's vital to soak them overnight, rinse them and change the water several times to get rid of chemicals that can upset your digestion.

ONION AND GARLIC

My friend Musa Dağdeviren, the scholar-chef who sparked the revival of regional Anatolian cooking (see the Dinner chapter), was once asked to name the three ingredients he would take with him to a desert island. He said: 'Onions, garlic, and spring onions, because as long as I have them, I can make a delicious meal with anything else I find on the island.'

Onion was the key flavour-booster in Anatolian food long before the arrival of peppers from the Americas, and it remains dominant. Every home-style Turkish appetiser or main course has onion or garlic or both at its heart, often with leek as well.

My preference is to use red onions in salads, and white or brown onions in cooking, and always to sauté onions for 5 minutes longer than garlic.

It's common in Turkey to use the green shoots of fresh garlic, which are most readily available in spring. They look like thin spring onions (scallions). In some recipes, we've suggested garlic shoots, but if you can't find them, toss whole spring onions in equal amounts of olive oil and finely crushed garlic for a similar flavour.

We love leeks in winter, particularly braised in olive oil as part of a meze spread, or as wrappers instead of pastry around mince or rice parcels.

PARSLEY AND OTHER HERBS

Anytime I talk about parsley in this book, I mean the flat-leaf kind English-speakers call continental or Italian parsley. You never see the curly type in Turkey, but you see the flat-leaf kind everywhere. Don't feel compelled to follow the Turkish habit of sprinkling it on anything savoury. I know parsley is good for you, but I fear it is used too often as decoration, and in my restaurant I have to spend a lot of time picking it off dishes my cooks send out of the kitchen.

Mint is our second favourite herb, used fresh in salads and dried as decoration on soups and dumplings. It is hardly ever associated with lamb—Turks regard that as an English eccentricity, preferring to use oregano or thyme (which in the southeast is also used to make an invigorating tea). We like to use bay leaves with fish, marjoram with chicken, and wild weeds (nettles) with eggs and pastries—but only on the west coast.

Herbal teas are central to Turkish life, seen as suitable treatments for colds, anxiety and stomach upsets. Wild thyme (*zahter*) tea is popular in the southeast for aiding digestion; you'll also find teas made with linden, mountain sage and wild nettles.

THE EQUIPMENT YOU SHOULD HAVE

- Big sharp knife for mincing (ideally a *zırh* or a mezzaluna knife)
- Large, thick wooden board
- Long tongs for the barbecue
- Mortar and pestle
- Baking trays for pastries
- Plastic wrap
- Paper towel
- Baking paper
- Aluminium foil
- Skewers—bamboo and three sizes of metal (round, narrow-flat, wide-flat)
- Small and large clay pots for baking
- Wooden spoons
- Mixer/ blender/ food processor
- Whisk
- Regular rolling pin
- Thin (stick) rolling pin
- Wide heavy-based saucepans
- Pizza stone or unglazed terracotta tile
- Charcoal grill (broiler) or wood-fire barbecue
- Muslin (cheesecloth), for straining
- Ideally, a pomegranate seeder
- Turkish coffee pot (*cezve*)
- Spice grinder
- Sealable jars (for pickles and preserves)

Turkish home cooking is about doing what's comfortable with the equipment that's available, so if you don't have any of the above, adapt with what's in your cupboard.

THE WINES OF ANATOLIA

It is believed that the first place in the world where wine was made was Anatolia—by those reliable old Hittites, around 6000 years ago. The Hittites used the Sumerian term *viyana* for the alcohol derived from grapes—a word which some Turkish scholars think was the origin of a name to the capital of Austria (just as the Persian word for grapes, *ungur*, gave a name to the capital of Turkey, Ankara).

Jewish and Muslim texts tell us that the first crop planted by Noah after he got off the ark was grapes, so his family could celebrate with a cup of wine. That supposedly happened on the southeastern side of Anatolia. Nowadays, excellent red wines are still made in that hot, dry climate.

The Greeks who conquered Troy thought the west-coast town of Nysa was the birthplace of white wine—and of the drunken demigod known to them as Dionysos (Dionysius) and to the Romans as Bacchus. Around 3000 years ago, white wines from western Anatolia were exported all around the Mediterranean in giant two-handled jugs called *amphoras*, some with a capacity of 75 litres (over 15 gallons). Thousands of *amphoras* have been found in ships that sank in the Aegean Sea, stamped with details of the wine's quality, including a recommendation that it be diluted in the proportion two cups wine to five cups water, or improved by the addition of honey.

Wine became a key component of celebrations for every ethnic, tribal or religious group that ever ruled Anatolia. Even some Ottoman sultans, supposedly devout Muslims, consumed vast quantities at palace banquets, while publicly disapproving of it for their subjects.

But in the nineteenth century the Turkish wine industry went into a decline, as drinkers decided they preferred to swallow *rakı* with their *meze*. By the time I was at university and ready to start my drinking life, wine (sold in bottles with plastic stoppers) was regarded as a poor man's tipple, suitable only for alcoholics who couldn't afford *rakı*.

The comeback started in the 1990s (despite a government determined to tax it out of existence), when some visionary Turkish companies sought the help of French winemakers to make better use of ideal climatic conditions in particular regions of Anatolia. Nowadays, if you visit a wine-tasting shop such as Sensus, near Istanbul's Galata Tower, you'll be surprised how many Turkish wines can match the best of America, Australia, Italy and France.

Many Turkish winemakers simply replicate the international clichés of chardonnay, sauvignon blanc, cabernet sauvignon and shiraz. They taste fine, but for the visitor they don't represent a uniquely Anatolian experience. You should look for wines made from the local white grapes called *emir* (from the cold middle of the country), *narince* (from Tokat in Central Anatolia), and *misket* (from the Aegean coast). My favourite whites are Suvla Kınalı Yapıncak and Sevilen Isabey Narince.

I think Turkish reds are much more advanced and complex than Turkish whites. My favourites are Sevilen Plato Kalecik Karası and Kavaklıdere Prestige Boğazkere.

The red grapes to look for are *öküzgözü* (literally 'ox-eye', grown in Eastern Anatolia near Malatya) and *boğazkere* ('savoury throat', grown in the southeast, near Diyarbakır). I'm particularly pleased to see *kalecik karası* making a comeback in the vineyards near Ankara. That was the grape used by the Hittites (and probably Noah), so it could well be the oldest wine in the world. Dionysos would approve.

Somer's mum Ülkü with her signature fava *meze*.

A BEGINNER'S GLOSSARY

Here are a few terms you'll encounter in Turkey that might not turn out to be quite as you expect:

Ayran (pronounced 'eye-run'): The other national drink (after *rakı*), made with *yoğurt*, salt and water.

Baklava: A sweet made with filo pastry layered with pistachios (sometimes walnuts) and soaked in sugar syrup (not honey).

Börek: Savoury pastry (called *yufka*) that has been rolled, stuffed or layered with (usually) feta, spinach and/or lamb mince.

Çay (pronounced 'ch-eye'): Tea, served with all shopping experiences and much more popular than Turkish coffee.

Çorba (pronounced 'chorba'): Soup, served for breakfast, lunch and dinner, sometimes approaching the thickness of stew.

Dolma: Anything stuffed, most often peppers, eggplants (aubergines) and zucchini (courgettes), but occasionally lamb ribs, intestines and melons.

Dondurma: Ice cream, the best kind being the stretchy *maraş* (pronounced 'marash') made with mastic gum and *salep* (wild orchid stems).

Gözleme (pronounced 'goz-lem-eh'): A kind of savoury pancake, usually stuffed with feta, spinach and/or lamb mince.

Helva: A sweet, often made with semolina or flour (at home) or with tahini and soapwort root (in shops, where it's sold in sticky blocks).

Kahve (pronounced 'kah-weh'): Turkish coffee, and please wait for the grounds to settle (see the Afternoon Tea chapter).

Kaymak ('keye-muk'): Clotted cream, made with buffalo, cow's or sheep's milk.

Kebap: Char-grilled meat, usually on a skewer. *Döner kebap* is the vertical version.

Köfte (pronounced 'kof-tuh'): Usually translated as 'meatball'—minced meat kneaded into various shapes, often with bulgur wheat.

Kokoreç (pronounced 'koko-rezh'): A kind of char-grilled sausage made with lamb offal wrapped in lamb intestines, often sold in street stalls.

Lokanta: A casual eatery, ideal for a cheap lunch, where most dishes are displayed on counters and served lukewarm.

Lokum: Turkish delight.

Mantı (pronounced 'mantuh'): Dumplings usually stuffed with beef mince and served with garlic *yoğurt* and pepper sauce.

Meyhane (pronounced 'may-huh-neh'): A bar that serves small tasting plates called *meze*, accompanied by aniseed-flavoured alcohol called *rakı*, or wine if you insist.

Muhallebici (pronounced 'moo-hah-lebee-zhee'): A pudding shop, selling milk- and rice-based desserts.

Pastane (pronounced 'pas-tah-neh'): a pastry shop, selling biscuits and syrupy sweets.

Pastırma: Dried spiced beef, usually served in thin slices as a cold cut.

Pide ('pee-deh'): A kind of bread roll, often stuffed with cheese or minced meat, sold in shops called *pideci* ('pee-day-zhee').

Restoran: Less casual than a *lokanta*, open for lunch and dinner, where you're likely to see a menu and a wine list.

Salça (pronounced 'salcha'): A flavouring paste, usually made with tomatoes or peppers.

Salep: A hot drink for winter, made with powdered orchid tubers, thought to be an aphrodisiac.

Sucuk (pronounced 'soo-jook'): A spicy dried sausage, usually made of beef and usually fried.

Tarator: A paste of walnuts, garlic and day-old bread, usually served with fried seafood.

THE TEN TOP TECHNIQUES

DOLMA AND SARMA (STUFFING AND ROLLING)

Most English-speakers are familiar with a Greek dish called dolmades, which they take to be vine leaves filled with seasoned rice. In Turkey, that's not a *dolma*, that's a *sarma*. *Dolma* means 'stuffed' and *sarma* means 'rolled'. Turks will stuff anything that can be made to have a space in the middle, and anything they can't stuff (like leaves from grapevines, spinach or cabbage) they will roll.

Records from the sultan's palace show that in the fifteenth century Turks were stuffing onions, apples and intestines; in the sixteenth century, zucchini (courgettes), eggplants (aubergines) and butternut pumpkins (squash); in the seventeenth century, mackerel, watermelon and *barbunya* (red mullet); in the eighteenth, leeks, spinach and quince; and in the nineteenth, melon, okra and lamb ribs.

You'll find most of those recipes in this book, though we've occasionally expanded upon the two standard fillings (rice, onion and lamb mince; or rice, cinnamon, currants and pine nuts).

SALÇA (PASTE-MAKING)

The array of dishes that can be called 'Turkish cuisine' evolved in a time-rich, cash-poor society. Because of harsh climate variations in the eastern half of the country, people had to find ways to make ingredients last across four seasons. So they perfected techniques for drying, pickling, brining, preserving and pulverising products that were plentiful in late summer.

The pulverising process is called *salça* in Turkish—a word that entered culinary dictionaries only in the nineteenth century, even though it is derived from the Latin *salsa*. Before that, the word *palude* was used for pastes, sauces and reductions that were thickened with starch. For me, *salça* means a concentration of one ingredient—a paste, perhaps with salt as a preservative.

The most popular *salça* is made with peppers. On the farm of my traditionalist friend Musa, they pick the peppers in the morning, remove the stalks and seeds, and toss them into a purpose-built pepper mincer. Then they simmer the minced peppers in huge pots over a wood fire until most of the water has evaporated.

To make your own pepper salça (pepper paste):
Remove the stulks and seeds from your capsicums (peppers) and boil the chopped pieces in a little water for 1 hour, with the lid on the pot. Strain the capsicum and purée the pieces in a blender, then simmer the purée for 1 hour with the lid off.

For every kilogram of capsicum, stir in 2 tablespoons of olive oil and 1 teaspoon of salt. Pour the paste into clean glass jars while still warm, top with olive oil and seal.

FIRIN (BAKING)

The local baker in an Anatolian village is the home cook's best friend. You can send him any dish and he will cook it for you in his wood-fire stone oven, taking a share of the food as payment if you're not flush with funds.

In the southeastern town of Gaziantep, I spent a morning in the bakery of Aydın Kilitoğlu, who's had more than thirty years' experience with heat. His place is as big as the average bedroom, but he produces 3000 pides a day. His eleven-year-old son Samet (opposite) works as an apprentice during school holidays—just as Aydın did with his own father.

Locals kept coming in with trays of eggplants (aubergines), peppers and even *kebaps* that would normally be done over charcoal, but which he quickly finishes in his oven. He charges 1 lira per tray, regardless of what the customer has put on it. Some people were bringing him 'new' dishes, such as pizzas they'd constructed at home, and he was enjoying the challenge of deciding where in the oven the pizza tray should go, and how long it should stay there.

If you don't have a stone wood-fire oven, the best way to get close to Aydın's effect is to turn your oven up to full blast for at least 30 minutes before you put in your baking tray (or pizza stone, or unglazed terracotta tile).

If you're using a metal oven tray, the best way to avoid your pide dough sticking is to spread a bit of flour on the tray and bake it for about 5 minutes before putting the ball of dough on the flour.

Samet, eleven-year-old son of the owner of Asri Bakery in Gaziantep, learning how to make pide.

The 'Spice Girl', Bilge Kadıoğlu, in her shop in 'Area 51' of Istanbul's Spice Market.

TENCERE (STEWING)

Turks don't make stocks or reductions for storage. We simmer whatever meat we need on the day we're going to eat it, and boil the accompanying rice in that water when the meat is removed. We might make a second dish from the leftovers, but essentially it's all consumed within 24 hours.

But we do love slow cooking. The tradition of *güveç* (clay pot) cooking started in rural households, which would have a fire pit outside the house—a hole in the ground called a *tandır*. You would light a fire in the bottom and hang a clay pot over the fire, slowly simmering a mixture of any ingredients you could find. If you could afford it, you would line the sides of the pit with clay, and bake dough on the hot sides, making a loaf that was called *nan* in Ottoman.

In the nineteenth century, an iron device called a *kuzine* became the centrepiece of every Turkish home. It was a wood-fire stove, useful for warming the house, but also used for stewing, brewing tea, even roasting chestnuts. The cook would leave a clay pot full of ingredients on the top all day long and everybody tucked in when they got home at night.

The trick with *güveç* cookery is layering the pot so that the ingredient that will take the longest is at the bottom, while the one needing least heat is at the top.

KURUTMA (DRYING)

In delicatessens called *şarküteri* all over Turkey, you'll see red tubes that look like salami and red slabs that look like leather hanging from hooks. The sausage is called *sucuk*, spiced beef inside a lamb intestine, and the leather is a marinated beef fillet called *pastırma*.

The word *pastırma* (adapted to *basturma* in Greece and *pastrami* in New York) simply means 'pressed', but that reveals nothing of the long and complex process of drying and coating in paste that produces Turkey's ubiquitous answer to prosciutto.

Kayseri in central Anatolia is the capital of *pastırma*-making. It is thought to be the first place in the world meat was wind-dried, some time before the Romans arrived. These days the master-driers are said to be people of Armenian background. Afyon on the Aegean coast is the capital of *sucuk*-making.

In this book we've given a few recipes for non-traditional *pastırma* and a suggestion for *sucuk* without the intestine, but we're happy for you to use store-bought general versions.

In food markets across the land you will see small purple pouches hanging on strings from the roof beams. They are dried eggplants (aubergines), waiting to be stuffed. Most likely they came from the Oğuzeli area in southeastern Anatolia, where summer is perfect for growing baby eggplants and drying them. In the season, they pick the eggplants (and zucchini) early in the morning, scoop out the flesh and leave them to hang in the 35°C (95°F) heat for 24 hours. That's all it takes. But if it rains, the eggplants will become spotted and unsellable, and the grower will need to start again.

BAHARAT (SPICING)

For 1000 years Constantinople was the end point of the spice route. Some spices were literally worth their weight in gold because they were thought to be miracle cures for a variety of ailments. Now they are flavour boosters.

In a quiet corner of Istanbul's spice market, identified as number 51, you'll encounter a shop called Ucuzcular (Cheapies), run by Bilge Kadıoğlu (opposite). She'll tell you her first name is pronounced 'like Bill Gates—but without the money'. She'll tell you she doesn't mind being called the 'Spice Girl'. She'll tell you the term 'Area 51' is appropriate, echoing the section of a US air force base where UFOs are allegedly hidden, because in the marketplace she's an alien—the only woman to run a shop, and the only shopkeeper to charge the same prices to locals as to visitors. She's an honest broker in one of the world's oldest professions.

When I'm there, I always buy my *salep* powder (made from orchids) and *mahlep* powder (made from white cherry seeds) from Bilge. She also turns her spices into perfumes and oils for the skin.

Bilge's two most traditional spice mixes are spot on: *dolma baharı* (a blend of cinnamon, allspice, black pepper and pimento, to be stirred through rice) and *köfte baharı* (a mixture of cumin, black pepper, pimento, dried oregano and dried coriander, to be kneaded into minced meat). They are extraterrestrial. In this book we'll try to show you how to replicate their effect.

TURŞU (PICKLING)

A local movie called *Happy Days*, made in the 1970s, exposes one of the most divisive issues in Turkish society. It shows a married couple at odds over the best way to pickle vegetables. The husband says lemon, the wife says vinegar. They divorce and then get back together, but never reach agreement. Both as a chef and as a married man, I know you can never win an argument with a woman, so I mostly go with vinegar.

That also puts me on the side of the first published picklers. A fourteenth-century nutrition book contains recipes for preserving cucumber, eggplants, onions and beetroot in a vinegar marinade. In the seventeenth century, Greek *meyhanes* started pickling a fish called *lakerda*, its saltiness probably boosting alcohol sales.

To pickle your own vegetables, Turkish style:
For every 1 litre (35 fl oz/4 cups) of water you need 100 ml (3½ fl oz) of vinegar and 3 tablespoons of natural rock salt (not iodised). But the devil is in the detail—you must make sure your glass jar is sterilised, the vegetables are of premium quality, not over-ripe, and evenly placed in the jar, and you must wait at least 5 weeks before eating them. You can throw in a few chickpeas to speed fermentation, but be sure to remove them

after 1 week. The ideal temperature of the room where you store your pickles is 20°C (about 70°F). For every two degrees Celsius below that, wait another week.

REÇEL (PRESERVING)

There are more jams in Turkey than there are fruits, because we often make several types from the one ingredient—for example, orange rind marmalade and orange jam, or unripened fig jam, fresh fig jam and dried fig marmalade.

Some recipes are simple—as in, boil 1 kg (2 lb 4 oz) of berries with 800 g (1 lb 12 oz) of sugar for 30 minutes, adding the juice of half a lemon to prevent crystallisation. Some are more elaborate, such as rose petal jam.

The word *reçel* (jam) comes from the Persian *ricar*, which suggests an origin a little to the east of Anatolia. But we know the Romans were making marmalade with fruit and honey before they arrived in Byzantion, so we could also credit an influence from the West. The crusaders supposedly took jam-making recipes from Istanbul to northern Europe in the thirteenth century, and by the sixteenth century the futurologist Nostradamus was using them to impress the French royal family. Eat jam with pide and clotted cream.

KÖFTE (KNEADING)

This is what they do for entertainment in the southeastern town of Şanlıurfa: watch an expert make *çiğ* (chee) *köfte*. While a band plays and singers emote, the master sits on the floor and kneads a mixture of raw veal, bulgur and spices in a large tray for up to an hour. Moving his shoulders in time to the music, he produces hundreds of meatballs, which are served to the guests sitting around the musicians. The guests roll the pieces of *köfte* in lettuce leaves, and munch on them as they watch the floor show. The sweat from the master's hands has become part of the flavour. In a sense, sweat is the most important ingredient in any *köfte*, because it symbolises how much effort you've put into the kneading.

Köfte is often translated as 'meatball', but it comes from a Persian word that simply meant 'mashed'. The name implies no particular ingredient, which can be raw or cooked, meat, fish or veg. You work with shoulders and (thoroughly washed) hands for as long as it takes to produce a smooth patty. When you think it's ready, knead it for another 10 minutes.

In the centre of Sultanahmet Square, just near the Topkapı Palace, you will see rows of *köfte* sellers claiming to be 'the original', 'the historical' and 'the traditional'. The best, the first and the original does not display any of those adjectives. It's called Selim Usta (Selim the Master) and it dates from 1920. Selim's *köfte* is made from spiced beef and served with bean and onion salad.

KEBAP (GRILLING)

A common folk myth goes that *kebap* cooking was invented in the twelfth century by Turkish soldiers who skewered meat on their swords and cooked them over a fire. But an archaeological dig in Santorini, Greece, found *kebap* cookers called 'fire dogs' (with a hotbox carved into the shape of a dog) that were in use 3700 years ago. So it's one of humanity's most ancient forms of cooking, now evolved into a fine art.

First you must decide the form in which your lamb, beef or chicken will be cooked—whole, in lumps, or minced into patties. Any mincing must be done with a giant sharp knife called a *zırh*. Then you must blend in your flavouring—a sophisticated mix of herbs, peppers, onions, spices and (with meat *kebaps*) lamb fat, which will drip out of the meat and turn into a fragrant smoke that will further complicate the ultimate flavour.

And it's not just a matter of sticking it on a fire. The wood or charcoal must be lit 1 hour in advance and allowed to die down to embers, so there will be no flames in contact with the meat.

Turks do make *kebaps* at home, but they prefer to go out to specialist *kebap* houses for their charcoal hits, sitting around a fiery pit and watching a master *kebapçi* carefully turning his skewers. You should join them if you're visiting Turkey.

Many other cultures (such as Australia and the southern states of America) think of themselves as barbecue kings, so *kebap* cooking at home should be easy for them. If you don't own a charcoal grill, this book offers some *kebap* recipes that can be cooked in the oven at high temperatures.

At Karadeniz in Istanbul's Beşiktaş market, the *döner kebap* starts the morning as a 100 kilo ball of meat and slims down as the day proceeds.

BREAK FAST

LIGHT STARTS & BANQUETS

BREAKFAST

They love a big breakfast banquet in the far east of Anatolia. In the city of Van (pronounced 'wahn'), they'll take three hours to consume as many as forty-one courses, and then eat nothing else for the rest of the day. Most of the courses will be small—like a dish of olives, a few slices of watermelon, a pot of rose jam and bread rolls in various shapes—but they add up to a feast. There's a famous Turkish romantic poem, written by Yılmaz Erdoğan in 2002, in which an ardent suitor tells his sweetheart: 'I'd love the chance to have breakfast with you in a breakfast salon in Van.'

Now please don't imagine this is typical of all of Turkey—or even that it's an ancient tradition. Our word for breakfast is *kahvaltı*, which literally translates as 'coffee after'. It implies that breakfast is something that puts a layer on your stomach before your first coffee of the day, and in most Istanbul homes most mornings that means white cheese, fruit, *yoğurt* and bread from the local bakery. The egg dishes will come out at weekends.

Even the wealthy Ottomans of the sixteenth century didn't go in much for breakfast, preferring to have some soup and leftovers from last night's banquet around 11 am, in what these days we would call brunch.

Outside of Istanbul today, there is huge regional variation in morning behaviour. In the gourmet town of Gaziantep, in southeastern Turkey, they like to eat liver *kebap*s or a fiery soup of lamb, rice and chilli. Along the Black Sea they dip their bread into a kind of cheese fondue. In central Anatolia they love *börek*s—pastries usually stuffed with feta and spinach. In ancient Tarsus, they serve warm *humus* with bread for dipping. All of them drink tea with their first meal of the day, and have coffee after.

And in Van, they've only been doing the big breakfast since the 1940s, when it was introduced in a salon called Sütçü Kenan (which we could translate as 'Milkman Ken') to showcase the vast variety of cheeses from the region. Milkman Ken's breakfast banquet was quickly copied by other cafés in his town, and then by breakfast salons (*kahvaltı evi*) in Istanbul.

To educate Australians about Turkey's diversity, I decided to offer a 'Van breakfast' on Saturdays and Sundays at my restaurant Efendy in Sydney. It's been a huge success. This chapter shows how you can create your own Van breakfast, or any part thereof, at home. For the record, these are the courses I serve in my version. Now you can make your own.

1. Pide bread
2. Pomegranate molasses
3. Bazlama bread
4. Poğaça pastry
5. *Simit* (a kind of pretzel)
6. *Kaymak* (clotted cream)
7. Honey
8. Rose jam
9. Sour cherry jam
10. Fig jam
11. Quince jam
12. Feta (goat's cheese)
13. *Kashkaval* (sheep's cheese)
14. *Tulum* (sheep's cheese aged in goat skin)
15. String cheese
16. *Lor* (a kind of ricotta)
17. Labne balls (*yoğurt* cheese)
18. Unsalted butter
19. *Sucuk* (sausage)
20. Cigar *böreks*
21. Spinach *böreks*
22. *Paçanga* (pastırma böreks)
23. Cracked green olives
24. Black olives
25. Sliced tomatoes
26. Cucumbers
27. Olive paste
28. Tomato ezme (crushed with chilli)
29. *Muhammara* (pepper dip)
30. *Pastırma* (cold cuts of spiced beef)
31. Barbecued haloumi
32. *Menemen* (scrambled eggs)
33. Watermelon
34. Melon
35. Grapes
36. Mulberry leather (dehydrated grape molasses)
37. *Katmer* (sweet börek)
38. Red grapes
39. Turkish delight
40. Baklava
41. Tahini *helva*

The Sunday Van
breakfast at Efendy
restaurant in Sydney.

What pretzels are to New Yorkers, *simit* are to Istanbulians, who buy them from street stalls all day long and munch them between appointments.

They are at least 600 years old—Topkapı Palace documents from 1593 include bulk orders for *simid-i halka* (round *simits*). They have entered the language of metaphor. A Turk who hates his job will say: 'I'd be better off selling *simit*'. Protesters trying to dissuade police from breaking up a demonstration will shout: 'Sell *simit* and leave with honour.'

There are bakeries that cook nothing but *simit* ... in wood-fire ovens, of course, at 300°C (570°F). And there are cafés, usually with titles such as 'Palace of Simit', that serve them with melted cheese, tomato and other unnecessary additions. Personally, I would never sit down to eat *simit*, and I would never cook them at home if I was in Istanbul. But outside my homeland, you need a recipe.

SİMİT
SESAME RINGS

SERVES 8

2 teaspoons dried yeast

2 teaspoons sugar

300 g (10½ oz/2 cups) plain (all-purpose)
   flour, plus extra for dusting

1 tablespoon vegetable oil, plus extra
   for greasing

45 ml (1½ fl oz) thickened (whipping)
   cream

1 teaspoon salt

350 g (12 oz/1 cup) grape molasses

140 g (5 oz/1 cup) sesame seeds

butter and feta, to serve (optional)

Mix the yeast and the sugar in a bowl with 250 ml (9 fl oz /1 cup) of lukewarm water and then set aside for 5 minutes. The mixture should start to form bubbles. Add another 125 ml (4 fl oz/½ cup) of water and combine.

Sift the flour into a mixing bowl, make a well in the middle, and pour in the yeast mixture, vegetable oil and cream. Knead the mixture for 5 minutes to make a soft and stretchy dough, adding more flour if the dough is sticky. Cover the bowl with a damp cloth and rest for 1 hour; the dough should expand.

Preheat the oven to 230°C (450°F).

Add the salt to the dough and knead for 3 minutes. Sprinkle some extra flour on your work surface. Divide the dough into eight pieces and roll into balls. Rest for 3 minutes. With floured hands, pull each ball in half and roll each half into a strip about 50 cm (20 in) long. Twist the two strips around each other into braids. Pull the braided dough around into a circle. Stick the ends together, wetting the dough if necessary to help it hold.

Dilute the grape molasses in 170 ml (5½ fl oz/⅔ cup) of water.

Place a frying pan over low heat. Add the sesame seeds and toast, tossing constantly, until the seeds turn golden brown. Turn onto a tray and set aside

Pour the grape molasses into a shallow bowl. Dip the braided dough into the molasses, one at a time. Turn to coat both sides. Shake off the excess liquid, then toss each braid in the sesame seeds, making sure both sides are evenly coated.

Line a baking tray with baking paper and brush with oil. Arrange the *simit* on the tray and bake for 20 minutes, until golden brown and crusty.

Serve warm with butter and feta, or at room temperature as part of a breakfast spread.

BAZLAMA
PAN-FRIED BREAD

Bazlama is the simplest form of bread in the world—it doesn't even require an oven. The technique is probably at least 3000 years old. In Turkish villages, lumps of dough are spread on a *sac* (pronounced 'sazh'), which is like an upturned wok resting over hot coals. You could try that, or use a frying pan instead.

Unlike most breads, *bazlama* involves little preparation time. You could leave it to rise overnight, or you could wake up on a Sunday morning, decide 'Lets do a *bazlama* brunch', invite your friends, leave the dough to rise while you're showering and tidying up, and fry your bread while your guests are sitting down.

Because it contains *yoğurt* it has a rich flavour and an interesting texture—soft inside and crunchy outside. You'd serve it with jams or cheeses (which you would need to make earlier).

SERVES 4

2 teaspoons dried yeast
1 teaspoon sugar
600 g (1 lb 5 oz /4 cups) plain
    (all-purpose) flour, plus extra
    for dusting
125 g (4½ oz/½ cup) plain *yoğurt*
1 teaspoon salt
vegetable oil, for frying
butter, jam or cheese, to serve

Put the yeast and sugar in a bowl with 250 ml (9 fl oz/1 cup) of lukewarm water, then set aside for 5 minutes. The mixture should start to form bubbles.

Sift the flour into a mixing bowl, make a well in the middle, and pour in the yeast mixture. Knead the dough for 1 minute, then add the *yoğurt*. Knead for a further 10 minutes, or until the dough has reached, as we say in Turkey, 'the softness of an earlobe'. Cover the bowl with a damp cloth and rest in a warm place for 2 hours. The ball of dough should double in size.

Add the salt to the dough and knead for 3 minutes. Sprinkle some flour on your work surface and divide the dough into four balls. Return the dough to the bowl, cover with a damp cloth and rest for 10 minutes.

Place one ball of dough on the work surface and, using floured hands or a rolling pin, flatten into a round about 10 cm (4 in) wide and 1 cm (½ in) thick. Repeat with the remaining dough balls.

Heat 1 tablespoon of vegetable oil in a frying pan for 1 minute over medium heat and swirl gently to coat. Add one round of dough and cook for 1 minute. Turn the round over and cook for 1 minute more, or until golden brown, then transfer onto paper towel. Repeat with the remaining three rounds, adding more oil to the pan as required.

Serve the *bazlamas* with butter, jam or cheese.

TIRNAKLI PİDE
FINGER PIDE

Let me say it again—pide bread is different from pita, which is a Greek term for the unleavened bread that wraps around *kebaps* (better known as *lavaş* in Turkish). In Istanbul, pide is a treat you enjoy for one month of the year—when you break your fast after sunset during the month of Ramadan. In lucky southeastern Anatolia they get to have pide all year round, because it's their main form of bread. The cooks augment it with a coating of *yoğurt*, deposited on the top with dancing fingers, like concert pianists—hence the name 'finger pide'. The accompaniments for pide are infinite; jam is only the beginning.

SERVE 4

3 teaspoons dried yeast
500 g (1 lb 2 oz/3⅓ cups) plain (all-purpose) flour, plus extra for dusting
50 ml (1½ fl oz) sunflower oil
½ teaspoon *mahlep* powder (ground white cherry seeds) (optional)
2 teaspoons salt
25 g (1 oz) plain *yoğurt*
1 tablespoon nigella seeds
1 tablespoon sesame seeds
50 g (1¾ oz) wholemeal flour (if using a baking tray)

Dissolve the yeast in a bowl with 250 ml (9 fl oz/1 cup) of lukewarm water. Set aside for 5 minutes. The mixture should start to form bubbles.

Sift the flour into a mixing bowl, make a well in the middle and pour in the yeast mixture. Add 375 ml (13 fl oz/1½ cups) of water, the sunflower oil and *mahlep* powder, and knead for 5 minutes to form a soft dough. Cover the bowl with a damp cloth and rest in a warm place for 1 hour. The ball of dough should double in size.

Add the salt to the dough and knead for 3 minutes. Sprinkle some extra flour on your work surface. Divide the dough into five pieces and roll into balls. Return the dough to the bowl, cover with a damp cloth and leave to rest for 30 minutes.

Preheat the oven to its maximum temperature (as close to 300°C/570°F as possible). If you have a pizza stone or unglazed terracotta tile, place it in the oven to heat.

Place one ball of dough on the work surface and, using floured hands or a rolling pin, flatten into a round about 10 cm (4 in) wide and 2 cm (¾ in) thick. Repeat with the remaining dough balls.

Mix the *yoğurt* and 25 ml (¾ fl oz) of water together in a bowl. Dunk both your hands in the mixture and then, using four fingers of each hand joined together, hop your fingertips across the dough vertically and then horizontally to make indentations across the top of each round. Dip your fingers into the *yoğurt* regularly to keep them wet.

Mix the nigella and sesame seeds together and sprinkle them evenly onto each round. Put the bread on the pizza stone or tile and place on the middle rack of the oven. If you don't have a stone or tile, sprinkle the wholemeal flour on a baking tray lined with baking paper and place the rounds on the flour. Cook until brown on top and golden on the sides—about 5 minutes at 300°C (570°F), or 6 minutes at 250°C (500°F), or 7 minutes at 200°C (400°F).

Serve warm as part of a breakfast spread.

POĞAÇA
BALKAN-STYLE BRIOCHE STUFFED WITH POTATO AND CHILLI

SERVES 4

1 teaspoon dried yeast
2 teaspoons sugar
70 g (2½ oz) butter, at room temperature
1 egg
125 g (4½ oz/½ cup) plain *yoğurt*
300 g (10½ oz/2 cups) plain (all-purpose) flour, plus extra for dusting
3 boiling potatoes (such as desiree)
2 teaspoons salt, plus extra for boiling the potatoes
1 teaspoon freshly ground black pepper
2 teaspoons chilli flakes
1 heaped tablespoon shredded *kaşar* (or mozzarella)
1 tablespoon vegetable oil
1 egg yolk
1 tablespoon nigella seeds
1 tablespoon sesame seeds

Mix the yeast and the sugar in a bowl with 125 ml (4 fl oz/½ cup) of lukewarm water and set aside for 5 minutes. The mixture should start to form bubbles.

Whisk the butter, egg and *yoğurt* together in a bowl. Sift the flour into a mixing bowl, make a well in the middle, pour in the yeast mixture and stir through. Add the *yoğurt* mixture and knead vigorously for 10 minutes to make a soft, stretchy dough. Cover the bowl with a damp cloth and rest in a warm place for 2 hours to expand.

Preheat the oven to 200°C (400°F).

Peel and quarter the potatoes, then place in a large saucepan, cover with salted water and bring to the boil. Cook for 15 minutes, or until the potatoes are tender, then drain well. Add half the salt, and all the pepper, chilli flakes and cheese, and roughly mash.

Add the remaining salt to the rested dough and knead to combine. Sprinkle some extra flour on your work surface. Divide the dough into eight pieces and roll into balls. Place one ball of dough on the work surface and, with floured hands or a rolling pin, flatten into a round about 10 cm (4 in) wide and 1–2 cm (about ½ in) thick. Repeat with the remaining dough. Add 1 tablespoon of the mashed potato mixture in the middle of each round. Fold over one side to create a half-moon shape. Press lightly around the edges to seal.

Line a baking tray with baking paper and brush with vegetable oil. Arrange the *poğaças* on the tray. Brush the pastry with more oil and the tops with egg yolk, and sprinkle on the seeds. Bake for 30 minutes, or until golden brown.

Serve warm, two per person.

The Turkish word *poğaça* (pronounced 'poe-uchah') comes from the same root as the Italian word focaccia: the Latin *panis focacius,* which means bread cooked in the hearth. That suggests it must have been a favourite of the Romans during their time in Constantinople. In the mid-seventeenth century, the travel writer Evliya Çelebi reported in his memoir *Seyahatname* (Tales of the Journey) that a sweet version of *poğaça* had been popular in the sultan's palace 100 years earlier, but was introduced as street food by Balkan immigrants, who would heap hot ashes over the dough, let it bake, then scrape the bread clean and serve it with cheese or lamb mince. (The description sounds rather like damper, a favourite of Australian bushies in the nineteenth century.)

My version of this recipe could not have been eaten by the Emperor Constantine, since potatoes only reached Turkey from South America in the eighteenth century. I think *poğaça* tastes even better when the mash melts into the dough.

When I led my first gourmet tour of Turkey in 2013, we visited the tranquil Istanbul suburb of Anadolu Kavaği, the last stop for the Bosphorus ferries, lined with casual seaside restaurants looking out to the Black Sea and up to Yoros Castle. We sat down to a fish feast.

Walking back to the ferry, we passed an unassuming bakery, and one of my guests noted a snack I'd never seen before—cornbread that seemed to be stuffed with sardines and leeks. He bought some for everyone and they declared it the highlight of the day. So I researched it and recreated it for this book.

Hamsi is the most prized fish of the Black Sea— somewhere between an anchovy and a sardine. I decided to substitute baby whitebait, because *hamsi* don't swim far beyond the Bosphorus and sardines might be too strong for breakfast.

BALIKLI EKMEK
BLACK SEA CORNBREAD WITH LEEKS AND WHITEBAIT

SERVES 8

½ bunch silverbeet (Swiss chard)
½ bunch dill
½ bunch flat-leaf (Italian) parsley
2 leeks
2 onions
2 tablespoons butter
2 tablespoons dried mint
500 g (1 lb 2 oz) whitebait
2 teaspoons baking powder
1 kg (2 lb 4 oz) maize flour
250 ml (9 fl oz/1 cup) olive oil,
   plus extra for brushing
1 egg
1 tablespoon salt

Wash the silverbeet and remove the stalks; finely chop the leaves. Remove the stalks from the dill. Pick the leaves from the parsley. Remove the roots and green outer layer from the leeks, then rinse to remove any dirt. Finely chop the leeks, parsley and onions separately.

Melt the butter in a frying pan over high heat. Add the onion and cook for 3 minutes, or until soft. Add the leek and cook for 3 minutes, then add the silverbeet and cook for a further 5 minutes. Remove from the heat, turn into a bowl and leave to cool.

Preheat the oven to 180°C (350°F).

When the silverbeet mixture has cooled, stir in the parsley and dried mint. Add the whitebait and mash together with a fork.

Mix the baking powder with 300 ml (10½ fl oz) of warm water. Sift the maize flour into a mixing bowl, make a well in the middle and pour in the baking powder mixture. Stir thoroughly and then add the whitebait mixture, olive oil, egg and salt. Knead for 5 minutes, or until the mixture forms a rough dough.

Line a 30 x 20 x 4 cm (12 x 8 x 1½ in) baking tray with baking paper and brush with olive oil. Press the dough into the tray. Sprinkle the dill over the top and press it in. Brush the top with oil and bake for 45 minutes.

Take the tray out of the oven and make three knife cuts across the top of the bread to ensure even cooking. Brush the top and the slits with more oil and bake for a further 45 minutes, or until golden brown.

Turn off the heat, leaving the bread in the oven, and rest for 30 minutes.

Slice or break the warm cornbread into chunks and serve.

The harbour at Bodrum,
on the Aegean coast.

LABNE
MINTED YOĞURT BALLS

MAKES ABOUT 15 BALLS

1 garlic clove
1¼ tablespoons salt
1.4 kg (3 lb 2 oz) plain *yoğurt*
juice of ¼ lemon
1 mint stalk
500 ml (17 fl oz/2 cups) extra
   virgin olive oil
3 tablespoons dried mint
3 teaspoons ground sumac
2 teaspoons chilli flakes
1 tablespoon dill tips (or dried dill)

Crush the garlic with 1 teaspoon of the salt, then mix with the *yoğurt* and lemon juice.

Place the *yoğurt* mixture on a sheet of muslin (cheesecloth), tie up the corners and hang over a pot for 12 hours to drain. The *yoğurt* should thicken to a cream cheese consistency.

Mould the thickened *yoğurt* into spheres about the size of a ping-pong ball. This quantity should make about fifteen balls.

Gently place the labne into a large jar with the fresh mint. Cover with the olive oil, seal the jar and then set aside to rest for at least 24 hours.

When you're ready to serve, combine the dried mint, sumac, chilli flakes and remaining salt on a plate and roll the balls in the mixture, one at a time.
Serve on a platter in the middle of the table for people to help themselves.

NOTE
Labne can be kept in the fridge for up to 1 month.

When I first heard of a Middle-Eastern cheese called *labne* I was intrigued, but I refrained from using it in my restaurant because I thought it was Lebanese. Then I discovered that the name comes from *laban*, an Egyptian-Arabic word for 'milk', that it is just strained *yoğurt*, treated with a little lemon and salt; and that it can be found all over Turkey under the name *süzme*. The Lebanese like to dip their labne in zaatar, and the Egyptians dip them in dukka, but I thought I'd be Turkish and use mint and sumac.

This is the first of two recipes for *böreks,* the pastries that got their name from a Turkish verb meaning 'to twist'. You can tie yourself in knots trying to fold the pastry as neatly as a Turkish cook. We suggest you just relax and try to make shapes that vaguely resemble cigars (this recipe), or spirals (the next recipe), or square parcels.

The word *börek* is very old—there's a reference to a sugar *burek* in a twelfth-century book called *Danişmendname,* about the conquest of Anatolia by the Turks, which presumably means we can call *böreks* 'the breakfast of conquerors'.

The cigar *börek* is the simplest form, and can be made with commercial *yufka* (or two layers of filo) instead of rolling out your own pastry. From one sheet of *yufka* you can make eight to twelve cigars, which you could freeze and then deep fry (without defrosting) when you need them.

Normally *sigara böreği* are stuffed with just feta and parsley, but I find mint a refreshing addition.

SİGARA BÖREĞİ
ROLLED PASTRY CIGARS WITH FETA AND PARSLEY

MAKES 8

1 sheet *yufka*, about 80 x 80 cm
   (31½ x 31½ in); if you cannot buy
   yufka, or prefer to make your own,
   see page 27; alternatively, use
   2 layers of filo pastry
1 egg white
sunflower oil, for frying

CHEESE FILLING
1 bunch flat-leaf (Italian) parsley
1 bunch mint
300 g (10½ oz) sheep's feta
1 egg
1 tablespoon sweet paprika

First, make the cheese filling. Pick the parsley and mint leaves (discarding the stalks) and finely chop. Mash the feta with a fork. Break the egg into a small bowl and whisk. Add the feta, parsley, mint and paprika, and stir to a chunky paste.

Place the *yufka* on a board and cut across four times to create eight wedges (or cut eight times, into 16 wedges, to make *cigarillos*). Next, fill and fold your cigars. Place the egg white in a bowl and lightly beat. With the round edge of one *yufka* segment facing towards you, place a strip of filling across the pastry, about 5 cm (2 in) from each edge. Fold the round edge over the strip of filling and press down. Then, fold over about 5 cm (2 in) of pastry from the left side, leaving a straight edge. Finally, fold over a 5 cm (2 in) flap from the right side, leaving a straight edge. Using a pastry brush, brush the top triangle of pastry with egg white and roll the folded part tightly over to make a cigar shape.

Repeat this process with the seven other *yufka* segments.

Place a deep frying pan over high heat and add enough sunflower oil to cover the *böreks* (about 3 cm/1¼ in deep). Add a drop of water to the oil: if it sizzles, the oil is ready. Carefully add four *böreks* and fry for 2 minutes, or until lightly golden. Remove the *böreks* from the pan with a slotted spoon and place on paper towel to absorb the excess oil. Repeat with the remaining *böreks*.

Serve immediately.

ROLLED PASTRY WITH SPINACH AND FETA

SERVES 8

250 g (9 oz) English spinach
1 onion
4 spring onions (scallions)
120 ml (4 fl oz) sunflower or vegetable oil
1 tablespoon dried mint
1 tablespoon chilli flakes
1 tablespoon salt
1 teaspoon freshly ground black pepper
150 g (5½ oz) feta
80 ml (2½ fl oz/⅓ cup) milk
1 egg
1 tablespoon plain *yoğurt*
2 sheets *yufka*; if you cannot buy
   yufka, or prefer to make your own,
   see page 27; alternatively, use
   4 layers of filo pastry

Wash the spinach thoroughly. Remove the stalks, then finely chop the leaves. Finely slice the onion. Wash the spring onions, then remove the roots and green outer layer. Finely chop.

Put 2 tablespoons of the oil in a frying pan over medium heat. Add the onion and cook for 3 minutes. Add the spring onion and cook for 3 minutes more. Add the spinach and cook for a further 3 minutes, then remove from the heat. Mix in all the dried herbs and spices and leave in the frying pan to cool. Grate the feta into the cooled spinach mixture.

Preheat the oven to 180°C (350°F).

Whisk the milk, egg, *yoğurt* and another 2 teaspoons of the oil in a mixing bowl.

Unfold a sheet of *yufka* and slice it down the middle to create a half-moon shape.

Brush a quarter of the egg mixture onto each half-moon of *yufka*. Spread a quarter of the spinach mixture along the flat side of the half-moon, making a strip about 5 cm (2 in) wide. Fold the strip over and tightly roll the *yufka* into a tube about 80 cm (31½ in) long.

Brush a 20 cm (8 in) wide baking tray with the remaining oil. Place the rolled *börek* onto the tray and pull it around into a circle, with the ends overlapping. Make another *börek* and join that to the inside end of the previous circle, so that it forms a smaller ring inside the first one. Add two more *börek* tubes so you have a spiral of smaller and smaller rings.

Bake for 20 minutes, or until the *börek* are golden. Turn off the heat, leaving the tray in the oven, and rest for 10 minutes.

Cut across the spiral four times to make eight wedges, and serve.

The Turkish word *kol* means 'arm', and presumably gets into the Turkish name for this *börek* because each roll of pastry is bent to look like an arm coming round to hug you. It would make more sense to call this a spiral or a labyrinth, since that is how it looks when all the arms are linked together.

My maternal grandma, who came from Yugoslavia, was a master of the 'arm *börek*', and she made giant spirals to feed a large family. In later life, she used an electric *börek* cooker, called a drum oven, which was a cylinder with doors on the side and shelves onto which you could place multiple layers of *börek*.

Spinach is the traditional filling, but you can use kale, silverbeet or even minced lamb.

MENEMEN
SMASHED EGGS WITH BULLHORN PEPPERS AND TOMATO

Menemen is a famous breakfast dish in Turkey—the nearest thing we do to scrambled eggs—but nobody can agree on the perfect version. It varies from village to village and from house to house—even in the Aegean town called Menemen, which is not necessarily its place of origin. There is constant debate among chefs and domestic cooks on whether to use butter or oil, whether to include onions or garlic, whether to include peppers or tomatoes, and whether to leave the eggs whole for the eater to smash, or scramble them as part of the cooking process.

I prefer to use oil, because I want to cook the onions and peppers without burning the butter. I add the tomatoes at the last minute so they taste fresh. And I prefer my eggs stirred not scrambled. You can join the debate and vary the dish to your taste.

SERVES 4

4 ripe tomatoes
2 green bullhorn peppers
   (or 1 large green capsicum/pepper)
1 red onion (optional)
2 tablespoons olive oil
4 eggs
1 teaspoon salt
1 teaspoon freshly ground black pepper
1 tablespoon chopped flat-leaf (Italian)
   parsley

Score a shallow cross in the base of each tomato. Put the tomatoes in a heatproof bowl and cover with boiling water. Leave for 30 seconds, then transfer to a bowl of cold water and peel the skin away from the cross. To seed, cut the tomato in half and scoop out the seeds with a teaspoon. Chop the tomatoes into 1 cm (½ in) dice.

Cut the bullhorn peppers in half and discard the stems and seeds. Chop the peppers into 1 cm (½ in) pieces. If you are using an onion, finely slice it.

Heat the olive oil in a frying pan over medium heat. Add a drop of water to the oil: if it sizzles, the oil is ready. Add the onion, if using, and cook for 5 minutes. Add the chopped peppers and cook for a further 5 minutes, or until soft. Break the eggs into the pan and cook for 30 seconds. Add the chopped tomatoes, salt and pepper. Stir two or three times to mix in the eggs, but don't blend. Cook over medium heat for a further 3 minutes, until the egg whites are set.

Sprinkle with the parsley and serve the *menemen* in the pan, for people to help themselves.

KUYMAK
BLACK SEA FONDUE

This is a speciality of the Laz people who live along the Black Sea in northern Anatolia. People from other parts of Turkey say two things about the Laz people: the women are very beautiful and the men are very smart before midday. The Laz are famous for creating hundreds of recipes from a fish, similar to a sardine, called *hamsi*, but this is one of the few sardine-free recipes. It's a kind of fondue into which you dip bread, but the maize flour gives it more of a hearty porridge consistency than a Swiss fondue. It prepares you to face the harsh climate along that windy coast.

SERVES 4

2 tablespoons butter
½ teaspoon salt
½ teaspoon freshly ground black pepper
100 g (3½ oz) maize flour
115 g (4 oz/¾ cup) shredded mozzarella
1 tablespoon grated parmesan
½ teaspoon smoked paprika
pide bread, to serve (to make your own,
    see page 45)

Combine the butter, salt, pepper and 500 ml (17 fl oz/2 cups) of water in a saucepan over high heat and bring to the boil. Reduce the heat and add the maize flour. Cook for 10 minutes, stirring constantly. Add the cheeses and stir in to melt.

Top with paprika and serve hot in the pot, with pide for dipping.

Pestil is fruit juice that has been dried into strips. Although the process originated as a way of preserving summer ingredients to last through winter, it has now become the candy bar of central Anatolia. Rolled around nuts, it goes in a kid's backpack to be consumed at school as a nutritious morning snack. We're suggesting you make *pestil* from grape juice, but you can also get tasty results with mulberries, plums or apricots.

If you're planning to keep your *pestil* strip for any length of time, roll it up in baking paper so it does not stick.

PESTİL
GRAPE LEATHER STUFFED WITH WALNUTS

MAKES 16

GRAPE LEATHER
500 g (1 lb 2 oz) red grapes
1 star anise
1 cinnamon stick
3 cloves
1 heaped tablespoon cornflour
   (cornstarch)

WALNUT AND FIG FILLING
5 dried figs
150 g (5½ oz/1⅓ cups) walnuts

Start by making the grape leather. Wash the grapes and remove any stalks. Place a large saucepan over low heat and then add the grapes, star anise, cinnamon stick and cloves. (Don't add any water.) Press down with a potato masher to push out some of the juices. Bring the grape mixture to the boil, and then simmer for 15 minutes, pressing down regularly to release the juices.

Take the grape mixture off the heat and leave to cool. Put a sheet of muslin (cheesecloth) over another saucepan and pour all the grape pulp into the muslin. Tie the edges of the muslin together and squeeze the bag to extract all the juice—it should yield about 300 ml (10½ fl oz).

Preheat the oven to 100°C (200°F).

Place the grape juice in a saucepan over medium heat and bring to the boil. Put the cornflour in a bowl, mix in 250 ml (9 fl oz/1 cup) of the hot grape juice, and then pour the mixture back into the pan. Continue to cook for 15 minutes, stirring regularly, until the mixture thickens to a custard-like syrup.

Line a baking tray, including the sides, with baking paper. Pour the syrup into the tray; it should be about 5 mm (¼ in) deep.

Tap the tray to remove any air bubbles from the syrup. Bake for 5 hours, checking every hour to ensure the edges are not becoming too dry. If they appear crusty, use a pastry brush to apply a little water.

Remove the tray from the oven and leave to cool slightly. When the grape leather is cool enough to handle, carefully lift the baking paper edges to remove it from the tray, and transfer to a board to cool completely.

To make the filling, put the figs in a bowl, cover with hot water and leave to soak for 15 minutes. Transfer the figs to paper towel and leave to drain for 10 minutes, and then remove the stalks. Put the figs in a food processor, add the walnuts and coarsely combine.

Cut across the grape leather to make four equal strips. Spoon a line of filling along the middle of each strip. Roll each strip, lengthways, to create a log about 20 cm (8 in) long, pressing down to keep it sealed. Slice the log into four equal pieces and serve as part of a breakfast spread.

KATMER
PISTACHIO PANCAKES WITH CLOTTED CREAM

SERVES 4

2 sheets of chilled filo pastry, about
    40 x 27 cm (16 x 10¾ in) each
2 tablespoons ghee (to make your own,
    see page 18)
2 tablespoons thick (double) cream,
    or *kaymak*
2 heaped tablespoons ground pistachios
1 tablespoon sugar

Take the filo sheets out of the fridge and leave to warm to room temperature for 1 hour. Spread one sheet out on a large work surface, then overlap with the other sheet, to create a 40 x 40 cm (16 x 16 in) square of filo. Paint a little ghee where the sheets overlap, and join them together.

Leaving a margin of about 10 cm (4 in) around the edges, dot nine dobs of cream onto the filo to make a square about 20 cm (8 in) wide. Sprinkle the pistachios and sugar over the cream, and then fold the four edges of pastry over to make a square parcel about 20 cm (8 in) wide.

Pour 1 tablespoon of ghee into a frying pan and swirl to coat. Place the pan over medium heat and let the ghee warm for about 10 seconds. Drop the filo parcel into the pan (wrap-side down) and cook for 2 minutes, or until golden. Using two spatulas or large knives, turn the pancake over and cook for 1 minute more.

Cut the *katmer* into eight squares and serve two per person as part of a breakfast spread.

Mehmet Özsimitci, third-generation master of the art of *katmer* making.

When the suffix *-ci* (pronounced 'zhee') is added to a Turkish noun, it means 'a maker of' that thing. Thus a *katmerci* is a maker of *katmer*, the crunchy pancake that is a speciality of Gaziantep. The supreme *katmerci* in that foodie city is a man named Mehmet Özsimitci, whose surname translates as 'maker of genuine simits'. That tells you one of his ancestors was a specialist in the pretzel/bagel that every Turk consumes as a street snack. Somewhere along the line, Mehmet's family swapped from making *simits* to making *katmers*,

adding greatly to the world's happiness. Outside his shop, at the end of an arcade in the modern part of the city, Mehmet displays a slogan that translates as '*Katmer* is not a product of a pastry shop but a culture of master Zekeriya'. Zekeriya is Mehmet's father, who these days sits at the cash register while Mehmet supervises his team of young pastry rollers and dances around the outside tables, taking orders, chatting to customers, and arranging home deliveries by moped and plane (to international customers).

At Zekeriya Usta, the art of *katmer* making begins with sprinkling and tossing sheets of buckwheat dough to make the thinnest possible filo. *Katmer* is traditionally served to newlyweds as the first breakfast of their honeymoon, to keep up their strength.

You've got to get up pretty early to catch Ali Haydar. Around 6 am should do it. By 8 am, he might have gone home, having sold out of his speciality, lamb liver *kebaps*—another breakfast tradition of southeastern Anatolia that baffles visitors from Istanbul.

Ali opens his little *kebap* shop, just down the hill from Gaziantep Castle, immediately after the dawn prayer: around 5 am in summer, and 6 am in winter. Gradually customers arrive to sit on the tiny stools outside the shop. Some sit at an angle that suggests they are on the way home from a night of drinking. Inside, Ali risks setting fire to his moustache as he fans the coals of his charcoal grill with a sheet of cardboard. He watches his skewers and, at the moment the exterior turns crunchy, lifts them off the coals and wipes the meat into a mitten of flatbread. When all his livers (and hearts, lungs and kidneys) have been consumed by customers, he heads home, naps briefly, then visits the offal market for the ingredients he'll prepare overnight for tomorrow's feast.

CARTLAK KEBABI
LIVER KEBAPS

SERVES 4

2 lamb livers, about 300 g (10½ oz)
250 ml (9 fl oz/1 cup) milk
4 mild green or red chillies
1 teaspoon ground cumin
1 teaspoon hot paprika
1 teaspoon chilli flakes
1 teaspoon salt
250 g (9 oz) butter, softened
4 store-bought pita breads (or make
    a *lahmacun* base and fold it over,
    see page 91), to serve

PARSLEY SALAD
1 bunch flat-leaf (Italian) parsley
1 red onion
1 tablespoon ground sumac
1 teaspoon chilli flakes
2 teaspoons pomegranate molasses
    (to make your own, see page 24)
1 tablespoon olive oil

Soak the lamb livers in the milk overnight, covered in the fridge.

Remove the bowl of livers from the fridge and set aside.

To make the parsley salad, pick the leaves off the parsley and roughly chop; discard the stems. Finely slice the red onion and place in a salad bowl. Add the parsley, sumac, chilli flakes, molasses and olive oil, and mix well.

When you're ready to cook the livers, remove them from the bowl of milk, pat dry with paper towel and clean off the membrane and sinews. Roughly cut each of the cleaned livers into 16 cubes about 2 cm (¾ in) across—the size of a bird's head, as we say in Turkey.

Preheat the barbecue grill to very high. If using bamboo skewers, soak in water for 15 minutes.

Slit down one side of each chilli and remove the seeds. Slice across each chilli to make six pieces about 1 cm (½ in) wide. Mix the cumin, paprika, chilli flakes and salt in a bowl, then stir in the softened butter. Using your hands, rub the pieces of lamb liver in the spiced butter to coat well.

Next, make the *kebaps* by alternately threading four pieces of liver and three chilli chunks onto each skewer—with the chilli keeping the liver pieces apart. Repeat to make eight *kebaps*.

Put the skewers on the grill and cook for 2 minutes on each side, turning the skewers once. The liver chunks are ready when they start to form a crust.

Partly slit through the pita bread so that it can open like jaws. Spread any leftover spiced butter inside the bread. Next, holding a skewer in your left hand and a pita bread in your right hand, use the pita like a baseball mitten to wrap round the skewer and pull the row of liver and chilli pieces off. Repeat so each pita contains the liver from two skewers. Open the bread again and add a heaped tablespoon of salad between the two strips of liver. Close the bread and serve immediately.

İNCİR UYUTMASI
THE SLEEPING FIGS

SERVES 4

10 dried figs
500 ml (17 fl oz/2 cups) milk
2 fresh figs
2 tablespoons grape molasses
60 g (2 oz/½ cup) walnuts

Put the figs in a bowl, cover with hot water and leave to soak for 15 minutes. Transfer the figs to paper towel, leave to drain for 10 minutes, then remove the stalks. Roughly chop each fig into about six pieces and then set aside.

Warm the milk in a saucepan over low heat until it reaches a low simmer, preferably using a simmer mat, being careful not to let the milk start to boil. If you have a food thermometer, try to keep the temperature around 70°C (160°F).

Add the chopped figs and, using a hand-held blender, mix to a purée. Simmer for a further 5 minutes. (If you don't have a stick blender, pour the mixture into a blender and pulse until smooth, then pour it back into the saucepan and warm for a further 7 minutes.)

Half-fill four small bowls with the fig purée. Put the bowls in a cool spot, cover with a tea towel and rest for 2 hours. Cover the bowls with plastic wrap and place in the fridge overnight.

When you're nearly ready to serve, preheat the oven to 180°C (350°F).

Cut each fresh fig into quarters. Place them on a baking tray with the skin side down. Brush each fig piece with grape molasses, then bake for 5 minutes, until slightly soft but still semi-firm.

Roughly chop the walnuts using a food processor, or by hand. Remove the fig purée cups from the fridge. Place two fig quarters on each cup, sprinkle the crushed walnuts over the top, then serve.

'While shepherds watched their flocks by night, all seated on the ground, they also soaked their figs in milk, and then some sleep they found.'

That's essentially the back story of this dish. I love its name—the Sleeping Figs—because it suggests the gentle process of warming the milk and resting the pudding overnight.

A version of this dessert, called *teleme*, has been a typical goat herder's snack popular for thousands of years in northwestern Anatolia. They would milk their goats, add a few drops of sap from fresh figs to the milk, mix it for a few minutes, and let it set into *yoğurt*. Then they would slice fresh figs through it, using fig leaves to scoop it to their mouth. Of course, that restricted the pleasure to early autumn, when figs are at their best.

Our version uses cow's milk, walnuts and dried figs to make a healthy breakfast for all seasons.

In Ottoman times, *çılbır* was the generic term for poached eggs, done all sorts of ways. Palace records from the fifteenth century show that a version of *çılbır* containing poached eggs and onion was cooked for the mighty sultan Mehmet II. The imperial cooks kept improving on it over the years. This recipe, with garlic *yoğurt*, was a favourite of the second-last sultan in the empire, Abdulhamid II, in the early twentieth century, and became the gold standard for *çılbır* in homes and restaurants across Anatolia.

ÇILBIR
POACHED EGGS IN GARLIC YOĞURT AND PAPRIKA

SERVES 4

1 garlic clove (or 3 chopped garlic shoots)
500 g (1 lb 2 oz/2 cups) plain *yoğurt*
½ small red capsicum (pepper)
125 ml (4 fl oz/½ cup) white vinegar
8 eggs
2 tablespoons butter
½ tablespoon aleppo red pepper flakes (or chilli flakes)
4 teaspoons smoked paprika
pide bread, to serve (to make your own, see page 45)

Crush the garlic and mix it with the *yoğurt*. (If the taste of raw garlic in the morning is too strong for you, leave out this step, and instead fry a little garlic or chopped garlic shoots later with the capsicum.) Set aside at room temperature.

Remove the seeds from the capsicum and finely chop the flesh.

Divide the *yoğurt* mixture among four bowls.

Put the vinegar and 1 litre (35 fl oz/4 cups) of water in a deep frying pan over high heat. Bring to the boil, then reduce the heat to a gentle simmer. Carefully break in the eggs, one at a time, with a maximum of three eggs poaching at a time. Cook for 2–3 minutes, or until the whites are set and the yolks are still soft and runny.

While the eggs are poaching, melt the butter in a saucepan, add the red pepper flakes, paprika and capsicum (and garlic, if you've saved it for this step) and cook for 3 minutes.

When ready to serve, scoop the eggs out of the simmering water with a slotted spoon and place two in each bowl, on top of the *yoğurt*. Pour a light stream of the melted butter and peppers over the eggs. Serve with pide.

KAYGANA
CRETAN EGGS WITH WILD WEEDS

SERVES 4

1 mixed cup of any or all of these:
  nettles, curly endive, chicory (but
  not witlof), dandelion greens, round
  radicchio, beetroot (beet) leaves,
  wild rocket (arugula)
3 spring onions (scallions)
1 onion
80 ml (2½ fl oz/⅓ cup) olive oil
1 teaspoon salt
1 teaspoon freshly ground black pepper
1 teaspoon hot paprika
4 eggs
pide bread, to serve (to make your own,
  see page 45)

If you are using nettles, use gloves to handle them. To remove the sting, put them in a heatproof bowl and cover with boiling water for 30 seconds. Transfer to cold water for 30 seconds. Pick the green leaves and discard the stems.

Clean and finely chop the endive and the chicory, discarding the woody stems. Wash the spring onions, then remove the roots and green outer layer. Finely chop the onion.

Heat the olive oil in a non-stick frying pan over medium heat, then add the onion and brown for 5 minutes. Add the spring onions and cook for another 3 minutes, then add the wild leaves in this order (from toughest to softest): endive, chicory, radicchio, nettle, dandelion, beetroot leaves, wild rocket. Lightly fry for about 5 minutes to let any excess water evaporate.

Add the spices and stir. Make four wells in the mixture and break an egg into each well. Continue to cook until the whites are set, but the yolks are still runny.

Serve the *kaygana* in the pan for people to help themselves. If the yolks spread into the mixture, so much the better. Serve with pide.

There's a joke about a salad farmer who is having a tea in the village café. A neighbour comes in and says: 'There's a goat in your field.' The farmer says: 'Don't worry, he won't eat much'. Shortly afterwards, the neighbour returns and says: 'There's a cow in your field.' The farmer keeps sipping his tea and says: 'Don't worry about it.' Then the neighbour returns and says: 'There's a man from Crete in your field.'

The farmer leaps up and rushes back to save his field before everything green has been stripped.

People of Cretan background are famous for eating the dark-green weeds that grow wild along the Aegean coast and that were ignored for centuries by Turkish cooks. This egg dish uses the kind of wild (and tame) greens the Cretans have taught the Turks to love.

Mustafa Hasırcı preparing mutton for *beyran* soup at Metanet, Gaziantep.

Take a whole sheep, skin it and gut it. Boil it for 12 hours. Shred all the meat. Boil the same weight of rice. Put some rice, a handful of meat and a hell of a lot of garlic and chilli into a bowl. Put it over an open flame so the fat on the surface catches fire. Serve.

That's not the recipe we're suggesting for *beyran*, but it's what Mustafa Hasırcı and his team do every day at Metanet, just behind the central spice market in Gaziantep. The restaurant's name means 'endurance', which is presumably what you need to eat this spicy

soup every day for breakfast, as many Gaziantep citizens do; only tourists think of having *beyran* for lunch.

Mustafa certainly has endurance. For the past forty years he's been rising every day at 4 am to make his soup, following in the footsteps of his father, the founder of Metanet. Mustafa has earned the title *usta*, meaning 'master of your craft'. He has no equal in Gaziantep.

Our soup is a modified version of Mustafa's masterwork, and we won't tell anybody if you decide to have it for lunch or dinner.

BEYRAN
FIERY LAMB AND RICE SOUP

SERVES 4

1 lamb neck, about 1 kg (2 lb 4 oz)
220 g (7¾ oz/1 cup) medium-grain rice
2 teaspoons salt
4 garlic cloves, crushed
1 tablespoon chilli flakes

Put the lamb neck in a large saucepan with 1 litre (35 fl oz/4 cups) of water. Cover and bring to the boil, then reduce the heat and simmer for about 1½ hours.

Lift out the neck and place it on a rack or plate to cool; do not discard the cooking water. When the lamb is cool enough to handle, strip off the meat and discard the bones. Shred the lamb into small strips and set aside.

Pour the rice into the pot of lamb-flavoured water and bring it back to the boil over medium heat. Cook the rice for 15 minutes, then add the salt, garlic, chilli flakes and shredded lamb. Increase the heat to very high and boil rapidly for 1 minute to spread the red chilli colour through the liquid. Serve immediately, while very hot.

Lunch heaven: one of Musa Dağdeviren's three Çiya restaurant in Kadiköy, Istanbul.

LUNCH

CASUAL & REGIONAL

LUNCH

Traditionally in Turkey, lunch was no big deal. People ate before they went out to work in the fields, and carried with them simple snacks such as bread, olives and cheese. In the late nineteenth century, cheap eateries started appearing in the cities, where tradesmen and shopkeepers could grab a soup, a stew, and maybe a *börek* or a *kebap*. These places came to be called *lokanta* (from the Italian word *locanda*).

In the 1980s, the lunchtime habit of going quick and casual made Turks in Istanbul an easy target for the American fast-food chains, and for a while it looked as if the midday formula of soup-stew-*kebap* was going to turn into Coke-fries-Big Mac.

Then Musa Dağdeviren appeared and went in exactly the opposite direction. He travelled round the countryside and spoke to farmers, bakers, butchers, picklers, pastrymakers and home cooks, and figured out how to recreate Turkey's vast regional diversity in a commercial kitchen.

Now his three *lokantas* Çiya, Çiya Sofrası and Çiya Kebap, in the Istanbul port suburb of Kadıköy, are packed every lunchtime with people desperate to test how many of the fifty dishes on display can be crammed into their bellies, and looking forward to returning three months later to find that the new season has brought a different array of 'forgotten' recipes. Young chefs have been inspired by Musa's 'rediscoveries' to open bistro-style *lokantas* across Istanbul.

Musa grew up in a family of bakers in southeastern Anatolia, and moved to Istanbul in the late 1970s to operate the wood-fire oven in his uncle's *kebap* house. He became obsessed with preserving the great regional repertoire that seemed to be disappearing in the rush towards 'modernisation'.

Here's a rough translation of his philosophy:

I travel all over the country to cook with people in their homes and also study old books to find new leads. I get very excited when I discover new poor-people's dishes, because I believe only poor people can create great food. If a man has money, he can buy anything, but a person who has nothing must create beauty from within.

Since he opened his first Çiya in 1987, Musa has regularly found himself in dispute with the Turkish food establishment, which is prone to engage in nationalist myth-making and wishful thinking about our cuisine. He fights fantasies with facts, publishing a quarterly magazine called *Yemek ve Kültür* (Food and Culture), which funds scholarship on the origins of Anatolian dishes. He's setting up a cooking school and research centre, with a seed bank that will preserve native ingredients.

Luckily for me, Musa opened his first restaurant close to my father's tailor shop in Kadıköy, back when I was a teenager who carried a McDonald's cup to school to show how cool I was. Çiya became my favourite eating place, and Musa my food hero.

Many of the dishes in this chapter, whether rustic, regional or urban, were inspired by Musa's food philosophy. You would be more likely to find them in Turkish homes far from Istanbul rather than in restaurants—unless you were lucky enough to live in Kadıköy.

Musa at one of his Çiya restaurants, with candied pumpkin, eggplants and olives.

Vegetarians are always surprised by how many interesting dishes the land of lamb lovers can offer.

In season, this stew appears regularly on the famous 'Fifty Bowl' display table at Çiya restaurant in Istanbul's Kadıköy market, using the kind of grains humans have been boiling for millennia. While it is likely that lentils and chickpeas originated in Anatolia, black-eyed peas are recent arrivals—brought from Africa in the fifteenth century for palace chefs eager to surprise the sultan.

The sour-salty green purslane, which contains more omega-3 than any other leafy vegetable, is Turkey's favourite weed, usually consumed fresh in summer and dried in winter. In the first great work on botany, written in the fourth century BC, the Greek philosopher Theophrastus advises sowing purslane in mid-spring, so you can enjoy it in summer.

If you can't find purslane, the best substitute is baby rocket (arugula).

PİRPİRİM AŞI
PURSLANE AND ANCIENT GRAINS STEW

SERVES 4

95 g (3¼ oz/½ cup) dried chickpeas
95 g (3¼ oz/½ cup) black-eyed beans
110 g (3¾ oz/½ cup) green lentils
45 ml (1½ fl oz) olive oil
1 onion, chopped
2 garlic cloves, chopped
1 tomato
½ tablespoon capsicum (pepper) paste
    (see page 32)
90 g (3¼ oz/½ cup) coarse bulgur
2 teaspoons freshly ground black pepper
1 bunch purslane (or baby rocket/arugula)
juice of ½ lemon
1 teaspoon ground sumac
1 tablespoon butter
2 teaspoons dried mint
2 teaspoons chilli flakes
pide bread (to make your own,
    see page 45), to serve

Cover the chickpeas with water and soak overnight. Cover the black-eyed beans with water and also soak overnight.

Strain, then rinse the chickpeas and black-eyed beans. Rinse the lentils. Boil the chickpeas in plenty of water for 20 minutes, covered, and then add the black-eyed beans and lentils and boil, covered, for another 40 minutes.

Heat the olive oil in a saucepan over medium heat. Add the onion and cook for 3 minutes, then add the garlic and cook for 1 minute more. Cut the tomato in half and then grate it into the onion, discarding the skin.

Add the three pulses to the onion mixture. Dilute the capsicum paste in 250 ml (9 fl oz/1 cup) of warm water and add it to the mix. Add the bulgur and the pepper. Bring to the boil, then reduce the heat to a simmer.

Pick the leaves from the purslane and add them, whole, to the stew. Simmer, covered, for 10 minutes. Add the lemon juice and stir in the sumac, then turn off the heat.

Melt the butter in a frying pan over medium heat. Add the dried mint and stir for 1 minute. Add the chilli flakes and stir for 1 minute more.

Divide the stew among four bowls and drizzle with the mint butter. Serve with pide.

ANALI KİZLI
'MOTHER AND DAUGHTER' (DUMPLING AND CHICKPEA STEW)

SERVES 4

50 g (1¾ oz/¼ cup) dried chickpeas
400 g (14 oz) lamb leg meat
2 onions
1 tablespoon butter
1 tablespoon olive oil
1 tablespoon capsicum (pepper) paste
(see page 32)
10 flat-leaf (Italian) parsley leaves,
finely chopped
juice of ½ lemon

STUFFING
1 onion
1 tablespoon butter
150 g (5½ oz) minced (ground) lamb
½ tablespoon tomato paste
(to make your own, see page 24)
½ tablespoon capsicum (pepper) paste
(see page 32)
½ teaspoon salt
½ teaspoon freshly ground black pepper
½ teaspoon ground cumin

SHELLS
250 g (9 oz) fine bulgur
200 g (7 oz) lean minced (ground) beef
1 egg
1 tablespoon tomato paste
(to make your own, see page 24)
1 tablespoon butter
½ tablespoon cornflour (cornstarch)

TOPPING
2 tablespoons butter
½ tablespoon dried mint
½ tablespoon chilli flakes

Cover the chickpeas with water and soak overnight.

Strain and rinse the chickpeas, place in a saucepan with 500 ml (17 fl oz/2 cups) of water and simmer, covered, for 1 hour.

While the chickpeas are simmering, make the stuffing. Finely chop the onion. Melt the butter in a saucepan over medium heat, add the onion and cook for 3 minutes, or until soft. Add the minced lamb and cook for 2 minutes more.

Put the remaining stuffing ingredients in a bowl and mix with 125 ml (4 fl oz/½ cup) of water. Stir the mixture into the onion and minced lamb, and bring to the boil, then simmer, with the lid on, for 5 minutes. Set the stuffing aside.

Next, make the shells. Put all the ingredients in a mixing bowl. Slowly add 45 ml (1½ fl oz) of warm water. Wet your hands and knead for 5 minutes to make a smooth paste.

Mould the shell mixture into spheres about the size of a ping-pong ball. Put a ball in your palm and with the fingers of the other hand, make a well in the mixture. Place a teaspoon of stuffing in the middle and fold the shell back around it. Repeat to make sixteen balls. With the rest of the bulgur mixture, make about forty smaller chickpea-size balls.

Chop the meat from the leg of lamb into small cubes, removing any sinews and most of the fat. Finely chop the onions. Melt the butter in a frying pan over medium heat. Add the olive oil and, when sizzling, cook the onion for 5 minutes, or until translucent. Add the capsicum paste and fry for 1 minute. Add the cubed lamb. Cook for 2 minutes, then add 250 ml (9 fl oz/1 cup) of water. Bring to the boil and simmer for 5 minutes.

Add the small balls (daughters) and the large balls (mothers), chickpeas and parsley to the lamb mixture. Bring back to the boil, then reduce the heat and simmer for 10 minutes. Add the lemon juice. Divide the mothers and daughters among four serving bowls, with the cubed lamb underneath.

For the topping, place a frying pan over medium heat and melt the butter. Add the dried mint and chilli flakes and sizzle for 4 minutes. Drizzle the mint and chilli butter over the *analı kızlı* and serve.

This complex combination of large and small dumplings in a lamb and chickpea stew comes from Malatya in eastern Anatolia, an area best known for apricots. The 'mothers' are a mixture of beef and bulgur stuffed with minced lamb. The 'daughters' are not big enough to have stuffing.

You won't find this dish in many restaurants—only home cooks (and my friend Musa) have the time to do it properly.

For the mums' outer coating, it's important to choose beef with a low fat content, and to knead it thoroughly so it dissolves into the bulgur.

İMAM BAYILDI
'THE PRIEST FAINTED' (BRAISED EGGPLANT STUFFED WITH PEPPERS AND TOMATOES)

Why did this dish (first discussed in an 1844 cookbook) make the priest faint? Some say it was with pleasure, some say because of the extravagant amount of oil in it, and some say because it used up every ingredient in his pantry. The story I like comes from *Moveable Feasts: The History, Science and Lore of Food,* where Gregory McNamee says the imam married the daughter of an olive oil seller. Every day after the wedding she made him an eggplant dish cooked in her father's olive oil. On the thirteenth day the oil ran out and her husband collapsed in shock.

Most Turkish cooks would start this dish by frying the eggplant, but the famous Istanbul chef Şemsa Denizsel of Kantin showed me what she says is the original method—steaming the eggplants in a pot with the stuffing mixture before filling them. This makes them a lot lighter, and more delicious. With this recipe, the imam might have lasted a few more days.

SERVES 4

4 tomatoes
25 flat-leaf (Italian) parsley leaves
4 onions
1 teaspoon salt
1 teaspoon sugar
4 long eggplants (aubergines)
150 ml (5 fl oz) olive oil, plus extra
    for greasing
16 garlic cloves, whole and peeled
1 red bullhorn pepper (or ½ large
    red capsicum/pepper)

Score a shallow cross in the base of the tomatoes, then transfer to a heatproof bowl and cover with boiling water. Leave for 30 seconds, then plunge in cold water and peel the skin away from the cross. Cut the tomatoes in half and scoop out the seeds with a teaspoon. Roughly chop.

Finely chop the parsley leaves and onions. Put the chopped parsley, onion, tomato, salt and sugar in a large saucepan and knead the mixture for 2 minutes.

Slice three strips off the skin of each eggplant, starting about 2 cm (about 1 in) below the top and finishing 2 cm (about 1 in) above the base. The eggplants should now look like they're wearing striped pyjamas. Put them on top of the mixture. Pour in the olive oil and simmer over low heat for 30 minutes, with the lid on. Add the garlic cloves and simmer for another 20 minutes.

Remove the eggplants from the pan and slit lengthways, starting 2 cm (¾ in) from the tip and finishing 2 cm (¾ in) from the base. With the slit facing upwards, use the back of a tablespoon to push the slit open and give the eggplant a canoe shape. Brush a baking tray with oil. Put the eggplant boats onto the greased tray. Remove the garlic cloves from the pan and set aside. Spoon the onion mixture from the pan into each eggplant.

Remove the stalk and seeds from the bullhorn pepper and cut into four slices, lengthways. Place one slice of pepper and four garlic cloves on top of each canoe. Spoon the remaining sauce over the top, then set aside until you're ready to serve.

Serve the *İmam bayıldı* at room temperature, or do what I do in my restaurant and reheat them in a 180°C (350°F) oven for 10 minutes before serving.

PAPARA
GRANDMA'S BREAD AND BEEF STEW

I learned this dish from my mother's mother, who died in 2010 at the age of 103. Living through two world wars and three military coups, she raised three kids by herself. She knew how to survive, how to improvise and how not to waste a single grain.

I remember when she made *papara* the first time, from leftover bread, rice and a handful of minced meat. The origin of the dish is uncertain, but it is part of the peasant culture of Anatolia and the Balkans. In Istanbul during the seventeenth century, there were shops that sold 'papara cubed bread' as an ingredient for this dish—because, of course, the rich gourmands didn't have stale bread of their own.

SERVES 4

375 g (13 oz/1½ cups) plain *yoğurt*
1 onion
2 tablespoons vegetable oil
200 g (7 oz) minced (ground) lamb or veal
500 ml (17 fl oz/2 cups) beef stock
1 tablespoon tomato paste (to make
    your own, see page 24)
3 slices stale bread
2 tablespoons butter
185 g (6½ oz/1 cup) leftover rice
    (optional)
2 garlic cloves
1 teaspoon chilli flakes
1 teaspoon sweet paprika
1 tablespoon dried mint

Preheat the oven to 180°C (350°F).

Place the *yoğurt* on a sheet of muslin (cheesecloth) and tie up the corners. Hang the muslin over a pot for 3 hours to allow the *yoğurt* to thicken.

Finely chop the onion. Heat the vegetable oil in a frying pan over medium heat. Add the onion and sauté for 3 minutes. Add the meat and cook for 5 minutes. Add the beef stock and bring to the boil. Mix in the tomato paste and simmer for 15 minutes.

Chop the stale bread into 2 cm (about 1 in) cubes. Melt half the butter in a frying pan over medium heat. Brush the bread with the melted butter, reserving the remaining butter, then toast in the oven for 5 minutes, or until golden.

Add the bread to the minced meat and mix it through. If you want to thicken it with leftover rice, stir that into the mixture now. Simmer for 5 minutes.

Pour the *papara* into a serving bowl.

Crush the garlic into a smooth paste using a mortar and pestle (or in a bowl with a wooden spoon) and fold it into the *yoğurt*. Pour the garlic *yoğurt* over the dish.

Melt the remaining butter in a small frying pan, add the chilli flakes and paprika, and sizzle for 2 minutes. Pour the butter mixture onto the *yoğurt*. Top with the dried mint and serve.

As a chef, I often get asked: 'What would be your last meal?' I always reply: 'My grandmother's *karnıyarık*. She put something in there that I have never been able to replicate.

This dish first appeared in the nineteenth century on palace menus, but now it's a *lokanta* favourite. The name 'split belly' is not a reference to what the dish will do to you, but what you need to do to the eggplant.

There's a mistaken belief that the previous recipe, *İmam bayıldı* ('The priest fainted'), is just a vegetarian version of this one. The recipes both include eggplant and they look alike, but the other ingredients and the cooking methods are different. And the priest fainted years before the belly got split.

KARNIYARIK
'SPLIT BELLY' (BAKED EGGPLANT STUFFED WITH BEEF)

SERVES 4

4 long eggplants (aubergines)
135 ml (4½ fl oz) vegetable oil,
    plus extra for greasing
1 onion
1 garlic clove
250 g (9 oz) minced (ground) beef
1 tomato
2 tablespoons tomato paste
    (to make your own, see page 24)
½ tablespoon sugar
4 cherry tomatoes, halved
4 long sweet chillies (or 1 green
    bullhorn pepper)
½ tablespoon capsicum (pepper) paste
    (see page 32)
½ teaspoon freshly ground black pepper
½ teaspoon salt
10 flat-leaf (Italian) parsley leaves
rice pilav (see page 27) or boiled rice,
    and plain *yoğurt*, to serve

Slice three strips off the skin of each eggplant, starting about 2 cm (¾ in) below the top and finishing 2 cm (¾ in) above the base. The eggplants should now look like they're wearing striped pyjamas.

Heat 125 ml (4 fl oz/½ cup) of the vegetable oil in a frying pan over high heat. Add a drop of water to the oil: if it sizzles, the oil is ready. Carefully add the eggplants and cook for 2 minutes on each side, or until the exposed flesh is golden. Place the eggplants on paper towel to absorb the excess oil.

Preheat the oven to 180°C (350°F).

Finely dice the onion and slice the garlic. Heat the remaining ½ tablespoon of vegetable oil in a saucepan over medium heat. Add the onion and cook for 5 minutes, or until translucent. Add the garlic and cook for 2 minutes more. Add the beef and cook for 3 minutes, stirring regularly.

Cut the tomato in half and grate it over the mixture, discarding the skin. Dilute 1 tablespoon of the tomato paste in 1 tablespoon of water and stir it into the beef. Cook for 3 minutes more, stirring regularly.

Slit each eggplant lengthways, starting 2 cm (¾ in) from the tip and finishing 2 cm (¾ in) from the base. With the slit facing upwards, use the back of a tablespoon to push the slit open and give the eggplant a canoe shape. Brush a baking tray with oil. Put the eggplant boats onto the greased tray. Add a pinch of sugar to each eggplant and fill each boat with the beef mixture. Cut the chillies in half (or cut the bullhorn pepper in quarters) and remove the stalks and seeds. Place 1 sweet chilli (or a slice of bullhorn pepper) and 1 halved cherry tomato on top of the beef stuffing in each eggplant.

Dilute the remaining 1 tablespoon of tomato paste and the capsicum paste in 250 ml (9 fl oz/1 cup) of boiling water. Spoon the liquid over the eggplants to prevent them drying out while baking. Put the *karnıyarık* in the oven and bake for 20 minutes, until the pepper starts to brown.

Serve one boat per person, hot, with rice pilav or boiled rice, and *yoğurt* on the side.

YUVALAMA
'STORYTELLER SOUP'
(LAMB AND BEEFBALL SOUP)

SERVES 4

95 g (3¼ oz/½ cup) dried chickpeas
440 g (15½ oz/2 cups) medium-grain rice
1 tablespoon salt
750 g (1 lb 10 oz) plain *yoğurt*
250 g (9 oz) lean minced (ground) beef
1 teaspoon ground white pepper
165 g (5¾ oz/1 cup) rice flour
2 onions
2 tablespoons vegetable oil
400 g (14 oz) lamb (preferably lamb leg),
    trimmed and cubed
1 egg
2 tablespoons butter
1 tablespoon dried mint
½ tablespoon chilli flakes

Cover the chickpeas with water and soak overnight. Cover the rice with water, add half the salt, and also soak overnight.

Place the *yoğurt* on a sheet of muslin (cheesecloth) and tie up the corners. Hang the muslin over a pot for 3 hours to allow the *yoğurt* to thicken.

Strain and rinse the chickpeas, place in a saucepan with 500 ml (17 fl oz/2 cups) of water and simmer, covered, for 1 hour.

Strain and rinse the rice, then blend in a food processor or blender. Transfer the rice to a mixing bowl and add the beef and white pepper. Knead the mixture with wet hands for at least 5 minutes, or until it becomes a thick paste—almost like a dough.

Spread the rice flour onto a baking tray. Shape the dough into chickpea-size balls, regularly dipping your hands into the rice flour on the tray to keep them dry. You can roll the balls between your palms three or four at a time. Even so, this will take a long time, so enlist other family members to help, or have a storyteller ready. When all the mixture has been made into balls, space them out on the rice flour so they don't stick together.

Roughly chop the onions. Heat the vegetable oil in a saucepan over medium heat. Add the onion and cook for 2 minutes. Add the cubed pieces of meat and brown for 5 minutes, stirring regularly. Add 1 litre (35 fl oz/4 cups) of water, bring to the boil and simmer, covered, for 20 minutes.

Toss the rice balls lightly in the flour and add them to the meat. Simmer, covered, for another 15 minutes.

Whisk the thickened *yoğurt* and egg in a bowl, then whisk in 250 ml (9 fl oz/1 cup) of the meat cooking liquid. Slowly pour the *yoğurt* mixture into the pan, whisking constantly. Add the simmered chickpeas. Bring the liquid back to the boil and simmer, covered, for 5 minutes.

Melt the butter in a frying pan over medium heat. And the mint and chilli flakes and stir for 2 minutes.

Ladle the soup into four bowls, drizzle the mint and chilli butter over the top and serve.

Hatice Kalan and friends tell stories and prepare tiny *yuvalama* at Yörem restaurant, Gaziantep.

Because this dish takes a long time, it was traditional in the town of Gaziantep to hire a professional storyteller to keep the cooks entertained while they rolled hundreds of tiny balls of meat and rice. *Yuvalama* is consumed in vast quantities during the three-day eating festival called *Bayram* that follows Ramadan.

The word *yuvalama* means 'rolled', and it is said that it takes one person four hours to roll 1 kilo of meatballs. Few restaurants serve *yuvalama* these days, because their kitchen staff just don't have the time, but it remains a signature dish at the Gaziantep restaurant Yörem. Hatice Kalan, a rare female restaurateur in this male-dominated town, sits rolling and storytelling through the afternoon with a bunch of friends and employees. The meatballs they make go into her soup (decorated with a yin and yang of mint oil and paprika oil) and also get sold as takeaway to locals who add them to their own soups at home—grateful not to do all that rolling themselves ...but missing out on the stories.

When I say thin-crust pizza is Italy's answer to *lahmacun* (pronounced 'lah-mahjun'), I'm not trying to start a fight. The idea of putting spiced mince on a disc of dough would have occurred to human beings long before there were nations called Italy or Turkey, or for that matter Armenia, Greece or Syria—all of whom have claimed to be the originators of this addictive pastry.

What we do know is that nowadays *lahmacun* is a speciality of the town of Şanlıurfa, in southeastern Turkey, where they pride themselves on the crispness of their bases. *Lahmacun* should not be confused with the heavier *kıymalı* pide, well known for the thickness of its dough and the coarseness of its meat topping. For *lahmacun* you need a light touch.

In Şanlıurfa, they turn out hundreds of *lahmacun* every lunchtime from big stone ovens. The best way to get the same effect at home is to use a pizza stone or an unglazed terracotta tile, and to ensure your oven is preheated to the max.

LAHMACUN
THIN-CRUST PIDE WITH SPICY LAMB TOPPING

SERVES 4

200 g (7 oz/1⅓ cups) plain (all-purpose) flour, plus extra for dusting
1 teaspoon salt
70 g (2½ oz/½ cup) wholemeal flour (if using a baking tray)

TOPPING

2 tomatoes
1 red capsicum (pepper)
75 g (2½ oz) capsicum (pepper) paste (see page 32)
5 garlic cloves
½ bunch flat-leaf (Italian) parsley
2 teaspoons chilli flakes
1 teaspoon freshly ground black pepper
1 teaspoon salt
200 g (7 oz) minced (ground) lamb (about 25 per cent fat)

RED ONION AND SUMAC SALAD (OPTIONAL)

½ red onion, finely sliced
1 teaspoon salt
1 tablespoon ground sumac
1 tablespoon extra virgin olive oil
juice of ½ lemon, plus extra to serve

Preheat the oven to its maximum temperature (as close to 300°C/570°F as possible). If you have a pizza stone or tile, place it in the oven. Or leave your baking tray in the oven so it will preheat.

Sift the flour into a mixing bowl and add the salt. Make a well in the middle and slowly pour in 125 ml (4 fl oz/½ cup) of lukewarm water. Knead the dough for 5 minutes. Sprinkle some more flour on your work surface and then divide the dough into four balls. Cover the bowl with a damp cloth and leave to rest.

To make the topping, score a shallow cross in the base of the tomatoes, then transfer to a heatproof bowl and cover with boiling water. Leave for 30 seconds, then plunge in cold water and peel the skin away from the cross. Cut the tomatoes in half and scoop out the stalks and seeds with a teaspoon. Roughly chop. Remove the seeds from the capsicum and roughly chop the flesh. Coarsely blend the chopped tomato and capsicum with the capsicum paste, garlic, parsley, chilli flakes, pepper and salt. Combine the mixture with the lamb mince and stir thoroughly.

Place a ball of dough on the floured work surface and, with floured hands or a rolling pin, flatten into a round about 25 cm (10 in) wide and less than 5 mm (¼ in) thick. Repeat with the remaining dough balls.

Using a tablespoon, thinly spread the lamb mixture onto the rounds. Then press it in with your hands.

If you are using a baking tray, take it out of the oven and put a piece of baking paper over it. Dust the baking paper with a little wholemeal flour. Place the rounds of dough on the baking paper and bake for about 5 minutes, or until the edges are crisp.

Meanwhile, if you are making the salad, finely slice the onion and place in a bowl. Sprinkle with salt and sumac, add the olive oil and lemon juice, and then mix together with your hands.

Sprinkle the salad, if using, over each *lahmacun*, squeeze on some lemon juice, and serve.

SAMSUN PİDE
PIDE WITH FOUR CHEESES

SERVES 4

1 tablespoon dried yeast
1 teaspoon sugar
300 g (10½ oz/2 cups) plain (all-purpose)
    flour, plus extra for dusting
150 g (5½ oz/1 cup) strong flour
50 ml (1¾ fl oz) milk
1 teaspoon salt
spoon salad (see page 108), to serve

FOUR-CHEESE FILLING

4 tablespoons each of four different
    cheeses—such as feta, *kaşar* (or
    provolone or mozzarella or any
    semi-hard yellow cheese), *tulum*
    (or aged ricotta or any sharp crumbly
    white cheese) and gorgonzola
    (or any piquant mouldy cheese)
1 egg
2 teaspoons chopped oregano

TOPPING

2 large tomatoes
2 green bullhorn peppers
    (or 1 large green capsicum/pepper)
4 eggs
2 tablespoons vegetable oil

Dissolve the yeast in 50 ml (1¾ fl oz) of lukewarm water. Stir in the sugar and set aside for 5 minutes. The mixture should start to form bubbles.

Sift the flours into a mixing bowl, and make a well in the middle. Pour in the yeast mixture, milk, and 250 ml (9 fl oz/1 cup) of water. Knead the dough for 10 minutes, or until it reaches earlobe softness. Cover the bowl with a damp cloth and rest for 30 minutes to let the dough rise.

Add the salt to the dough and knead for 3 minutes. Place the dough on a floured work surface and form it into a cylinder, then cut it into four equal pieces. Rest for another 10 minutes.

Meanwhile, preheat the oven to 200°C (400°F). If you have a pizza stone or tile, place it in the oven. Or leave your baking tray in the oven so it will preheat.

To prepare the filling, crumble the four cheeses together in a mixing bowl. Break the egg into the bowl and fold it through the cheeses. Pick the oregano leaves off the stalk and finely chop, then stir the oregano through the cheese mixture.

Place a piece of the rested dough on the floured work surface. Using floured hands or a rolling pin, flatten it into an oval about 30 x 20 cm (12 x 8 in) wide and 5 mm (¼ in) thick. Repeat with the remaining dough.

Spoon a thick strip of cheese filling into the middle of each oval, leaving a 5 cm (2 in) gap around the edge. Fold over the two longer edges so they touch the filling but don't cover it. Join the folded edges at the top and bottom to make a boat shape. Press each end into a point and twist to close tightly.

To prepare the topping, finely slice the tomatoes. Halve the bullhorn peppers, remove the stalk and seeds, and finely slice. Put six slices of tomato and four slices of pepper on each pide, and break an egg into the middle.

If you are using a baking tray, take it out of the oven and put a piece of baking paper over it. Dust the baking paper with a little flour. If you are using a pizza stone or tile, sprinkle a little flour on it. Place the pides on the baking paper (or stone or tile) and brush the tops with teh vegetable oil. Bake for 15 minutes, or until golden brown.

Serve warm, with a spoon salad.

Samsun is a city on the Black Sea famous for its pide—a thick form of flatbread that's not the same as pita or pizza. The defining qualities of a Samsun pide are: the dough contains the highest-quality flour, cheese and eggs; it is rolled out by hand, not with a rolling pin; it is pulled into a boat shape that can hold a stuffing; and it is baked in a wood-fire oven.

In this case, the passengers on the boat are cheeses, tomatoes and a fried egg, but don't get hung up on finding four different cheeses—three or even two will do, as long as they contrast in texture and flavour.

And by the way, we do not agree with the claim by some bold Turks that our pide gave birth to Italy's pizza.

My ancestors are Tartars who moved to central Anatolia from an area that is now close to Russia on the Black Sea. This is one of their dishes. Using raw beef (the meaning of the word *çiğ* in the Turkish name), you must knead it tenderly before stuffing it inside *yoğurt* pastry in a half-moon shape. It is vital to seal the pastry tightly, so the meat steams inside, without making contact with the frying oil.

ÇİĞ BÖREK
HALF-MOON PASTRY WITH BEEF AND CHILLI

SERVES 4

2 tablespoons plain *yoğurt*
100 ml (3½ fl oz) vegetable oil
2 teaspoons salt
juice of ½ lemon
1 egg
750 g (1 lb 10 oz/5 cups) plain
    (all-purpose) flour, plus extra
    for dusting
500 ml (17 fl oz/2 cups) vegetable oil

STUFFING
1 brown onion
250 g (9 oz) minced (ground) beef
1 tablespoon chilli flakes
1 tablespoon freshly ground black pepper
½ tablespoon salt
5 ice cubes

Mix the *yoğurt*, vegetable oil, salt and lemon juice in a bowl. Break the egg into the mixture and whisk. Sift the flour into the mixture, add 250 ml (9 fl oz/1 cup) of water and knead for 10 minutes into a soft dough. Cover the bowl with a damp cloth and let it rest for 30 minutes.

Sprinkle a little extra flour on your work surface. Divide the dough into ten pieces, then roll into balls. Return the dough to the bowl, cover again with a damp cloth and rest for 15 minutes.

Meanwhile, make the stuffing. Finely chop the onion, then combine it with the minced beef, chilli flakes, pepper and salt.

Wrap the ice cubes in a tea towel and crush into small pieces. Add the crushed ice to the meat mixture and knead until it dissolves. The meat mixture should be very moist, but not runny. If it seems watery, pour off the excess water.

Place a ball of dough on the floured work surface and, with floured hands or a rolling pin, flatten into a round 25 cm (10 in) wide and about 2 mm (about 1/16 in) thick. Imagine each round is two half-moons joined together. Put 2 tablespoons of the stuffing in the middle of the right half-moon, leaving a 5 cm (2 in) gap around it. Fold the other half of the dough over. Dip your fingers in water and press down all around the edges to tightly seal the package. Fold 1 cm (½ in) of the outer edge over to 'double lock' it. This ensures the filling will stay moist when cooked. Repeat with the remaining dough and stuffing.

Heat the vegetable oil in a deep frying pan over high heat. Add a drop of water to the oil: if it sizzles, the oil is ready. Add the *böreks*, two at a time, and cook for 2 minutes, until they start to puff up. Turn over and cook for 1 minute more, or until the *böreks* have golden-brown spots. Scoop the *böreks* out of the oil and rest on paper towel. Repeat with the remaining pastries.

Serve two *böreks* per person, with a glass of *ayran* or basil lemonade.

SU BÖREĞI
WATER PASTRY WITH FETA AND KALE

SERVES 4

8 kale leaves
1 bunch flat-leaf (Italian) parsley
3 garlic shoots (or 1 garlic clove)
1 heaped tablespoon plain *yoğurt*
250 g (9 oz) hard feta
4 eggs
2 teaspoons salt
500 g (1 lb 2 oz) strong flour,
    plus extra for dusting
2 tablespoons olive oil
300 g (10½ oz) butter

Put the kale in a heatproof bowl and cover with boiling water. Leave for 30 seconds, then plunge in cold water. Remove the white stalks and finely chop the leaves.

Discard the parsley stalks and finely chop the leaves. Finely chop the garlic shoots (or crush the garlic) and mix in a bowl with the *yoğurt* and chopped kale. Crumble the feta into the mixture.

Whisk the eggs in a deep mixing bowl. Add 1 tablespoon of water and the salt. Sift the flour into the bowl and mix well. Knead for 10 minutes, or until the mixture becomes a hard dough. Dust your work surface with extra flour and divide the dough into eleven balls. Dust the dough with flour and let it rest in a bowl, covered with a damp cloth, for 15 minutes.

Flour a board and, using a thin rolling pin, roll each ball into a 30 cm (12 in) wide round. (Turning the dough on the work surface 90 degrees at a time will ensure a circular pastry.) You can stack the eleven sheets while you do the next step, but be sure to scatter plenty of flour between the sheets so they don't stick together.

Pour the olive oil into a large non-stick frying pan and brush to coat. (The pan should be at least 25 cm/10 in across and 10 cm/4 in deep.) Warm the butter in a small saucepan.

Fill a deep saucepan with water and bring to the boil. Using a thin rolling pin or the handle of a long wooden spoon, lift one round of dough at a time and dunk it into the boiling water for 2 minutes. Lift out and pat dry on a clean cloth. Repeat with the remaining rounds of dough.

Place a round of dough in the large oiled non-stick frying pan and brush with butter. Slice around it to remove any overlap, and scatter the sliced-off bits on top of it. Place another dough round loosely on top, and brush with butter. Continue to stack to make six layers. Spread the kale and cheese mixture on the sixth layer, then continue to stack another four buttered layers. Cut the final (eleventh) layer to fit as a round over the top (discarding any leftover pastry). Pour the remaining butter on top.

Place the pan over medium heat and cook for 10 minutes, constantly tilting the pan to prevent the bottom layer sticking. Place a large plate over the frying pan and, with one hand on the plate and the other hand on the handle, upend the pastry onto the plate.

Brush the inside of the pan again with olive oil and slide the upturned *börek* into the pan—with the cooked layer now on top. Cook for 8 minutes.

Cut across the *börek* to make four quarters (with one wedge per person). Serve in the pan, with glasses of *ayran* to accompany the meal.

Although the *börek* translated as 'water pastry' is usually credited to the central Anatolian cities of Ankara and Çorum, ancient cookbooks reveal the Romans were layering lasagne, under the name *laganum*, in the first century—which was when they moved into Byzantion in northwest Anatolia. So we should probably credit the Romans with starting the fad for layering dough with cheese and greens between. Getting it right is a laborious process, because you must boil and butter each of the eleven layers, then fry or bake the whole thing. But the result is worth the effort, as our Italian culinary cousins would agree.

Normally in my restaurant I cook water *börek* in the oven in a rectangular tray, and slice it into squares (as shown above). For this recipe though, I suggest you use a round, deep frying pan, and slice the *börek* into wedges, which makes it look less like lasagne, but is easier to work with.

Here's another dish with an Italian connection. Italians are known in Turkey as *makarnacı*, which literally translates as 'macaroni maker' or 'pasta maker', because the suffix -ci means 'maker of' or 'doer of'. On the same principle, an Argentinian is a *tangocu* (a tango maker) and Brazilians are *sambacı*.

What the Turks call *erişte* is a flat ribbon pasta the macaroni makers call tagliatelle or fettuccine. We can trace the Turkish version back to the fifteenth century, when a central Anatolian doctor called Şirvani wrote

that *erişte* should be made from flour kneaded with egg whites, cut into thin strips and dried in the sun. In the sixteenth century, palace chefs were boiling it in soup.

Turks like to eat their pasta bland, usually just tossed with butter. I've boosted the flavour with dried mullet roe —what the Italians call *bottarga* and Turks call *mumlu havyar* (which sounds like caviar for a reason). The best *havyar* is from the beautiful Dalyan region, where the Mediterranean and Aegean coasts meet. There they eat their bottarga with bread, and take their *erişte* straight.

CEVİZLİ ERİŞTE
EGG PASTA WITH WALNUT AND BOTTARGA

SERVES 4

3 eggs
150 ml (5 fl oz) milk
500 g (1 lb 2 oz) plain (all-purpose) flour
   (preferably durum wheat), plus extra
   for dusting
1 teaspoon salt, plus extra for cooking
   the *erişte*

WALNUT SAUCE
1 tablespoon butter
100 g (3½ oz) walnuts
1 teaspoon ground turmeric
45 ml (1½ fl oz) thickened (whipping)
   cream
100 g (3½ oz) sharp white cheese
   (such as barrel-aged feta)
1 tablespoon chopped tarragon
1 tablespoon finely grated bottarga
   (or 2 tablespoons fresh mullet roe)

Whisk the eggs and milk together with a fork. Sift the flour into a mixing bowl, make a well in the middle and add the salt. Pour in the egg mixture and knead for 10 minutes, until the mixture is stretchy. Cover the bowl with a damp cloth and rest for 30 minutes.

Knead the pasta dough for 5 minutes, making sure there are no bubbles. Dust your work surface with flour and divide the dough into three balls. With floured hands or a rolling pin, flatten a ball of dough into a round 30 cm (12 in) wide and less than 5 mm (¼ in) thick. Repeat with the remaining dough. Rest in a warm spot (preferably in direct sunlight) for 30 minutes. (You could drape them over your clothesline, or over a rolling pin between two chairs.)

Place the rounds on the floured work surface and cut into strips about 5 mm (¼ in) wide and 5 cm (2 in) long. Don't worry if the shapes are irregular. If you have a pasta machine, you can follow the same process and make the strips as if they were fettuccine.

Bring a large saucepan of salted water to the boil. Add the *erişte* and boil for 2 minutes.

Meanwhile, make the walnut sauce. Melt the butter in a large frying pan over low heat, then add the walnuts, turmeric and cream.

Toss the cooked *erişte* in the sauce for 1 minute over low heat. Transfer to a bowl and grate the cheese over the top. Sprinkle on the tarragon. Finely grate the bottarga over the top and serve.

KAYSERİ MANTI
TWICE-COOKED MINI BEEF DUMPLINGS

SERVES 4

375 g (13 oz/2½ cups) plain (all-purpose)
    flour, plus extra for dusting
½ teaspoon salt
2 eggs
1 tablespoon dried mint
1 tablespoon ground sumac

BEEF MINCE STUFFING
2 onions
250 g (9 oz) lean minced (ground) beef
½ teaspoon ground nutmeg
1 teaspoon salt
1 teaspoon freshly ground black pepper

COOKING WATER
1 tablespoon butter
2 tablespoons olive oil
1 tomato
1 tablespoon tomato paste
    (to make your own, see page 24)
1 tablespoon salt

YOĞURT SAUCE
2 garlic cloves
500 g (1 lb 2 oz/2 cups) plain *yoğurt*

PAPRIKA BUTTER
4 tablespoons butter
2 tablespoons smoked paprika
1 tablespoon chilli flakes

Sift the flour into a mixing bowl, make a well in the middle and add the salt. Break in the eggs. Add 3 tablespoons of water and knead for 10 minutes, until the dough is stretchy. Cover the bowl with a damp cloth and rest for 30 minutes.

Meanwhile, to make the stuffing, grate the onions into a bowl, add the remaining ingredients and knead for 3 minutes to combine.

Dust your work surface with flour and divide the dough in half. Using a thin rolling pin, roll out each piece as thinly as you can, using plenty of flour to prevent sticking. Using a sharp knife or a rolling wheel, cut each dough sheet into 3 cm (1¼ in) squares.

Have a bowl of water handy for dipping your fingers. Using the tip of a teaspoon, place a lump of the beef stuffing, about the size of a chickpea, into the middle of one square. Wetting your fingers, pull the four corners of each square together above the filling and press the points together. Repeat with the remaining dough sheets. You should end up with about 200 small dumplings (50 per person). Warning: this will take a long time ...

Preheat the oven to 180°C (350°F).

Sprinkle some flour on a wide baking tray. Place each *manti* on the tray as you finish them, making sure they don't stick to each other. Put the tray in the oven for 10 minutes to dry the *manti* but not completely cook them.

To prepare the *manti* cooking water, heat the butter and olive oil in a large saucepan over medium heat. Halve the tomato and grate it into the oil, discarding the skin. Add the tomato paste and stir for 2 minutes. Add 1 litre (35 fl oz/4 cups) of water and the salt, and bring to the boil. Reduce the heat to medium, add the *manti* and boil for 8 minutes.

While the *manti* are cooking, make the *yoğurt* sauce by crushing the garlic and mixing it with the *yoğurt*.

To make the paprika butter, melt the butter in a small frying pan. Stir in the smoked paprika and the chilli flakes and sizzle for 2 minutes.

Use a serving spoon to scoop the *manti* into four bowls. Discard the cooking water. Pour 3 tablespoons of garlic *yoğurt* into each bowl, drizzle with paprika butter, top with a pinch of dried mint and sumac, and serve.

If I had to nominate three dishes that I am confident originated with the ethnic group called the Turks (who arrived in Anatolia from Central Asia in the eleventh century), I would say *yoğurt, pastırma* and the wrapped dumplings we call *mantı* (pronounced 'mant-uh').

Mantı are often labelled 'the Turkish ravioli', but given their Asian origin, it would be more appropriate to call them 'the Turkish wonton'. Versions are served all around Turkey, as well as in several countries to the northeast, but the most famous are the ridiculously small ones from Kayseri in central Anatolia. Apparently they were designed as a torture test by mothers-in-law, because 'a good bride should be able to make *mantı* so small you can fit 40 of them on one spoon'.

So I'm not being cruel here by asking you to cut the dough into 3 cm (1¼ in) squares—the usual size in Kayseri is around 1 cm (½ in) square.

MARRIED AND FEASTED IN ANATOLIA

The next three dishes are served at wedding feasts in rural Turkey. Here's what happens first ...

Boy meets girl. Boy tells his mother this girl might be the one for him. Mother makes inquiries in the village to check out girl's suitability, then contacts her mother, saying, 'We would like to visit you for a good reason.' Girl's mother has a pretty good idea what this means, and replies: 'Would you like to come over for afternoon tea?'

Girl's mother asks the girl if she's interested in the boy, and if she gets the reply 'It's up to you', she tells the father there may be an offer to consider. (If the girl is not interested, the afternoon tea would still go ahead, but it would not end happily.)

On the appointed day, boy's family brings Turkish delight and baklava, beautifully packaged. Girl's family serves tea and other pastries, on the principle '*Tatlı ye, tatlı konuş*' ('Eat sweet, talk sweet').

Girl is not present during the family chat, but if the conversation goes well, her mother will ask her to make coffee for everybody. She might then put salt instead of sugar into the cup intended for her suitor, in order to test his manners. If he compliments her on the coffee, he will be a patient husband.

Assuming everybody is getting on well, boy and girl will now be allowed to go out together, accompanied by a chaperone,

of course. This will progress to a small ring, which means they are 'promised', followed by a bigger ring, which means they are engaged. Girl's family will pay for the engagement party.

On the day before the wedding, girl will have her hands coloured with henna, and on the morning of the wedding, boy will be shaved by the town barber. Everyone in the village—and anybody who happens to be passing through town—will be invited to the festivities.

After the imam has conducted the formalities, the bride will then ride into the town square on horseback, carrying the possessions she will bring to the marriage and accompanied by drummers, clarinet players and car horns. And so the feasting begins.

This was where we came in. Photographer Bree Hutchins and I were chatting to a farmer selling peppers and eggplants in the markets at Bodrum, on Turkey's west coast. The young farmer took a liking to us (to be honest, more to Bree) and asked if we'd like to come to his cousin's wedding feast. We said of course.

We arrived on the third day of a five-day festival. The food was cooking in huge pots all around the square. They'd slaughtered cattle and sheep specially for the occasion, which they were roasting over open fires. The three dishes you are about to read about were a tiny part of the banquet.

The bride and her brother at a Yörük wedding in the Aegean village of Milas.

This is a yoğurt soup with chicken or lamb meat, usually cooked over an open fire and served early in a wedding feast for up to 1000 invited guests from surrounding villages. A wedding feast can continue for five days, with cooking duties alternating between the bride's family and the groom's family. This dish takes 24 hours to prepare, so better hope the bride doesn't change her mind.

DÜĞÜN CORBASI
WEDDING SOUP WITH CHICKEN AND YOĞURT

SERVES 8

50 g (1¾ oz/¼ cup) dried chickpeas
500 g (1 lb 2 oz/2 cups) plain *yoğurt*
1 small chicken
220 g (8 oz/1 cup) medium-grain rice
1 teaspoon salt
1 egg
2 tablespoons plain (all-purpose) flour
2 tablespoons butter
2 teaspoons dried mint
2 teaspoons paprika

Cover the chickpeas with water and soak overnight.

Strain and rinse the chickpeas. Place the *yoğurt* on a sheet of muslin (cheesecloth) and tie up the corners. Hang the muslin over a pot for 3 hours to allow the *yoğurt* to thicken.

Put the chicken and chickpeas in a large saucepan, cover with water and boil, with the lid on, for 30 minutes. Take out the chicken and remove the skin. Strip off the meat and shred, then set aside. Put the chicken bones and skin back in the pan and boil for a further 15 minutes, with the chickpeas, to make a stock.

Pour 500 ml (17 fl oz/2 cups) of the stock into another saucepan. Rinse the rice. Add the rice and salt to the pan and bring it to the boil. Boil for 10 minutes, until not quite soft.

Whisk the egg and flour together in a bowl. Add the *yoğurt* and 2 tablespoons of the warm chicken stock and combine.

Take the carcass and skin out of the stock, and discard. Add the *yoğurt* mixture to the stock and slowly simmer for 5 minutes, stirring constantly. Slowly pour in the strained rice and continue to stir. Bring to the boil over medium heat and add the shredded chicken. Reduce the heat and simmer for another 10 minutes.

Divide the soup into four bowls. Heat 1 tablespoon of butter in a frying pan. Once it sizzles, add the mint and stir for about 30 seconds. Drizzle it over the soup in splashes. Heat the remaining butter and add the paprika. Sizzle for 30 seconds, then drizzle it over the soup in spaces not covered by the mint butter.

Serve with pide and pride.

EZO GELİN
'EZO THE BRIDE'
(RED LENTIL AND BULGUR SOUP)

Ezo the Bride is a famous figure in Turkish folklore. Her real name was Zöhre Bozgeyik, and she was born in 1909 in southeastern Anatolia. She married a local musician and, following the regional Berdel tradition, her brother married her husband's sister. A few years later, her brother divorced his wife, which meant that although Ezo dearly loved her husband, she had to follow local custom and separate from him. Beautiful Ezo was forced to travel to Syria and marry a distant relative and, according to a popular song, she died there in 1956 of sorrow and homesickness. Her deathbed wish was for her remains to be buried in her home village, Dokuzyol. This soup comes from a happy time in her life.

SERVES 8

1.5 litres (52 fl oz/6 cups) beef stock
2 onions
2 tablespoons sunflower oil
2 tablespoons tomato paste
   (to make your own, see page 24)
1 tablespoon capsicum (pepper) paste
   (see page 32)
1 teaspoon hot paprika
115 g (4 oz/½ cup) medium-grain rice
200 g (7 oz/1 cup red lentils
90 g (3 oz/½ cup) fine bulgur
2 teaspoons salt
2 teaspoons freshly ground
   black pepper
2 mint sprigs, chopped

PAPRIKA BUTTER
1 tablespoon butter
1 tablespoon hot paprika
1 bird's eye chilli, finely chopped
   (optional)

Pour the beef stock into a pot and bring to the boil. Reduce the heat to a simmer.

Meanwhile, finely chop the onions. Heat the sunflower oil in a frying pan over medium heat. Add the onion and cook for 3 minutes, until soft. Dissolve the tomato and capsicum pastes in 250 ml (9 fl oz/1 cup) of the beef stock, add the paprika, and then stir the mixture into the cooking onion. Pour the onion mixture into the simmering beef stock.

Rinse the rice, red lentils and bulgur, then add to the pot. Cover and cook for 20 minutes, or until the lentils are soft. Season with the salt and black pepper, then ladle the soup into four bowls.

To make the paprika butter, melt the butter in a small frying pan, add the paprika (and chopped chilli if you want extra heat), and sizzle for 1 minute.

Top each bowl with chopped mint and drops of paprika butter, and serve.

KEŞKEK
LAMB AND BARLEY PORRIDGE

Keşkek is now served at village weddings all over Anatolia, but it originated with the Yörük people (nomadic Turks from Central Asia). For the authentic version, you'd need a brass pot as big as a bathtub, a bonfire, and 200 single men with thick pounding poles. Traditionally, a whole sheep or cow is boiled with pearl barley, then pulled out of the pot so the bones can be removed, then put back in and pounded for about an hour by the single men of the village until it becomes a paste. This recipe is a compromise.

SERVES 8

1 kg (2 lb 4 oz) pearl barley
1 lamb neck, about 1 kg (2 lb 4 oz)
1 teaspoon salt
2 onions
1 tablespoon sunflower oil
3 tablespoons butter, melted
1 teaspoon ground cinnamon

TOMATO SAUCE
1 tablespoon butter
1 tablespoon tomato paste (to make
    your own, see page 24)
½ teaspoon salt
½ teaspoon freshly ground black pepper
1 teaspoon dried oregano

Cover the barley with water and soak for 8 hours.

Cut the lamb neck into four pieces and place in a large saucepan with the drained barley. Cover with water, bring to the boil and then cook for 1½ hours, or until the barley and meat are tender.

Scoop out the pieces of neck and remove the bones. Shred the meat. Strain the barley and combine it with the meat in a large bowl. Add the salt.

Dice the onions. Heat the sunflower oil in a frying pan over medium heat. Add the onion and sauté for 5 minutes, until translucent. Add the onion to the meat and barley, and pound the mixture with a wooden spoon until it reaches a paste-like consistency.

To make the tomato sauce, melt the butter in a frying pan over low heat. Stir in the tomato paste, salt, pepper and dried oregano. When the mixture sizzles, remove the pan from the heat.

Serve the *keşkek* in a big bowl in the middle of the table for people to help themselves. Drizzle the tomato sauce and the melted butter over the top. Sprinkle on the cinnamon and serve.

GAVURDAĞ
'SPOON SALAD' (CHOPPED TOMATO, WALNUT AND SUMAC SALAD)

SERVES 4

6 ripe tomatoes
1 red onion
1 bunch mint
½ bunch flat-leaf (Italian) parsley
115 g (4 oz/1 cup) walnuts
3 green bullhorn peppers
   (or 1 green capsicum/pepper)
1 green chilli
1 tablespoon ground sumac
2 tablespoons pomegranate molasses
   (to make your own, see page 24)
60 ml (2 fl oz/¼ cup) olive oil
1 teaspoon apple cider vinegar
1 teaspoon sea salt
150 g (5½ oz/½ cup) pomegranate
   seeds

Quarter the tomatoes, remove the white centres and then finely chop. Finely chop the red onion. Discard the mint and parsley stalks and finely chop the leaves. Finely chop the walnuts. Cut the bullhorn peppers and the chilli in half, and remove the seeds and stalks. Finely chop. Mix all the chopped ingredients together in a salad bowl.

Mix the sumac, pomegranate molasses, olive oil, apple cider vinegar and salt together, pour onto the salad and toss.

Sprinkle the pomegranate seeds on top and serve.

SUMMER VARIATION
Leave out the walnuts and replace the mint and parsley with two bunches of purslane (or baby rocket/arugula if you can't find purslane).

A couple of hours before you want to serve the salad, make a pomegranate granita. Here's how: put about eight ice cubes in a heavy-duty zip-lock bag with 150 g (5½ oz/½ cup) of pomegranate seeds and 2 tablespoons of pomegranate molasses. Wrap a thick kitchen cloth around the bag (to absorb the pressure, so the plastic doesn't tear with the impact), and give it a few good bashes with the back of a soup ladle. Pick out the pomegranate seeds. Keep the bag of crushed pink ice in the freezer until you are ready to serve.

Put the salad on the table in a big bowl. Scrape the pomegranate granita into a smaller bowl, sprinkle some extra pomegranate seeds on top and put it next to the salad. Let your guests serve themselves, with a heaped spoonful of granita on each plate, surrounded by four spoonfuls of salad. Eat slowly. Finish slurping the salad with a spoon.

This salad is served with *kebaps* all over Turkey, and is designed to be eaten with a spoon. It's just a finely chopped salad, with the tomato pieces no bigger than the pomegranate seeds, but you will see it on menus in Istanbul described as the famous '*Gavurdağ*' salad (apparently named after a mountain in southeast Anatolia).

My friend Musa points out in his scholarly journal *Yemek ve Kültür* (Food and Culture) that there's a trend in Turkey for chefs to give obscure names to standard dishes in an attempt to suggest authentic regional origins. This could well be one of those.

In summer, you can make this a salad that turns into a cold soup (a gazpacho, to be precise). I've given a variation that involves putting a pomegranate granita on top. It looks very trendy, but is actually very traditional.

This is my attempt to recreate a memory. As a teenager, I used to buy sandwiches from fishermen who would moor their boats next to one of the pillars of the Galata Bridge, just across the road from Istanbul's spice market. They would fillet their catch and cook fish pieces over a little charcoal grill, then shove them inside pide. Nowadays, this has turned into a tourist experience, where colourful boats, permanently moored, sell frozen fish cooked on flat griddles.

You can come close to the original experience by walking across to the other side of the Galata Bridge and turning left into the fish market.

There they sell genuine fish sandwiches from carts in the street. They use locally caught fish and cook them over charcoal. They then add salad and lemon—rather than the walnut tarator sauce in this recipe, which is my improvement on the memory.

BALIK EKMEK
WHITING SANDWICH WITH TARATOR

SERVES 4

8 school whiting
185 g (6½ oz/1¼ cups) plain
   (all-purpose) flour
2 teaspoons salt
1 teaspoon freshly ground black pepper
250 ml (9 fl oz/1 cup) soda water
250 ml (9 fl oz/1 cup) vegetable oil
pide bread, to serve (to make your
   own, see page 45)

TARATOR

15 g (½ oz/¼ cup) breadcrumbs
60 g (2 oz/½ cup) walnuts
2 garlic cloves
juice of ½ lemon
pinch of salt
60 ml (2 fl oz/¼ cup) extra virgin
   olive oil

ROCKET SALAD

12 large rocket (arugula) leaves
1 bunch flat-leaf (Italian) parsley
1 red onion
1 tablespoon chilli flakes
1 tablespoon red wine vinegar
60 ml (2 fl oz/¼ cup) extra virgin
   olive oil
2 teaspoons salt
juice of ½ lemon

First make the *tarator*. Soak the breadcrumbs in 60 ml (2 fl oz/¼ cup) of water for 5 minutes. Put the breadcrumbs, walnuts, garlic, lemon juice and salt in a food processor, and pulse. While you're pulsing, slowly add the olive oil—you are aiming for a spreadable paste like mustard, so add a little more water if it does not seem smooth enough.

Now make the salad. Remove the stalks from the rocket and the parsley. Finely chop the leaves. Finely chop the onion. Mix the leaves, onion, chilli flakes, red wine vinegar and olive oil together in a bowl, then add the salt and lemon juice.

Next, prepare the fish. Slice each fish through the stomach, removing the gut. Butterfly each fish and remove the spine and any bones. Cut off and discard the heads and tails and wash the fish thoroughly. Pat the fish dry and dust in about 35 g (1¼ oz/¼ cup) of the flour.

Put the remaining flour in a mixing bowl and add the salt and pepper. Make a well in the middle and whisk in the soda water to make a batter.

Heat the vegetable oil in a deep frying pan over high heat. Add a drop of water to the oil: if it sizzles, the oil is ready.

Dip the fish in the batter, allowing the excess to drip off. Carefully lower the fish into the hot oil and fry for 2 minutes on each side, or until golden. Using a slotted spatula, remove the fish from the pan and place on paper towel to absorb the excess oil.

Cut each pide in half. Spread the *tarator* on the top and bottom. Put the fillets from two fish on each sandwich, then 2 tablespoons of salad, then close the lid. Serve with a glass of *şalgam*.

KADINBUDU
'LADIES' THIGHS' (VEAL MEATBALLS WITH RICE AND EGGS)

Probably because of the puritanism of their governments over the centuries, Turks have expressed their fascination with anatomy in their approach to naming foodstuffs. There are treats called woman's bellybutton, vizier's finger, lady's lips, sluts' dumplings and brothel donuts. The plump patties in this recipe made from young cows obviously reminded some nineteenth-century chef of a pleasant experience. The first published mention of this kind of *köfte*, using mince, watercress and eggs, appears in a Persian dictionary published around 1800—under a more polite name.

SERVES 4

1 onion
2 garlic cloves
2 tablespoons vegetable oil
500 g (1 lb 2 oz) minced (ground) veal
115 g (4 oz/½ cup) medium-grain rice
2 teaspoons salt
1 teaspoon freshly ground black pepper
1 teaspoon ground cumin
1 teaspoon ground pimento
2 tablespoons chopped marjoram leaves
3 eggs
150 g (5½ oz/1 cup) plain
    (all-purpose) flour
250 ml (9 fl oz/1 cup) vegetable oil,
    for frying
Spoon salad (see page 108), to serve

Finely chop the onion and garlic. Heat the vegetable oil in a frying pan over medium heat. Add the onion and garlic and sauté for 3 minutes, until soft. Add half the veal mince and stir. Cook for 5 minutes, to evaporate any water it puts out. Transfer to a mixing bowl.

Wash the rice under cold running water. Pour 250 ml (9 fl oz/1 cup) of water into a saucepan. Add the rice and salt, and bring to the boil. Boil for 10 minutes, until soft. Strain.

Add the rice to the cooked mince, then add the spices and marjoram. Break 1 egg into the mixture.

Add the remaining raw veal mince. Knead with wet hands for 5 minutes to combine. Cover the bowl with a damp cloth or plastic wrap and rest in the fridge for 30 minutes. Divide the mixture into eight rounds, each about the size of an egg, then flatten each into a patty about 1–2 cm (½–¾ in) thick.

Put the flour in a bowl. Lightly beat the remaining eggs in a separate bowl. Coat both sides of each patty in the flour and dip in the egg.

Heat the vegetable oil in a frying pan over medium heat. Toss a drop of water into the oil: if it sizzles, the oil is ready. Carefully add four patties to the pan and cook for 3 minutes on each side, or until golden brown. Using a spatula, remove the patties from the pan and place on paper towel to absorb the excess oil. Repeat with the remaining patties.

Serve two *kadınbudu* per person, with the spoon salad.

ISLAK
KIDS' SOGGY BURGER

This is my adaptation of a relatively new street snack, usually found in takeaway joints around Taksim Square in Istanbul, and designed for consumption when you are drunk. It's a kind of slider, except the sauce is not inside the bun but all around it. When I first tried *islak*, I asked the shopkeeper what was in the sauce. He said it was a trade secret. I hung around for a while, and saw him pouring the fat that had collected under his *döner kebap* rotisserie into a mixture of tomato and peppers. I decided not to replicate this, and instead boosted the sauce with ground herbs, spices, and a plum.

My kids love soggy burgers because they are messy and full of flavour. This version won't give them heart conditions.

SERVES 4

100 g (3½ oz) breadcrumbs
1 tablespoon white vinegar
1 onion
2 tablespoons chopped flat-leaf
   (Italian) parsley
200 g (7 oz) minced (ground) lamb
   (preferably from breast)
400 g (14 oz) minced (ground) veal
1 egg
1 teaspoon salt
1 tablespoon vegetable oil
8 brioche or burger buns

SPICE MIX*

1 teaspoon dried oregano
2 teaspoons ground coriander
2 teaspoons ground cumin
¼ teaspoon ground pimento
1 teaspoon sweet paprika
1 teaspoon hot paprika
¼ teaspoon freshly ground black pepper
1 dried bay leaf

BURGER SAUCE

1 tablespoon butter
2 tablespoons tomato paste (to make
   your own, see page 24)
1 plum
500 ml (17 fl oz/2 cups) beef stock
1 teaspoon salt
1 teaspoon freshly ground black pepper
1 teaspoon dried mint

To make the spice mix, use a spice grinder or a food processor to grind the oregano into a powder. Mix all the spices together with the bay leaf. You can keep this powder in a sealed container for up to 3 months.

Put the breadcrumbs in a mixing bowl and moisten with 1 tablespoon of water and the vinegar. Finely grate the onion into the bowl. Stir in the parsley. Add the lamb and veal, break the egg in, then add the salt and ½ tablespoon of the spice mix. Knead with wet hands for 10 minutes, until the mixture turns into a paste.

Cover the bowl with a damp cloth or plastic wrap and rest in the fridge for 1 hour.

Divide the meat mixture into eight balls, about the size of billiard balls. With wet hands, flatten each ball into a patty about 2 cm (¾ in) thick.

To make the burger sauce, melt the butter in a saucepan over medium heat, add the tomato paste and stir for 1 minute. Finely chop the plum and add. Add the beef stock, salt, pepper and dried mint, bring to the boil, then reduce over low heat for 10 minutes.

To cook the *köfte*, heat the vegetable oil over medium heat. Fry four patties at a time for 4 minutes on each side, until brown, then place on paper towel to absorb the excess oil. Repeat with the remaining *köfte*.

Slice the buns in half. Put a patty in each bun. Dunk each bun into the hot sauce and squash down with a wooden spoon. Remove from the pan and serve two buns per person, with plenty of paper towels for wiping hands.

*NOTE
If you have a spice mill, buy coriander, cumin and pimento seeds, and grind them with the dried oregano. Alternatively, buy all ingredients except the bay leaf in powdered form.

TEKİRDAĞ KÖFTE
VEAL MEATBALLS WITH WHITE BEAN AND TAHINI SALAD

SERVES 4

KÖFTE

3 tablespoons breadcrumbs
½ teaspoon bicarbonate of soda (baking soda)
1 onion
1 garlic clove
500 g (1 lb 2 oz) minced (ground) veal (about 20 per cent fat)
1 teaspoon ground cumin
1 teaspoon salt
½ teaspoon ground pimento
½ teaspoon freshly ground black pepper
½ teaspoon chilli flakes
1 egg
½ tablespoon fine semolina

WHITE BEAN AND TAHINI SALAD

200 g (14 oz/2 cups) dried white cannellini beans
½ teaspoon sugar
1½ teaspoons salt
3 tablespoons tahini
3 tablespoons olive oil
juice of 1 lemon
2 tablespoons apple cider vinegar
½ bunch flat-leaf (Italian) parsley
½ bunch spring onions (scallions)
1 French shallot (eschalot), chopped
8 cherry tomatoes
8 quail eggs
2 teaspoons ground sumac
4 long yellow chillies

To make the *köfte*, put the breadcrumbs in a mixing bowl and moisten with 2 tablespoons of water. Stir in the bicarbonate of soda. Finely grate the onion and crush the garlic. Put the meat in the mixing bowl and then add the onion, garlic and the remaining *köfte* ingredients. Knead with wet hands for 15 minutes, until the mixture becomes a smooth paste. Cover the bowl with a damp cloth or plastic wrap and rest in the fridge overnight.

Meanwhile, make a start on the salad. Cover the dried cannellini beans with boiling water and leave overnight.

Strain and rinse the soaked beans, place in a saucepan with the sugar, cover with water and bring to the boil. Strain the beans and discard the water. Cover again with even more fresh water, add 1 teaspoon of the salt and boil, covered, for 1 hour.

Strain the beans, then transfer to a large salad bowl.

Dilute the tahini in 2 tablespoons of water. Add the olive oil, lemon juice, vinegar and the remaining ½ teaspoon of salt. Mix the tahini dressing through the beans.

Pick the leaves from the parsley and finely chop. Wash the spring onions, then remove the roots and tough outer leaves, and finely chop. Stir the parsley and spring onion through the salad. Finely slice the shallot. Sprinkle the pieces over the beans. Quarter the cherry tomatoes and spread them over the top.

Preheat the barbecue hotplate or a grill pan. Add a drop of water: if it sizzles, the grill is ready.

Meanwhile, bring a small saucepan of water to the boil, add the quail eggs and boil for 3 minutes. Remove the eggs with a slotted spoon and run them under cold running water. Remove the shells, slice in half and place the halves on top of the salad. Sprinkle a little sumac over the eggs.

Divide the ball of *köfte* into patties about 1 cm (½ in) thick and about 6 cm (2½ in) wide. Make indentations with your hand across the top. Put the patties on the barbecue and cook for 2 minutes on each side, until brown. (If you are using a grill pan, cook for 4 minutes each side.) Char the yellow chillies until the skin is slightly blackened.

Serve four *köfte* per person, with the bean salad and the grilled yellow chillies.

The west coast city of Tekirdağ is known for two things: its exceptional *rakı*, due to the grapes and water of the region; and its delicious *köfte*, which is consumed in eateries devoted to this one experience and recognised as the most beloved veal dish all across the land of lamb. Each *köfte* maker in town has a personal secret ingredient, a common one being lungs. You may be relieved to hear that my secret ingredient is not lungs, but semolina.

The accompanying salad comes from much further south—the sea resort of Antalya, where they add tahini to everything.

Chicken *kebaps* are mostly served with a rice pilav in Turkey. I find that a bit boring, and since I share the Ottoman taste for combining meat with dried fruits, I've added prunes. Sour plums are popular as summer fruits in Turkey, while the dried version (prunes) are handy in winter. We prefer damsin plums, which are named for their supposed point of origin—Damascus. They were brought to Byzantion by the Romans.

Instead of rice I've used a kind of pasta called *orzo* (the Italian word for barley), or *risoni* (which translates as 'big rice'). It's called *kritharáki* (little barley) by the Greeks and *arpa şehriye* (barley grains) by the Turks, but I most like the Arab name *lisân al-uşfür*, which translates as 'songbird tongues'.

TAVUK ŞIŞ

CHICKEN KEBAPS WITH PRUNE ORZO PILAV

SERVES 4

KEBAPS
8 chicken thigh fillets
4 thyme sprigs
250 g (9 oz/1 cup) plain *yoğurt*
100 g (3½ oz/½ cup) capsicum (pepper) paste (see page 32)
125 ml (4 fl oz/½ cup) olive oil
1 teaspoon ground cumin
1 teaspoon chilli flakes
1 teaspoon salt
1 teaspoon freshly ground black pepper

ORZO PILAV
80 g (2¾ oz/½ cup) blanched almonds
750 ml (26 fl oz/3 cups) chicken stock
2 tablespoons butter
2 tablespoons olive oil
280 g (10 oz/2 cups) orzo pasta
½ teaspoon salt
½ teaspoon freshly ground black pepper
10 prunes, seeded and chopped
200 g (7 oz) crumbly feta

To prepare the *kebaps*, cut the chicken thighs in half, crossways. Pick the leaves from the thyme sprigs and discard the stalks. Mix the *yoğurt*, capsicum paste, olive oil, cumin, chilli flakes, salt, pepper and thyme leaves in a large non-metallic bowl. Add the chicken and thoroughly coat in the *yoğurt* mixture. Cover the bowl with plastic wrap, transfer to the fridge and leave to marinate for at least 6 hours.

About 1 hour before serving, start making the orzo pilav. If you're using an oven rather than a grill, preheat it to 220°C (425°F).

Halve the almonds. Put the chicken stock in a saucepan over a low heat and bring to a simmer.

Meanwhile, melt the butter in a saucepan over low heat. Add the olive oil. When it begins to sizzle, add the almonds and half the orzo. Brown for 3 minutes. Add the remaining orzo and stir for another 3 minutes. Add the heated chicken stock. Stir and add the salt and pepper. Bring the orzo to the boil, and simmer, covered, for 8 minutes.

Preheat the barbecue hotplate or a grill pan. Add a drop of water: if it sizzles, the grill is ready.

Chop the prunes and stir them through the orzo mixture. Simmer, covered, for another 5 minutes. Turn off the heat and stir in the feta. Let the mixture rest, covered, for 10 minutes.

Meanwhile, cook the *kebaps*. Using eight metal skewers (ideally 1 cm/½ in wide), push each skewer through two pieces of chicken and place them on the hot grill. Grill for 7 minutes on one side, then 5 minutes on the other side. (If you are using the oven, put the chicken pieces on an oven rack and bake for 10 minutes.)

Divide the orzo pilav among four plates. Place two skewers on each and serve.

YENİ DÜNYA KEBABI
LOQUAT KEBAPS

SERVES 4

500 g (1 lb 2 oz) minced (ground) lamb
    (with about 25 per cent fat)
1 teaspoon salt
1 teaspoon freshly ground black pepper
20 loquats (or apricots)
2 spring onions (scallions)
3 garlic shoots (or 1 garlic clove)
8 cherry tomatoes
2 tablespoons pomegranate molasses
    (to make your own, see page 24)
1 tablespoon ground sumac
1 tablespoon olive oil
1 tablespoon chilli flakes
pita bread, to serve

If you're using a charcoal grill, you should light it 1 hour before you want to cook. Burn the charcoal for at least 45 minutes and when the flames have died down, and the coals are glowing with a covering of white ash, the barbecue is ready. (If you're using a gas barbecue, turn it on to medium heat about 5 minutes before you're ready to cook.)

Put the lamb in a mixing bowl. Add the salt and pepper, and knead with wet hands for 2 minutes. Divide the meat into twenty balls about the size of walnuts.

Slit each loquat (or apricot) down one side, pull the halves partly apart and remove the seeds and the surrounding membrane. Stuff a ball of meat into each loquat.

Preheat the oven to 180°C (350°F).

Using four flat metal skewers (ideally 1 cm/½ in thick), push five loquats onto each skewer. Each loquat should have the open side facing upwards, so the skewer passes through both sides of the fruit and also the meat.

Put the *kebap* skewers on the charcoal grill or barbecue, with the open sides of the loquats facing upwards. Cook for 3 minutes on each side, then remove from the heat. Remove the loquats from the skewers and put them in a round baking dish (preferably terracotta), leaving a space in the middle.

Wash the spring onions, then remove the roots and tough outer leaves. Roughly chop the spring onions and the garlic shoots (or garlic clove). Halve the cherry tomatoes and mix them with the spring onion and garlic shoots in a salad bowl. Add the pomegranate molasses, sumac, olive oil and chilli flakes. Toss the salad.

Make a mound of the tomato salad in the middle of the loquats (pushing the loquats to make it fit). Put the tray in the oven and cook for 15 minutes.

Serve with pita bread.

This is one of the many seasonal *kebaps* of Gaziantep in southeastern Anatolia, appearing at the beginning of spring and served for only three weeks. It uses loquats picked just before they are ripe (if you can't find loquats, try to use almost-ripe apricots). Usually a family will layer the fruit and meat in their own baking tray and get the kids to carry the tray to the nearest bakery to be cooked in a wood-fire oven.

At other times of the year they might layer garlic, shallots and eggplant (aubergine) with the meat.

There are two ways of cooking this dish: one over charcoal, the other in the oven. I mix both methods here, first giving the kebaps a smoky flavour on the barbecue, then finishing them off in the oven.

If you don't have a barbecue, do the whole thing in the oven.

The literal translation of the Turkish name for this dish is 'gentle Ali', leading to the theory that the creator was a chef named Ali. More likely, though, the name is a corruption of *ala nazik* (good and gentle) or *eli nazik* (gentle hand). In the land of dubious etymologies, the name is often said to have come from an event in the early 1500s, when Sultan Selim I ate a dish of eggplant and lamb and asked: 'What gentle hand made this?' Hopefully the answer was a good chef named Ali.

While I have adapted many of the regional recipes in this book to modern forms, this one is exactly as I first consumed it in Gaziantep. It won us the 'Best in Taste' award at the Taste of Sydney festival in 2012. Thanks, Ali.

ALİ NAZİK
'THE GENTLE KEBAP' LAMB AND SMOKED EGGPLANT)

SERVES 4

1 red capsicum (pepper)
700 g (1 lb 9 oz) lamb (at least 25 per cent fat), coarsely minced (ground)
1 teaspoon salt
1 tablespoon paprika
1 tablespoon chilli flakes
500 g (1 lb 2 oz/2 cups) plain *yoğurt*
4 large eggplants (aubergines)
juice of 1 lemon
4 garlic cloves
2 teaspoons salt
75 g (2½ oz) butter
1 piece pita bread, for holding the skewer

CHILLI AND CAPSICUM BUTTER
75 g (2½ oz) butter
1 red capsicum (pepper), chopped
50 g (1¾ oz) chilli flakes

Cut the capsicum in half and remove the stalk and seeds. Chop into quarters and pulse in a blender until finely minced. Transfer the capsicum to a mixing bowl and add the lamb, salt, paprika and chilli flakes. Knead the mixture for 5 minutes with wet hands to make a smooth paste. Cover the bowl with plastic wrap, transfer to the fridge and leave to marinate overnight.

Meanwhile, place the *yoğurt* on a sheet of muslin (cheesecloth) and tie up the corners. Hang the muslin over a pot overnight to allow the *yoğurt* to thicken.

In the morning, take the meat mixture out of the fridge and divide it into four balls, each about 180 g (6½ oz). Wrap the meat around four flat metal skewers (ideally 2 cm/¾ in thick). Squash each ball around the skewer, pressing the mixture so it spreads 5 cm (2 in) from the top to 10 cm (4 in) from the bottom. Once all four skewers are firmly covered, put them back in the fridge for at least 1 hour.

If you're using a charcoal grill, light it 1 hour before you want to cook. Burn the charcoal for at least 45 minutes and when the flames have died down, and the coals are glowing with a covering of white ash, the barbecue is ready. (If using a gas barbecue, turn it onto medium heat about 5 minutes before you're ready to cook.)

Char the eggplants on an open flame until the skin is blackened (see page 21). When they are cool, scoop out the flesh and put the pieces in a colander for 10 minutes to lose some of their water. Drizzle on the lemon juice to help them retain their colour.

Roughly chop the eggplant flesh into a chunky purée. Crush the garlic with 1 teaspoon of the salt. Mix the strained *yoğurt* with the crushed garlic. Set aside.

To make the chilli and capsicum butter, melt the butter in a frying pan over low heat. Add the capsicum and chilli flakes. Cook for 2 minutes, then set aside.

Melt the butter in a frying pan. Add the puréed eggplant and the remaining salt. Heat the mixture for 1 minute, then divide among four plates. Spread the garlic *yoğurt* over the eggplant.

Put the *kebaps* on the charcoal grill or barbecue. Cook for 2 minutes, until the meat on one side has seared, then turn over and cook the other side for 2 minutes. Turn again, and cook for 2 minutes on each side. The fat will drip on the charcoal and burn, but that smoke will add to the flavour. Constantly check to see if the meat is at risk of falling off the skewer, and if so, turn it over.

Use the piece of pita bread as a mitten to grip the meat and pull it off the skewer. Cut the meat from each skewer into three and place on the *yoğurt*. Pour the chilli and capsicum butter into a jug for people to help themselves. Serve immediately.

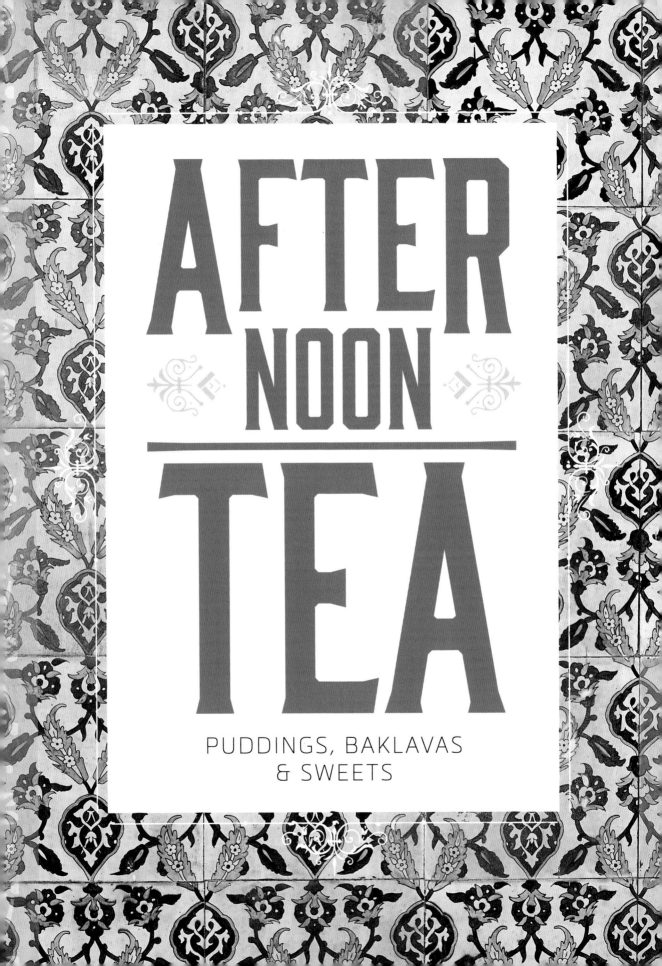

AFTER NOON
TEA

PUDDINGS, BAKLAVAS
& SWEETS

AFTERNOON TEA

If you've a sweet tooth like the average Turk, these are the signs you'll be looking for as you wander through the streets of any Turkish town. A *tatlıcı* will sell you *helva*, Turkish delight and ice creams; a *şekerci* will sell confectionery; a *muhallebici* will sell milky puddings; and a *pastane* will sell pastries (often including baklava, but if you're a connoisseur of the prince of pastries, you should look for a *baklavacı*, which serves nothing else). And at street stalls in Tarsus, on the Mediterranean coast, you'll find the iced rosewater pudding called *bici bici* (pronounced 'beegee beegee').

A Turk would drink tea with any of those desserts, but if you insist on coffee, you should look for a sign saying *Café*, which will offer a European mix of snacks. If you see the older word *Kahve*, you'll encounter a hole in the wall where men play cards and backgammon.

As you'll gather, Turks have a sugary treat for every occasion. For example, on the tenth day of the month of Muharram in the Islamic calendar, they share a dessert called *aşure*, which has up to forty-one ingredients, supposedly based on the dried fruits, nuts and pulses that Noah had in the cupboard when his ark finally settled on dry land. In Ottoman times, the fifteenth day of the month of Ramadan was associated with the gift of baklava to the janissaries—the soldiers of the sultan in the Topkapı Place. They were kept from staging military coups for two centuries by their annual sweet crunchy bonus.

There's even a pastry called *kerhane tatlısı*, which translates as 'brothel sweet' because it is sold outside houses of ill repute. If you buy one of these syrupy pretzels, the street seller won't wish you the usual *Afiyet olsun* (bon appétit), but rather *Beline kuvvet* (power to your back).

Sweet treats are more usually associated with the other end of the morality spectrum. In my parents' day, it was customary for a young man, seeking to get to know a young woman, to ask nervously: 'Would you like to meet me in the pudding shop?' The couple might bond over a *sütlaç* (rice pudding) and a house-made lemonade before he asked his mother to ask her mother if a marriage might be possible. Then the families would meet over pastries and Turkish delight. With tea, of course.

For 500 years, the Ottoman sultans were mad for rice puddings, but their chefs showed off by inventing micro-thin filo pastry and forty-layer baklava some time in the late fifteenth century. In the nineteenth century, the fad for cakes spread from the palace to the people as French *pâtissiers* arrived in Istanbul to serve the tourist trade from Europe.

Lokum (Turkish delight) is a vital element in Turkish hospitality, surrounded by rituals. You never eat it before midday, and it's better with coffee than with tea. And you should never arrive at somebody's house without a package of it to conclude an afternoon.

A sacred site for pastry lovers is the Markiz Pastanesi in the Istanbul suburb of Beyoglu—not for the pizzas and *kebaps* it serves nowadays, but because it started life in the 1880s as Café Lebon, a magnificent art-nouveau salon where the former chef of the French Embassy served crunchy creamy confections to passengers from the Orient Express. His slogan was '*Chez Lebon, tout est bon*'.

In the early twentieth century, Albanian *patissiers* took over from the French, opening Inci (specialising in profiteroles); Sariyer Muhallebicisi (specialising in *sütlaç*, *aşure* and *keşkül*); and Baylan in my suburb of Kadıköy (the first pudding shop I visited as a child—specialising in ice cream with caramel and bitter almonds).

Outside of Istanbul, certain regions are identified with certain desserts. The western town of Afyon is the place to go for *kaymak* (clotted cream). For the crunchy cheesy pastry *künefe*, you'd go south to Antakya (formerly Antioch). For *dondurma* (stretchy ice cream), you'd move east to Kahraman Maraş.

Or you could stay in your own kitchen and make this chapter your journey through the sweet history of Anatolia.

Contrary to popular belief, Turks drink more tea than coffee—7.5 kilos per person a year—especially if they're retired gents meeting in the local *kahve*.

This layered dessert is a speciality of the southeastern city of Gaziantep (best known for baklava). In the Turkish name, the word *sütlaç* (pronounced 'sutlatch') means 'milky rice pudding' and the word *astarlı* means 'the lining of a jacket'.

Saffron—either home-grown or imported from Persia—was an important ingredient in Ottoman cuisine, because it allowed the sultans to show off their wealth. Pretentious people got into the habit

of leaving the saffron threads in the pudding so their guests could say: 'Wow, that must have cost a bit!' There's actually no reason to leave the threads in, since all the flavour and colour you need is extracted by the warm water within 20 minutes.

I like to decorate my *astarlı sütlaç* with candied chickpeas, which you should be able to find in Middle Eastern food shops. But the dessert works perfectly well without them.

ASTARLI SÜTLAÇ
SAFFRON-LAYERED RICE PUDDING

SERVES 4

RICE PUDDING
100 g (3½ oz/½ cup) rice
1 piece of mastic crystal
 (less than 1 g/¹⁄₂₅ oz)
1 tablespoon sugar
750 ml (26 fl oz/3 cups) milk
2 tablespoons rice flour
pinch of salt

SAFFRON TOPPING
5 saffron threads
1 drop geranium oil (or rosewater)
1 tablespoon currants
1 tablespoon pine nuts
50 g (1¾ oz/¼ cup) rice
115 g (4 oz/½ cup) sugar
1 tablespoon rice flour

DECORATION (OPTIONAL)
20 candied or roasted chickpeas
4 tablespoons pomegranate seeds

To make the pudding, wash the rice in cold running water to remove the excess starch. Transfer to a saucepan, add 100 ml (3½ fl oz) of water, bring to the boil and simmer for 10 minutes. The rice will absorb most of the water.

Crush the mastic crystal into a powder, using a mortar and pestle or the handle of a knife, and then combine with the sugar. Heat the milk, mastic mixture and strained rice in a saucepan over medium heat, and bring to the boil. Combine the rice flour with 125 ml (4 fl oz/½ cup) of the boiling milk mixture, then add to the pan. Add the salt and simmer for 10 minutes, stirring constantly, to thicken. Remove the pan from the heat and leave to cool for 5 minutes, then divide the rice pudding equally among four 250 ml (9 fl oz/1 cup) glasses. Leave to cool completely at room temperature. Transfer to the fridge and chill for 30 minutes.

Next, make the topping. Put the saffron threads in a bowl and cover with 60 ml (2 fl oz/¼ cup) of warm water. Stir in the geranium oil and then leave to rest for 20 minutes. Discard the saffron threads and set aside.

Meanwhile, cover the currants in warm water, leave for 10 minutes and then strain. Toast the pine nuts in a frying pan over medium heat for 2 minutes, shaking the pan constantly to evenly brown.

Rinse the rice in cold running water to remove the excess starch. Transfer to a saucepan and add 125 ml (4 fl oz/½ cup) of water. Bring to the boil and simmer for 10 minutes. Add another 375 ml (13 fl oz/1½ cups) of water and half the sugar, and continue to simmer for 3 minutes, stirring constantly. Combine 125 ml (4 fl oz/½ cup) of the cooking liquid with the rice flour in a bowl. Discard the remaining rice mixture, and then pour the rice flour mixture into the pan. Add the remaining sugar and cook for a further 5 minutes, stirring occasionally. Add the saffron-infused liquid and simmer for a further 5 minutes, until it starts to thicken. Add the currants and pine nuts, remove from the heat and leave to cool.

Remove the rice puddings from the fridge, cover with the saffron topping, and then refrigerate again for 1 hour.

Decorate the chilled *astarlı sütlaç* with the chickpeas and pomegranate seeds, if desired, and serve.

YALANCI KAZANDİBİ
'TRICKSTER'S POTSTICKER' (BURNT MILK AND MASTIC PUDDING)

SERVES 8

1 piece of mastic crystal
   (less than 1 g/⅟₂₅ oz)
150 g (5½ oz) sugar
1 litre (35 fl oz/4 cups) milk
2 tablespoons rice flour
70 g (2½ oz) arrowroot powder
2 tablespoons butter, melted
100 g (3½ oz) icing (confectioners') sugar
1 tablespoon ground cinnamon

Crush the mastic crystal into a powder, using a mortar and pestle or the handle of a knife, and then mix with the sugar. Heat the milk and mastic mixture in a saucepan over medium heat. Meanwhile, add the rice flour and arrowroot to 250 ml (9 fl oz/1 cup) of water and stir to combine. Pour the arrowroot mixture into the milk and bring to the boil, then reduce to a simmer and cook, whisking constantly, for 5 minutes.

Brush a 30 x 40 x 4 cm (12 x 16 x 1½ in) baking tray with the melted butter. Sprinkle the icing sugar evenly over the tray. Place the tray over medium heat on the cooktop and gently shake so that the sugar caramelises evenly but does not burn. Pour the milk mixture over the caramelised sugar.

Remove the tray from the heat and tap it on a solid surface to make the pudding settle evenly. Put the pudding back over the heat and gently shake so that the mixture cooks evenly. Once all corners of the pudding have started to brown and the pudding starts to bubble, take the tray off the heat and sit it in a larger tray of iced water. Leave to cool to room temperature, then place the pudding tray in the fridge for 1 hour to chill.

Remove the pudding from the fridge and cut it into six slices (once lengthways and twice across). Fold each strip of pudding over to expose the burnt underside. Push a plastic spatula under one end and roll about a third of the strip over the top. Repeat with the remaining strips.

Dust each 'snail' with cinnamon and serve at room temperature.

In the Turkish name of this dish, the word *yalancı* (pronounced 'yalanjuh') means a liar or trickster— the kind of person who'd promise a pudding made with chicken breast, but leave out the chicken breast. In other words, me and most of the pudding shops in modern Istanbul.

What we have here is a variant of a classic Turkish pudding called *Tavuk göğsü*, which involved shredded chicken breast cooked with milk, sugar and mastic.

It was customary to scrape up the bits left at the bottom of the pan after the chicken breast pudding had been served, fold them over neatly, caramelise the outside, and present them as a new dessert called 'bottom of the pan' (*kazandibi*).

Nowadays, nearly all cooks leave out the chicken breast. I've followed the modern style because I wanted a dish suitable for vegetarians—or maybe just because I'm a trickster.

ÇİKOLATALI HURMA
CHOCOLATE DATES

Purists would say this is not a very Turkish dish, since dates tend to come from Arab countries to the south and east, and chocolate is a rare ingredient in our desserts (disappointing for a chocoholic like me). But we certainly use almonds and pistachios, so I've included them to appease the nationalists. *Çikolatalı hurma* has the great advantage of being easy to make with just a few minutes' notice—assuming your pantry is equipped with the right balance of Turkish and Arabic pleasures.

MAKES 16

16 dates (preferably medjool)
150 g (5½ oz/1 cup) slivered almonds
150 g (5½ oz) bitter chocolate
    (70 per cent cocoa)
70 g (2½ oz/½ cup) ground pistachios

Slit each date and remove the pit. Stuff the cavity with slivered almonds.

Bring 750 ml (26 fl oz/3 cups) of water to the boil in a large saucepan. Reduce the heat to a simmer and place a small metal mixing bowl over the pan, making sure it covers the sides like a lid, but doesn't touch the water below. Line a baking tray with baking paper and set aside. Break the chocolate into small pieces and gradually add to the bowl, stirring constantly so the chocolate melts but doesn't separate. Using tongs or a slotted spoon, place the dates, one at a time, in the hot melted chocolate and coat completely. Remove the dates, place on the lined tray, and leave to cool slightly.

Put the pistachios in a small bowl. Dip the still-warm chocolate-coated dates in the nuts to half cover, and then transfer to a clean tray. Put the tray in the fridge for 30 minutes for the chocolate to set, and then serve.

BADEM EZMESİ
BEBEK ALMOND TRUFFLES

Bebek, on the European side of the Bosphorus, is Istanbul's most expensive suburb, lined with elegant restaurants and bars that will charge you $25 for a cocktail. That was where I came across almond truffles, served in wooden boxes emblazoned with the golden logo of a shop called Meşhur Bebek Badem Ezmesi (Famous Bebek Almond Paste). It opened in 1904 and it sells only almond confectionery. If you make my version, you'll save a fortune—even when you include the orange blossom water and hazelnut liqueur.

MAKES ABOUT 10

50 g (1¾ oz) sugar
4 drops lemon juice
½ teaspoon orange blossom water
150 g (5½ oz/1 cup) blanched almonds
1 tablespoon Frangelico
    (or hazelnut liqueur)
50 g (1¾ oz) dark cocoa powder

Bring 50 ml (1¾ fl oz) of water to the boil over high heat. Add the sugar and stir to dissolve. Reduce the heat to a simmer, then add the lemon juice and the orange blossom water.

Put the almonds in a mixing bowl and gradually add the syrup, in four batches, pounding the mixture with a wooden spoon each time. Add the Frangelico and then knead the mixture for 5 minutes, until a smooth paste forms.

Roll the truffles into about ten walnut-sized balls, coat with cocoa powder and serve.

CEZERYE
MERSİN CARROT AND COCONUT BALLS

Every city in Turkey makes a sweet they claim is 'a natural Viagra'. *Cezerye* (pronounced 'jez-air-yeh') is the natural Viagra of Mersin on the southeast coast. It was once the ancient Greek city of Zephyrion, and now it's Turkey's largest port.

I have no evidence to support the alleged aphrodisiac value of carrots, but you could say that this is one of the healthier desserts you can consume from the region of excessive sugar and butter. I confess I have added turmeric mainly for visual impact, because carrots outside of Turkey have a less vivid colour—and presumably less potency.

MAKES ABOUT 20

75 g (2½ oz/½ cup) hazelnuts
4 carrots
1 teaspoon honey
1 tablespoon cornflour (cornstarch)
115 g (4 oz/½ cup) sugar
4 cloves
1 teaspoon ground cinnamon
½ teaspoon ground allspice
½ teaspoon ground ginger
½ teaspoon ground turmeric
30 g (1 oz/½ cup) flaked coconut

Preheat the oven to 180°C (350°F).

Place the hazelnuts on a baking tray and bake for 5 minutes. Remove the tray from the oven and set aside to cool, then rub off the hazelnut skins using your fingertips. Put the nuts in a food processor and coarsely grind.

Put the carrots and 250 ml (9 fl oz/1 cup) of water in a saucepan over high heat and boil for 10 minutes. Put 2 tablespoons of the boiling water in a bowl with the honey and cornflour and stir to combine.

Strain the carrots, then transfer to a blender. Add the sugar and blend into a purée.

Put the carrot purée back in the pan over low heat and stir in the spices. Add the honey and cornflour mixture and simmer for 10 minutes, stirring constantly. Remove the pan from the heat and discard the cloves. Add the hazelnuts and leave to cool to room temperature.

Using a teaspoon, shape the mixture into small walnut-sized balls; it should make about twenty balls. Spread the coconut flakes on a tray and then roll the balls in the coconut to evenly coat. Put the tray in the fridge and leave until you are ready to serve.

Put the *cezerye* on a plate (with toothpicks, if you like, so that people don't have to use their fingers) and serve.

In Mersin market (southeastern Anatolia), this stall specialises in every kind of confectionery—fruit candies, nougat, dried fruits, dried molasses stuffed with nuts, and *lokum* (Turkish delight).

This could well be the world's oldest pudding. The Turkish name *aşure* means 'ten' because you're meant to eat it on the tenth day of the first month of the Islamic calendar (which, being lunar, changes every year). It's staggering how many important events need to be remembered on that date—Moses crossed the Red Sea; Abraham's son Ishmael was born; Adam's plea for forgiveness was accepted by God; the prophet Jesus was born; and Noah's ark landed on Mount Ararat as the waters receded after the Great Flood.

It's the last event that explains why the full version of this pudding has forty-one ingredients. To celebrate his return to dry land after forty days on the water, Noah cooked up all the remaining supplies in the ark—nuts, pulses and dried fruits, but definitely no animals—and shared the resulting stew with everybody who had survived the flood.

We've simplified Noah's recipe, but the spirit of generosity remains: you're supposed to offer this dish to anybody who could smell it cooking.

AŞURE
NOAH'S ARK PUDDING

SERVES 16

100 g (3½ oz/½ cup) dried white
    haricot beans
100 g (3½ oz/½ cup) dried chickpeas
3 cloves
150 g (5½ oz) dried figs
200 g (7 oz) dried apricots
100 g (3½ oz) currants
100 g (3½ oz) sultanas
100 g (3½ oz) hazelnuts
50 g (1¾ oz/⅓ cup) blanched almonds
100 g (3½ oz) walnuts
350 g (12 oz/2 cups) pearl barley
880 g (1 lb 15 oz/4 cups) sugar
1 tablespoon cornflour (cornstarch)
250 ml (9 fl oz/1 cup) milk
1 tablespoon honey
zest of 1 orange

DECORATION
2 tablespoons ground cinnamon
4 tablespoons toasted sesame seeds
80 g (2¾ oz) walnuts, coarsely ground
80 g (2¾ oz) hazelnuts, coarsely ground
140 g (5 oz/1 cup) pistachios, coarsely
    ground
75 g (2½ oz/½ cup) dried apricots,
    finely chopped
200 g (7 oz) pomegranate seeds
zest of 2 oranges

Soak the dried haricot beans and chickpeas in water overnight, in separate bowls. Strain and rinse under cold running water, then place the beans and chickpeas, together, in a saucepan. Cover with water, bring to the boil over medium heat, then boil for 40 minutes, until the pulses are soft. Set aside.

Meanwhile, crack the cloves with a wooden spoon and soak in warm water for 1 hour. Finely chop the dried figs and apricots, and then place in a bowl with the currants and sultanas. Cover with lukewarm water and leave to soak for 30 minutes.

Preheat the oven to 180°C (350°F). Place the hazelnuts on a baking tray and bake for 5 minutes. Remove the tray from the oven and set aside to cool, then rub off the hazelnut skins using your fingertips.

Halve the hazelnuts. Halve the almonds. Put the walnuts in a food processor and coarsely grind. Set aside.

Wash the barley in cold running water to remove the excess starch. Half-fill a saucepan with water and bring to the boil over high heat. Add the barley and cook for 10 minutes. Strain the barley, half-fill the pan with fresh water and boil the barley again for 10 minutes. Strain the barley a third time, add to the pan with 1.5 litres (52 fl oz/6 cups) of water and boil for a further 40 minutes.

Add the strained chickpeas and beans to the barley and continue to boil for 10 minutes, stirring occasionally. Add the hazelnuts and almonds. Reduce the heat to a simmer and cook for 5 minutes, stirring slowly.

Next, add the strained dried figs, apricots, currants, sultanas and the sugar. Mix the cornflour in the milk, then add to the cooking mixture. Simmer for 3 minutes, stirring constantly. Add the strained cloves, honey and orange zest. Simmer for another 7 minutes, until the mixture starts to thicken.

Spoon the pudding into each serving bowl, then refrigerate for at least 2 hours.

Decorate the top of the puddings with the cinnamon, sesame seeds, nuts, apricots, pomegranate seeds and orange zest, and serve.

NOTE
Aşure will serve four people over four meals, and can be stored in the fridge for a week.

The cradle of civilisation, just north of the Garden of Eden, the Euphrates River in southeastern Anatolia, and the sunken city of Halfeti.

WHERE THE BEST BAKLAVA BEGINS

Undoubtedly, Anatolian cooks were playing around with dough, butter and beet-sugar long before the Ottoman Empire. The Romans in Constantinople and the Greeks in Byzantion loved their sweet pastries. But the ingredient that was added by the chefs in the Topkapı Palace in the fifteenth century was showmanship. They wanted their audience (the sultan, his family, his advisers and occasionally his bodyguards) to exclaim, 'My god, how can he roll out his filo so thin?' and 'My god, how does he have the patience to create forty layers, and still get it so light?' Nowadays, those questions are asked every day by the customers at İmam Çağdaş, the best baklava maker in Gaziantep, which is the best baklava town in Turkey.

Until I was twenty, I thought I was eating great baklava in Istanbul. Then the grandfather of one of my student friends arrived at our shared house with a beautifully wrapped box he'd bought in southeastern Turkey. As I tasted the contents, Şakir Dede, the grandfather, explained that the baklava at İmam Çağdaş was designed to satisfy the five senses:

The Look: High-domed with a golden top and glimpses of the fluorescent green of pistachio nuts;

The Smell: The richness of the butter and a hint of caramel and wood smoke from the baking;

The Touch: The syrup and butter should be so well absorbed that instead of being soggy, the filo is crisp enough to crumble under your finger;

The Sound: You should hear 'the tune of the crunch' when you bite; and of course

The Taste.

I had to make the pilgrimage to Gaziantep, where I met Telat Çağdaş and his son Burhan. Telat is the grandson of Hacı Hüseyin, who opened a bakery in Gaziantep in 1887 and began the legend. Telat spends all day in a fog of flour, supervising the thirty men who knead, roll out, sprinkle, layer, soak, bake and slice the precious product from 6 am to 3 pm every day.

While Telat runs the baklava factory upstairs, Burhan runs the 200-seat restaurant downstairs (which also serves excellent *kebaps*). Burhan's son, Telat Jr, looks after the cash desk.

The youngest workers are the twelve-year-old apprentices who come in before and after school to clean and carry, and bring cups of tea to the more senior workers. They can expect to rise, every two years or so, through these ranks: caretaker of ingredients; dough maker; dough roller (with the thinnest rolling pins in the world); baklava builder (layering with nuts and butter and sometimes clotted cream); wood-fire oven baker; slicer and folder; and syrup master.

The current syrup master has been working with the Çağdaş family for thirty years, and started at the age of twelve. Telat trusts him absolutely, but he still checks the syrup every day.

That perfectionism explains why the European Union has given the baklava of Gaziantep a 'Protected Geographical Indication' as a unique artisanal creation.

In Gaziantep, Telat Çağdaş and his grandson Telat Çağdaş Jr package their baklava to send all over the world.

The filo production room in Imam Çağdaş
Baklava House, where the pastry is rolled so
thin you can read a newspaper through it.

The next couple of recipes are forms of baklava, which Turks rarely make at home. We hate to seem defeatist, but honestly, you won't be able to make filo pastry to the standard of a place like İmam Çağdaş (see page 138) —even if you possess a huge marble table, a long thin rolling pin and the world's strongest shoulders.

At İmam Çağdaş, they aim to roll out the pastry so thin you could read a newspaper through it, but we don't expect you to manage that (although if you insist on trying, see page 27). For this recipe, just buy a couple of chilled packs of filo pastry. You'll need at least forty-two sheets to make true baklava.

The recipe assumes your baking tray is a 'quarter pan', which is 33 cm long, 22 cm wide and 2 cm deep (13 × 8½ × ¾ in), so try to find filo of similar dimensions. (If your tray is a different size, just cut the pastry to fit.) The most important ingredient of baklava is patience. Even with bought pastry, the recipe takes a long time—there are forty-two layers to butter and sprinkle. But the process is satisfying, and it's fun to get the kids to help.

BAKLAVA
TRADITIONAL PISTACHIO BAKLAVA

SERVES 8

400 g (14 oz) pistachio kernels
    (preferably Turkish or Iranian, and
    definitely not salted)
500 g (1 lb 2 oz) ghee (to make your own,
    see page 18) or clarified butter
375 g (13 oz) chilled filo pastry (at least
    42 sheets)
500 g (1 lb 2 oz) caster (superfine) sugar
juice of ¼ lemon

Put the pistachios in a blender and blend into a coarse powder. Gently melt the ghee in a frying pan (or microwave for 30 seconds).

Remove the top 12 layers of filo and place between two damp cloths, then set aside for the top of the baklava. Divide the remaining filo into two equal stacks and place each stack between damp cloths. Using a pastry brush, lightly brush the bottom and sides of a baking tray—traditionally measuring 33 x 22 x 2 cm (13 x 8½ x ¾ in)—with the warm ghee.

Place one filo sheet in the tray and lightly brush with ghee. Add two more layers, brushing with ghee each time, and then lightly sprinkle 1 tablespoon of ground pistachios over the third filo layer. Reserve 2 tablespoons of pistachios to decorate the top. Repeat the process six more times, to make a 21-sheet stack.

Top this layer with a thick, 5 mm (¼ in) layer of pistachios. Continue the layering process—three sheets, then a light sprinkling of pistachios—four more times to make a 33-sheet stack. (Any broken or offcut pieces of filo can be used to make the middle layer of any trio.) Take the remaining nine filo layers and continue to stack, brushing between each sheet with ghee, but not adding pistachios.

Using a sharp knife, cut the baklava seven times lengthways and six times across to make 42 portions. (The Turkish style is square, but you can also make rectangular blocks.) Reheat the remaining ghee and pour it between the cracks, and then set aside the pastry tray for 20 minutes, for the pastry to rest and absorb the ghee.

Preheat the oven to 180°C (350°F). Put the pastry in the oven and bake for about 30 minutes, rotating the tray after 15 minutes to ensure even baking.

Meanwhile, make the sugar syrup. Heat 600 ml (21 fl oz) of cold water and the sugar in a saucepan over medium heat. Add the lemon juice and bring to the boil, then reduce to a low simmer and cook for about 20 minutes, until the mixture becomes thick and syrupy, being careful not to let it caramelise. Check the pastry regularly and remove it once the top is golden brown.

Carefully place the baklava tray over medium heat for 1 minute, moving the tray around to ensure the base is evenly heated. Remove from the heat and pour the hot sugar syrup over the hot baklava. Leave to rest for 1 hour to absorb the sugar. Decorate the top with the reserved ground pistachios and serve.

NOTE
Leftover baklava can be kept for 4 days. Don't put it in the fridge, though, as this will ruin the texture.

BLACK SEA ROLLED BAKLAVA

The name of this Ottoman recipe literally means 'rolled turban'. In the sultan's kitchen the cooks would twist the pastry into a shape that resembled what they saw on the heads of the aristocrats around them. We're giving you a simpler version, but keeping the name.

We've already said Gaziantep has the greatest makers of baklava in Turkey and therefore the world, but other parts of Turkey approach baklava in different ways. On the Black Sea they use hazelnuts and their own butter, and they make the baklava into a roll shape. I've decided to use walnuts instead of hazelnuts, because I'm not from the Black Sea.

MAKES 50 PIECES

500 g (1 lb 2 oz) plain (all-purpose) flour
3 eggs
100 ml (3½ fl oz) milk
100 ml (3½ fl oz) vegetable oil
3 tablespoons plain *yoğurt*
pinch of salt
1 tablespoon baking powder
1 tablespoon white vinegar
150 g (5½ oz) butter
100 g (3½ oz) potato flour
600 g (1 lb 5 oz) walnut kernels,
    roughly ground
500 g (1 lb 2 oz) sugar
juice of ¼ lemon

Sift the flour into a mixing bowl and make a well in the middle. In a separate bowl, whisk the eggs, milk, vegetable oil, *yoğurt*, salt, baking powder, vinegar and 50 ml (1¾ fl oz) of water to combine. Pour the egg mixture into the flour. Knead for 10 minutes to make a smooth dough, then cover the bowl with a damp cloth and leave to rest for 15 minutes.

Melt the butter in a frying pan over high heat (or microwave for 30 seconds). Brush a baking tray with a little of the melted butter.

Divide the dough into ten billiard-sized balls. Dust your work surface with the potato flour to prevent sticking. Place a ball of dough on the work surface and flatten it using a thick rolling pin, being careful not to let the dough stick. Roll the dough out as thin as possible, stretching it into a square about 40 cm (16 in) wide, using your hands and a rolling pin. Brush the stretched dough with butter. Sprinkle with 50 g (1¾ oz) of walnuts.

Place a straightened wire coat hanger (or a very thin rolling pin at least 50 cm/20 in long) across the dough sheet, on the edge nearest you, and roll the sheet into a tight cylinder around the wire. Push the cylinder ends towards each other and squeeze into a crinkly concertina shape about 30 cm (12 in) long. Lift it onto the prepared baking tray. Gently pull the wire out. Repeat with the nine remaining balls of dough, tightly packing the concertinas into the tray. Preheat the oven to 180°C (350°F).

Cut across the row of concertinas four times to divide each cylinder into five rolls, each about 6 cm (2½ in) long. Reheat the remaining butter, then pour it over the pastry and between the cracks. Set aside for 10 minutes to rest and absorb the butter.

Bake for about 30 minutes, rotating the tray after 15 minutes to ensure even baking. Meanwhile, make the sugar syrup. Heat 600 ml (21 fl oz) of cold water and the sugar in a saucepan over medium heat. Add the lemon juice and bring to the boil, then reduce to a low simmer and cook for about 20 minutes, until the mixture becomes thick and syrupy, being careful not to let it caramelise. Check the pastry regularly and remove it once the top is golden brown.

Carefully place the baking tray over medium heat for 1 minute, moving the tray around to ensure the base is evenly heated. Remove from the heat and immediately pour the hot sugar syrup over the hot pastry. Leave to rest for 1 hour to absorb the sugar. Decorate the top with the remaining walnuts and serve.

KAVALA KURABİYESİ
KAVALA COOKIES

Kavala is a town in Greece, not far from the border of Turkey. I wanted to include what Turks call Kavala cookies in honour of one of my food idols—the Sydney chef Janni Kyritsis, whose grandparents were expelled from Turkey in the 1920s as part of a government policy of monoculturalism. They ended up living in Kavala (just as my grandparents were expelled from Greece and ended up living in the Turkish town of Mürefte, where Janni's parents had started). But when I asked Janni if he was familiar with Kavala cookies, he looked blank. The people of Kavala, it seems, just call them almond cookies, and are unaware of their city's fame throughout my country.

MAKES ABOUT 16

300 g (10½ oz/2 cups) plain (all-purpose) flour, plus extra for dusting
150 g (5½ oz/1½ cups) almond meal
150 g (5½ oz) butter
150 g (5½ oz) icing (confectioners') sugar
1 vanilla bean
1 tablespoon baking powder
2 eggs
50 g (1¾ oz/½ cup) coarsely ground almonds
1 tablespoon vegetable oil, for greasing

Mix the flour and almond meal together in a non-stick frying pan over low heat for 3 minutes until it begins to bake, then remove from the heat and set aside.

Gently melt the butter in a frying pan (or microwave for 30 seconds). Pour the melted butter in a bowl and add 50 g (1¾ oz) of the icing sugar. Slice the vanilla bean and scrape the seeds into the butter mixture. Add the baking powder and eggs, and whisk to combine.

Put the toasted flour mixture in a separate bowl. Make a well in the middle and pour in the butter and egg mixture. Knead for 5 minutes, to make a soft dough. (If it seems too moist, add a little more flour.) Add the ground almonds and knead for 5 minutes more, until the mixture forms a coarse paste. Cover the bowl with a damp cloth and rest for 15 minutes.

Preheat the oven to 170°C (325°F).

Place the dough on a floured work surface and roll out the dough, using a rolling pin, into a sheet about 30 cm (12 in) wide and 1 cm (½ in) thick. Use the rim of a glass to cut the sheet into rounds, then slice each round in half to make sixteen half-moons. (For a traditional shape, push the straight edge of the half-moon inwards to create a crescent.)

Line a baking tray with baking paper and brush with the vegetable oil. Add the half-moons and bake for 25 minutes, or until golden.

Remove the tray from the oven and leave to cool for 10 minutes, then sprinkle generously with the remaining icing sugar and serve.

TULUMBA
OTTOMAN DONUTS

MAKES ABOUT 20 DONUTS

LEMON SYRUP
440 g (15½ oz/2 cups) sugar
juice of ¼ lemon

DONUTS
50 g (1¾ oz) butter
pinch of salt
1 tablespoon sugar
300 g (10½ oz/2 cups) plain
   (all-purpose) flour
3 eggs
1 tablespoon semolina
1 tablespoon cornflour (cornstarch)
1 litre (35 fl oz/4 cups) vegetable oil

First, make the lemon syrup. Put 500 ml (17 fl oz/ 2 cups) of water and the sugar in a saucepan over medium heat and bring to the boil. Add the lemon juice, lower the heat and continue to simmer for 10 minutes. Remove from the heat and pour the syrup into a deep bowl. Set aside.

Now start on the donuts. In a separate saucepan, mix 500 ml (17 fl oz/2 cups) of water with the butter, salt and sugar, and bring to the boil over medium heat. Add the flour and continue to boil for 3 minutes, stirring constantly, to make a dough. Remove from the heat and stir to help it cool. Set aside.

Put the dough in a mixing bowl and stir in the eggs, one at a time, until combined. Knead for 3 minutes. Add the semolina and cornflour, and knead for a further 5 minutes to make a soft moist dough, adding 1 tablespoon of water if it seems dry. Cover the bowl with a damp cloth and set aside to rest for 15 minutes.

Push the dough into a piping (icing) bag fitted with a star nozzle. Squeeze out a long line of dough and cut it into 6 cm (2½ in) chunks.

Pour the vegetable oil into a deep heavy-based saucepan. Add the *tulumbas* and place the pan over low heat. Once the oil starts bubbling, simmer for 5 minutes, or until the donuts turn golden brown.

Remove the *tulumbas* with a slotted spoon and transfer to the bowl of lemon syrup. Leave to soak for 5 minutes, then remove from the syrup and serve.

This snack, from the late Ottoman period, is soft inside and crunchy outside. Fried batter soaked in syrup is a favourite in Greece and the Balkan countries. Or you might consider it similar to Spanish churros or Egyptian *balah el sham* (Damascus dates). *Tulumbas* are particularly popular during the fasting month of Ramadan, where they give a sugar and carbohydrate hit for people who haven't eaten all day.

This traditional dish is from Erzurum, in eastern Anatolia, where they stuff it with walnuts. I've reduced the amount of syrup and boosted the stuffing with apricots. It uses the crunchy 'string' pastry called *kadayıf*, which means there are interesting texture contrasts between the inside and the outside.

KADAYIF DOLMA
APRICOT AND WALNUT DOLMAS

MAKES 20

250 g (9 oz) chopped walnuts
50 g (1¾ oz) dried apricots,
    finely chopped
1 litre (35 fl oz/4 cups) vegetable oil

SUGAR SYRUP
500 g (1 lb 2 oz) sugar
¼ lemon

PASTRY
50 g (1¾ oz) butter
300 ml (10½ fl oz) milk
2 egg yolks
500 g (1 lb 2 oz) chilled fresh
    kadayıf pastry

DECORATION
2 tablespoons chopped walnuts

To make the syrup, put the sugar and 750 ml (26 fl oz/3 cups) of water in a saucepan over medium heat and bring to the boil. Reduce the heat, squeeze the quarter lemon into the water, and throw in the lemon skin. Simmer for 15 minutes, then remove the lemon skin and discard. Remove from the heat and set aside to cool. (Do not refrigerate.)

Meanwhile, put the walnuts and apricots in a bowl and mix together. Set aside.

Make a start on the pastry. Gently melt the butter in a frying pan over low heat (or microwave for 30 seconds). Transfer to a deep mixing bowl, add the milk and egg yolks and whisk to combine. Set aside.

Loosen the *kadayıf* pastry using your fingers, then roughly chop the strands. Using clean hands, take a handful of the *kadayıf* pastry and press together between your palms to make a round. Still holding the round in your palm, place 2 teaspoons of the walnut and apricot mixture in the middle; use your other hand to fold over the sides of the pastry and roll up the ends, and then squeeze into a tight tube. Dip your fist into the milk mixture, letting the pastry absorb some of the liquid through your fingers, pushing the pastry back inside your fist as it slightly expands. Shake off the excess liquid and then set aside on paper towel. Repeat with the remaining pastry to make about twenty rounds.

Heat the vegetable oil in a deep frying pan over high heat. Add a drop of water to the oil: if it sizzles, the oil is ready. Carefully add the *dolmas*, ten at a time, and then fry for 3 minutes, until golden and crunchy. Remove with a slotted spoon and transfer into the bowl with the syrup.

Leave to soak in the syrup for 2 minutes, then remove and serve, decorated with the chopped walnuts.

ŞEKERPARE
SEMOLINA DOMES

MAKES 20

½ lemon
550 g (1 lb 4 oz/2½ cups) sugar
125 g (4½ oz) butter
300 g (10½ oz/2 cups) plain (all-purpose)
    flour
95 g (3¼ oz/½ cup) fine semolina
1 egg
1 tablespoon baking powder
2 tablespoons vegetable oil
20 blanched almonds

First, make the syrup. Using a fine grater or a microplane, grate the lemon zest into a bowl and set aside. Squeeze the lemon juice into a cup. Mix 440 g (15½ oz/2 cups) of the sugar and 625 ml (21½ fl oz/2½ cups) of water in a saucepan over medium heat and bring to the boil. Add the lemon juice, reduce the heat and simmer for a further 15 minutes. Remove from the heat and set aside to cool.

Gently melt the butter in a frying pan over low heat (or microwave for 30 seconds).

Sift the flour into a mixing bowl and add the semolina. Make a well in the middle and pour in the butter. Break in the egg. Add the remaining sugar, then add the reserved lemon zest and the baking powder. Knead for 5 minutes. Cover the bowl with a damp cloth and set aside to rest for 15 minutes.

Preheat the oven to 180°C (350°F).

Knead the dough again for 5 minutes, then divide into about twenty ping pong-sized balls. Brush the vegetable oil onto a baking tray. Place the balls on the tray and push into a dome shape.

Push an almond into the top of each dome, then bake for 25 minutes.

Remove the *şekerpare* from the oven and pour the syrup over the top. Leave to cool for 15 minutes before serving.

This is a dish I learned from my grandma, who would make vast quantities of *şekerpare* (which means 'piece of sugar' in old Turkish) and invite twelve or more people at a time to share it for afternoon tea or dinner. I like it because semolina makes a lighter texture than you find in flour-based desserts.

It is vital to pour the syrup over the domes while they are hot, so there is maximum absorption, and also to leave plenty of space around each dome so they can expand—along with your waistline.

KAHVE—TURKISH COFFEE WITH ADDED PATIENCE

When I was growing up, Istanbul was changing, adapting to a faster way of life, but my grandma was determined to keep making perfect coffee. She used a *cezve* (a traditional copper pot), which she placed over burnt charcoal for 15 minutes but regularly removed from the heat to ensure it did not overcook.

In my grandmother's day, a prospective wife was judged by her coffee-making skills—not just her technique, but more importantly her patience. If she's patient with her coffee, she will be patient with her husband—or so the men thought at the time. Now it's possible to judge a Turkish café on the same principle. A second-rate place will boil the coffee too quickly, degrading the taste and producing little of the froth that needs to form gradually and cover the top of the liquid.

These days, you don't need charcoal to make a perfect Turkish coffee. An electric or gas stovetop works perfectly well—as long as you have the technique and the patience.

Here's how to order *Türk kahvesi* when you're in Turkey:

Sade ('sah-DEH'): plain, no sugar (fairly bitter)

Az şekerli ('AHZ sheh-kehr-lee'): a little sugar (takes off the bitter edge; half a teaspoon per cup)

Orta şekerli ('ohr-TAH sheh-kehr-lee'): medium (about a teaspoon of sugar per cup)

Şekerli ('sheh-kehr-lee'): sweet (two teaspoons of sugar per cup)

You never order coffee with milk. If you enjoy a milky coffee and you're lucky enough to be in the east of Turkey, you could ask for *menengiç* ('men-en-GITCH'), which is made with crushed wild pistachio nuts, milk and sugar. There's no caffeine, so you can drink it all day.

To make your own Turkish coffee, you will need a *cezve* (pronounced 'jezweh')—a heavy-based pot with a long handle, and you will need to buy finely ground medium-roast Arabica coffee. (Or, if you're a purist, you'd grind medium-roast beans in a cylindrical brass coffee mill called a *kahve değirmeni*.) Here's the process:

1. Pour cold water into the pot—one cup for each person you are serving, and an extra half cup 'for the pot'.
2. Add a heaped teaspoonful of the ground Turkish coffee for each cup and stir. The amount of coffee may be varied to taste, but don't forget, there should be a thick layer of grounds left at the bottom of each cup. Don't fill the pot too much.
3. If you need to add sugar, this is the time to do it. Check with your guests and if they say 'medium sweet', stir a teaspoon of sugar per cup into the cold water.
4. Heat the pot as slowly as you can—the lower the heat, the better it will be. Make sure you watch to prevent the *cezve* overflowing when the coffee boils.
5. When it boils, pour some—not all—of the coffee equally between the cups, filling each cup about a quarter to a third of the way. This will ensure everybody gets a fair share of the foam forming on top of the brew, without which, coffee loses much of its taste.
6. Put the pot back on low heat until the coffee boils again, which will be very soon. Distribute the rest of the coffee between the cups.

Since there is no filtering at any time during this process, you should wait for a few minutes before drinking your coffee while the grounds settle at the bottom of the cup.

In traditional cafés, coffee is cooked over charcoals that have been burning for more than an hour.

MEZE

SMALL PLATES
TO DRINK WITH

MEZE

Every great food culture has a tradition of small tasting plates served with a national drink. The Italians have antipasto, the French have hors d'oeuvres, the Spanish have tapas—all washed down with local wines. The Chinese have yum cha, served with tea. The Russians have *zakuski*, served with vodka.

And the Turks have *meze*, served with *rakı* (or occasionally wine or beer). *Mezes* are most likely to be served in a *meyhane*, which is a kind of bar/bistro/pub where people meet for a chat and a drink and a bite from sunset until well after midnight. During the Ottoman period, the *meyhanes* were often run by families of Greek or Armenian background, because those cultures do not have the Muslim aversion to alcohol.

There's an origin story for *meze* that sounds too good to be true. Supposedly the Ottoman sultans in the fifteenth century were a paranoid lot, fearful of being poisoned by foreign spies who sneaked into their kitchens, or by members of their own family. So they hired official food tasters, who would be given small helpings of every dish offered by the chef. They would have to be seen to swallow all of them and keep smiling before the sultan could begin his meal.

Other rich Turks thought they would look important if they followed the same ritual, even when they weren't in fear of death threats and couldn't afford official tasters. So they started serving small quantities on small plates and called them *meze*, from the Persian word for 'a taste'.

The reason I'm dubious about this tale is that there were *meyhanes* in the Middle East long before the Ottoman emperors built their kitchens. The eleventh-century Persian poet Omar Khayyam wrote this line: 'You say rivers of wine flow in heaven—is heaven a *meyhane* to you?' The rivers of wine would have flowed through Istanbul, a thriving trade hub, before the Muslims started cracking down on alcohol sales. Smart *meyhane*-owners would have served salty high-protein snacks to make their customers thirsty and to line their stomachs so they wouldn't fall unconscious before ordering another drink.

The need for stomach lining became more pressing in the seventeenth century, when the favoured drink in *meyhanes* changed to *rakı*. Like wine, *rakı* is made from grapes but, as it is distilled, it is much more alcoholic. Most people dilute *rakı* with water, which turns it white and explains its nickname—'lion's milk'. *Meyhanes* started boasting about the variety of *meze* they had available to keep the customer (relatively) sober.

The twentieth-century poet Nazım Hikmet wrote that a good *meze* table should feast the eye, the conversation should feast the brain, and the *rakı* should whet the palate: 'You can drink *rakı* with spicy or sweet, with cucumber, melon or cheese, with water or without water, in winter or in summer, in joy or in sorrow—the only thing you cannot drink *rakı* with is idiots.'

So here's a typical night out for me during my student years. You decide to meet your friends at a *meyhane* (a decision that might take a while, because the second most divisive question in Istanbul, after 'What's your soccer team?' is 'Which is the best *meyhane* in town?'). You find a table and order your *rakı* (aniseed-flavoured), which arrives with a jug of water and a bucket of ice. A waiter comes around with a tray displaying cold *meze*—maybe melon and white cheese, *yoğurt* and mint, spicy tomato salsa, eggplant salad, marinated fish, stuffed mussels—and you point at the ones you fancy. Musicians pass by and you might have to pay them to go away. Street sellers wander in and try to interest you in their wares. After an hour or so, the waiter returns and asks if you'd like any hot *meze*. He describes them, emphasising what's unique to the establishment, and maybe points to a tank from which a fish can be scooped out and grilled. You pick a few tastes and order another bottle of *rakı*. Suddenly it's midnight. You stagger out and buy some *kokoreç* (stuffed intestines that look like sausage) from a street stall to help you sober up.

This chapter gives you the tools to create your own *meyhane*, complete with cocktails. Turks think of *meze* as sharing food, to be placed in the middle of the table as part of a spread, but any of the dishes in this chapter could be served on its own as a starter or first course for lunch or dinner. We have suggested ingredient quantities that will make enough for four, when you want to serve the dish as a course by itself. If the dish is part of a *meze* platter or party table, then each guest is likely to take a smaller quantity. So if one of our 'serves 4' dishes is served as part of a platter of three *mezes*, for example, then you could say it will serve twelve (or six greedy people).

This is party food and party drink, served with conversation. The only thing you cannot serve it with is idiots.

A typical laneway *meyhene* in Istanbul, where friends gather to chat, sing, get tipsy on *rakı* and eat an array of *mezes*.

A well-made *humus* is a wonderful form of comfort food. But it's not Turkish. If you're offered it in Turkey, you're probably in a place run by someone with an Arabic background. (This is not to say that I'm taking a side in the *humus* war. You won't catch me making a declaration on whether its origin is Syrian or Israeli or Palestinian or Lebanese. All I know is it's not Turkish.)

At my restaurant in Sydney, we try to change our menu every three months. The discussion with my cooks and waiters begins with me saying: 'Let's lose the *humus*—it's not Turkish.' My manager, Fatih, always replies: 'Leave it alone. It's been seven years, and the customers love it.'

So I've compromised. I've turned an Arabic speciality into a Turkish dish by adding ingredients familiar to me—pomegranates to sweeten it, capsicum to colour it, and *sucuk* (spicy beef sausage) to give it heat. My customers are right.

SUCUKLU HUMUS
POMEGRANATE HUMUS WITH SPICY SAUSAGE

SERVES 6

200 g (7 oz/1 cup) dried chickpeas
1 teaspoon bicarbonate of soda
    (baking soda)
2 garlic cloves
60 ml (2 fl oz/¼ cup) lemon juice
1 tablespoon pomegranate molasses
    (to make your own, see page 24)
1 tablespoon capsicum (pepper) paste
    (see page 32)
4 tablespoons tahini
½ teaspoon salt
125 ml (4 fl oz/½ cup) olive oil
½ teaspoon paprika
pide bread (to make your own,
    see page 45), grilled, or pita crisps,
    to serve

TOPPING
1 small cucumber
½ small red onion
½ red capsicum (pepper)
100 g (3½ oz) *sucuk* (or chorizo)
2 slices day-old sandwich bread

Put the chickpeas in a saucepan, cover with water and bring to the boil over high heat. Boil for 1 minute, and then strain. Put the chickpeas in a bowl with the bicarbonate of soda, cover with water and soak overnight.

Strain the chickpeas and rinse under cold running water for 5 minutes. Transfer to a saucepan, cover with plenty of water, and bring to the boil over medium heat. Cook for 1½ hours, until the chickpeas are soft enough to mash with your fingers.

Put the cooked chickpeas in a food processor and blend into a smooth paste. Finely crush the garlic and stir into the chickpea paste. Add the lemon juice, pomegranate molasses, capsicum paste, tahini, salt, olive oil and paprika and blend into a smooth purée. Spoon the *humus* into a bowl.

Next, prepare the topping. Peel the cucumber and finely chop, along with the red onion. Slice the red capsicum, remove the seeds and stalk, and finely chop. Chop the *sucuk* very finely. Chop the day-old bread into small cubes.

Put the *sucuk* in a small frying pan over low heat and bring to a simmer, then cook until the fat begins to sizzle and release. Add the bread cubes and capsicum, then cook for 2 minutes, until crisp. Remove the *sucuk*, bread and capsicum from the pan and mix with the cucumber and onion.

Using a spoon, swirl the *humus* so it looks like a whirlpool, and then scatter the *sucuk* mixture into the swirls. Serve the bowl of *humus* with grilled pide or pita crisps.

PATLICAN SALATA
CHARRED EGGPLANT SALAD

SERVES 6

2 large eggplants (aubergines)
1 large red capsicum (pepper)
½ bunch flat-leaf (Italian) parsley
2 spring onions (scallions)
1 teaspoon salt
½ teaspoon freshly ground black pepper
60 ml (2 fl oz/¼ cup) extra virgin olive oil
2 tablespoons lemon juice
1 tablespoon apple cider vinegar

POMEGRANATE TOPPING
2 tablespoons pomegranate molasses
   (to make your own, see page 24)
1 tablespoon extra virgin olive oil
20 pomegranate seeds

Pierce the eggplants with a fork and char the skins by placing the eggplants directly onto the flame of a gas stove. Using tongs, move the eggplant around to evenly blacken and then remove from the flame. Peel off the skins and put the eggplant pieces in a colander to drain for about 10 minutes.

Blacken the skin of the capsicum over an open flame in the same way. Put the capsicum in a bowl and cover with plastic wrap to sweat. Leave to cool. Once the capsicum is cool enough to handle, peel off the skin under cold running water. Discard the stalk and seeds.

Pick the parsley leaves, discard the stalks, and finely chop the leaves. Wash the spring onions, remove the roots and tough outer leaves, and finely chop. Roughly chop the roasted eggplant into a chunky purée. Finely dice the roasted capsicum. Mix the vegetables and parsley together in a salad bowl. Add the salt, pepper, olive oil, lemon juice and apple cider vinegar and mix thoroughly.

For the topping, mix the pomegranate molasses and olive oil together in a small jug, to make a dressing. Serve the *patlican salata* at the table for people to help themselves. Swirl the pomegranate dressing over the eggplant and decorate with the pomegranate seeds.

If you've been in Turkey for more than a day, you've had a version of this salad, which would have arrived automatically when you sat down for lunch or meze. It's a candidate for the title of National Dish.

The flesh of the eggplant has a lovely texture, but does not have much flavour of its own. It's a great carrier of flavours, though—particularly the smokiness that comes when the skin is burnt on a barbecue or char-grill or open gas flame. The other key flavour here is apple cider vinegar.

Although Turks are notorious for their addiction to lamb, Turkey is highly congenial for travellers who are vegetarians or vegans. But if you're a vegetarian who happens to also be allergic to eggplant—like one of my closest friends—then eating out in Turkey can become a little difficult.

My mother, who was a great home cook, became a professional restaurateur when I was sixteen. It was great experience for me to work in her *meyhane* as a kitchenhand while I was studying. I became the fallback cook every time she sacked her chef, which, on average, was about once a month. I got a crash course in meze preparation, barely having time to learn one new recipe from each chef before they disappeared. One dish mum would never let anyone else touch was the *fava*, which she made with her own hands in spring, using a mixture of dried and fresh broad beans, and adding black olive paste because she liked the colour contrast. She said *fava* should be like a cake—able to endure a long sitting at a meze table. If the cake collapses, it's a dip, not a *fava*.

In this recipe I have used dried beans, so you can make it year round, but if you're making it in spring, you could include fresh double-peeled broad beans.

FAVA
MUM'S BROAD BEAN PÂTÉ

SERVES 4

200 g (7 oz/1 cup) dried split
   broad beans
1 small onion
1 teaspoon salt
1 teaspoon sugar
70 ml (2¼ oz) olive oil, plus extra
   for greasing
2 tablespoons black olive paste
3 dill stalks

TOPPING

1 red bullhorn pepper
   (or ½ red capsicum/pepper)
¼ red onion
8 black olives, pitted
2 tablespoons olive oil

Wash the broad beans and then transfer to a bowl. Add 750 ml (26 fl oz/3 cups) of water and soak overnight.

Rinse the soaked beans under cold running water. Heat the beans, onion, salt, sugar, 50 ml (1¾ fl oz) of the olive oil and 750 ml (26 fl oz/3 cups) of water in a saucepan over medium heat for 15 minutes. Reduce the heat and simmer for 15 minutes, stirring regularly.

Remove the pan from the heat and purée the mixture using a hand-held blender (or leave to cool slightly and blend in a food processor). Spoon half the purée into a bowl, add the olive paste and mix together thoroughly, then set aside.

Pick the leaves off the dill and discard the stalks. Fold the leaves into the remaining broad bean purée and leave to cool to room temperature. Brush four teacups (or rice bowls) with the remaining olive oil. Half-fill each cup with the broad bean and dill purée and refrigerate for 30 minutes.

Remove the cups from the fridge and fill the rest of each cup with the olive paste mixture. Refrigerate for a further 30 minutes.

Now make the topping. Slice the bullhorn pepper and discard the stalk and seeds. Finely chop the red onion and black olives. Mix the chopped ingredients in a bowl with the olive oil and then set aside.

Remove the cups from the fridge and upend each one onto its own plate. Use the back of a teaspoon to dent the top of each dome. Spoon on the topping, then serve.

ZEYTİN PİYAZI
GREEN OLIVE AND WALNUT SALAD

SERVES 6

125 g (4½ oz) green olives
2 garlic cloves
125 ml (4 fl oz/½ cup) extra virgin olive oil
½ bunch flat-leaf (Italian) parsley
4 spring onions (scallions), chopped
50 g (1¾ oz) walnuts
½ green apple
1 red bullhorn pepper
  (or ½ red capsicum/pepper)
juice of 1 lemon
2 tablespoons pomegranate molasses
  (to make your own, see page 24)
1 teaspoon chilli flakes
½ tablespoon dried thyme

Slice the olives into quarters, and remove the seeds. Squash the garlic cloves and remove the skin. Put the olive slices and garlic in a small container with half the olive oil, and leave to marinate overnight.

Finely chop the parsley leaves. Wash the spring onions, remove the roots and tough outer leaves, and finely chop. Roughly chop the walnuts. Slice the apple. Slice the bullhorn pepper, remove the seeds and the stalk, and finely chop.

Transfer the olives from the garlic marinade into a large bowl. Add all the other ingredients and mix thoroughly.

Serve the bowl of *zeytin piyazi* at the table for people to help themselves.

This dish appears on every meze table near the Aegean Sea. It's best made with what we call 'scratched green olives' (early harvested and lightly crushed before being soaked in salty water). They come from the Edremit area in the northwest.

The world's first known edible olives were cultivated in Anatolia 6000 years ago, long before anybody talked about nations called Greece or Turkey. These days Turkey is one of the largest olive oil producers in the world, and arguably the most enthusiastic eater of olives in the Mediterranean.

The word *piyaz* in the Turkish name comes from Ottoman times, and suggests a salad that contains onions. In fact, the onions are the least interesting part of this dish.

ANTEP EZME
CHILLI AND CAPSICUM SALSA

I've translated the word *ezme*, which literally means 'crushed', as 'salsa', because it's chunkier than a sauce but runnier than a dip, and because it contains the New World ingredients chillies and tomatoes. The secret to making a great *ezme* is never to use a food processor. Instead, you should chop it finely just before you take it to the table.

Ezmes are served in *kebap* houses to lubricate the palate before the meat arrives. The waiter just plonks a few small plates on the table when you sit down, and you spoon them up while you discuss what kind of *kebap* you might order. The spiciest *ezmes* are made in Gaziantep.

SERVES 6

6 ripe tomatoes
4 green bullhorn peppers
   (or 2 green capsicums/peppers)
1 bunch flat-leaf (Italian) parsley
3 red onions
3 garlic cloves
1 tablespoon *isot* (or chilli flakes)
1 tablespoon capsicum (pepper) paste
   (see page 32)
50 ml (1¾ fl oz) pomegranate molasses
   (to make your own, see page 24)
100 ml (3½ fl oz) extra virgin olive oil
juice of ½ lemon
1 tablespoon sea salt
pomegranate seeds, to decorate
   (optional)
pide bread (to make your own,
   see page 45), grilled, to serve

Score a shallow cross in the base of each tomato. Put the tomatoes in a heatproof bowl and cover with boiling water. Leave for 30 seconds, then plunge in cold water and peel the skin away from the cross. Cut the peeled tomatoes into quarters and scoop out the seeds.

Slice the bullhorn peppers and discard the stalks and seeds. Pick the parsley leaves and discard the stalks. Preferably using a mezzaluna, finely chop the tomatoes, parsley, peppers, red onions, garlic and parsley together into a chunky purée.

Drain off any excess water from the chopping board, then transfer the purée into a bowl. Add the *isot*, capsicum paste, pomegranate molasses, olive oil, lemon juice and salt, and stir well to combine.

Decorate the bowl of *antep ezme* with pomegranate seeds, if using, then serve with grilled pide.

MÜCVER
NETTLE AND FETA FRITTERS

Usually the classic dish called *mücver* is made with zucchini, dill and feta. In some parts of the country they add carrots or spinach. I decided to sharpen the flavour with the wild weeds that grow near Bodrum, the west-coast resort town where my mother had her restaurant.

Turks who use wild weeds in their cooking were probably originally taught by the descendants of the Cretans, who used to live along the Aegean coast (until they were expelled in the 1920s).

If you can't find nettles, you could substitute spinach.

SERVES 4

15 flat-leaf (Italian) parsley stalks
10 dill stalks
3 spring onions (scallions)
50 g (1¾ oz) hard feta
20 g (¾ oz) parmesan
1 egg
35 g (1¼ oz/¼ cup) plain
    (all-purpose) flour
1 teaspoon freshly ground black pepper
2 zucchini (courgettes)
½ teaspoon salt
30 nettle leaves (or 3 spinach stalks)
60 ml (2 fl oz/¼ cup) olive oil

MINT YOĞURT
1 garlic clove
130 g (4½ oz) plain *yoğurt*
1 teaspoon dried mint

Pick the parsley leaves, discard the stalks, and finely chop the leaves with the dill. Wash the spring onions, remove the roots and tough outer leaves, and finely chop. Grate the feta and parmesan.

Whisk the egg in a mixing bowl. Add the flour, feta, parmesan, dill, parsley and pepper, and mix together to make a runny paste.

Peel the zucchini, then finely grate. Place the zucchini shreds in a colander and sprinkle on the salt. Leave for 5 minutes—the salt will help extract the moisture from the shreds. Wrap the zucchini in muslin (cheesecloth) and tightly squeeze out the excess water.

If you are using nettles, use gloves to handle them. To remove the sting, put them in a heatproof bowl and cover with boiling water for 30 seconds. Transfer to cold water for 5 minutes. Pick the green leaves and discard the stems. Pat the leaves dry with paper towel and then roughly chop. (If using spinach instead, wash thoroughly and remove the stalks, then chop.)

Mix the zucchini and nettle (or spinach) with the flour and egg mixture. Divide this dough into eight small patties, flattening them in your palm.

Heat the olive oil in a frying pan over high heat. Add a drop of water to the oil: if it sizzles, the oil is ready. Add the patties, four at a time, and fry for 2 minutes on each side, until golden. Transfer to paper towel to drain the excess oil.

To prepare the mint *yoğurt*, crush the garlic and mix in a small bowl with the *yoğurt* and dried mint.

Place the patties on four plates and serve with the mint *yoğurt*.

ÇIĞ KÖFTE
NIMROD'S VENISON TARTARE

Çiğ köfte (raw meatball) is usually made with veal because of its low fat content. But I'm suggesting you try venison, because it is hallowed by history (and has an even lower fat content).

Let me take you back 4000 years to the city of Şanlıurfa in southeastern Anatolia. As the story goes, the ruler at the time was a man named Nemrut (translated as Nimrod in English), who was a great grandson of Noah. Nimrod became paranoid after a dream in which he was told he was about to be replaced by a leader named Abraham, who would try to persuade Nimrod to worship one god.

So he ordered his soldiers to collect all the wood they could find so they could burn Abraham at the stake. When a hunter returned home to his village after killing a deer, his wife was unable to cook it because she, of course, had no wood. Instead, she chopped the raw meat and kneaded it with spices and bulgur—thereby presenting a new dish to the world. (And God saved Abraham by turning the fire to water—the site of which is recognised today by the famous pond in the middle of Şanlıurfa, full of sacred carp.)

SERVES 4

250 g (9 oz) venison loin fillet
  (or veal loin), trimmed
2 onions
5 garlic cloves
2 tablespoons capsicum (pepper) paste
  (see page 32)
½ tablespoon tomato paste
  (to make your own, see page 24)
½ tablespoon salt
½ tablespoon freshly ground
  black pepper
4 heaped tablespoons *isot* (or chilli flakes)
1 tablespoon ground pimento
1 tablespoon ground cumin
½ tablespoon ground cinnamon
450 g (1 lb/2½ cups) very fine bulgur
15 ice cubes
5 flat-leaf (Italian) parsley stalks
5 mint stalks
3 spring onions (scallions)
lettuce leaves (or pita bread), to serve

Finely cut the venison. Put the meat in a food processor and blend into a coarse paste, then transfer to a round baking tray with indentations on the bottom (or a mixing bowl).

Finely grate the onions. Crush the garlic cloves. Add the onion, garlic, and capsicum and tomato pastes to the meat and combine. Stir in the salt, pepper and spices. Knead the meat mixture for 10 minutes to make a smooth paste.

Add 90 g (3 oz/½ cup) of the bulgur and three of the ice cubes, and continue to knead until the ice has melted. Repeat with the remaining bulgur and ice cubes, until all the bulgur is well combined with the meat.

Pick the parsley and mint leaves and discard the stalks. Finely chop the leaves. Wash the spring onions, then remove the roots and tough outer leaves. Finely chop. Add the mint, parsley and spring onion to the veal mixture and knead for 10 minutes, until it holds together as a large ball.

To make the *çig köftes*, take a handful of the mixture and squeeze tightly in your fist to make a log about 3 cm (1¼ in) across and 6 cm (2½ in) long. Repeat to make about thirty patties.

Place about three *köfte* in each lettuce leaf, and serve on a platter for guests to help themselves.

MERCİMEK KÖFTESİ
RED LENTIL MEATBALLS

Here's another dish with history. The Bible tells how Esau, a hunter who normally ate venison, saw his brother Jacob eating a bowl of red lentils and was so hungry he offered to give up his inheritance for it.

This is a rare vegetarian version of *köfte*, which is normally associated with raw veal or lamb, and is a staple winter dish in the eastern half of Turkey. Even if you love it as much as Esau, be careful not to overload, as bulgur will continue to expand in your stomach.

SERVES 6

400 g (14 oz/2 cups) split red lentils
175 g (6 oz/1 cup) fine bulgur
2 onions
2 tablespoons vegetable oil, for frying
1 tablespoon capsicum (pepper) paste
   (see page 32)
1 tablespoon tomato paste
   (to make your own, see page 24)
1 bunch flat-leaf (Italian) parsley
6 spring onions (scallions)
1 tablespoon ground cumin
1 tablespoon chilli flakes
1 tablespoon olive oil
2 teaspoons salt
1 cos lettuce
1 lemon

Wash the red lentils in cold running water, then place in a saucepan with 1 litre (35 fl oz/4 cups) of water and bring to the boil over high heat. Reduce the heat and simmer for 15 minutes, with the lid partly closed.

Put the bulgur in a large mixing bowl and pour over the hot lentils and the cooking water. Cover and rest for 15 minutes, to soften the bulgur.

Finely chop the onions. Heat the vegetable oil in a frying pan over medium heat, then add the onion. Cook for 5 minutes, until the onion is translucent. Mix the capsicum and tomato pastes in a small bowl with 1 tablespoon of water. Stir the mixture into the pan and cook for 3 minutes more, until the whole mixture is mushy. Remove the pan from the heat and set aside.

Pick the leaves from the parsley, discard the stalks, and finely chop the leaves. Wash the spring onions, then remove the roots and green outer layer. Finely chop.

Once the bulgur has softened, stir in the parsley, spring onion, cumin, chilli flakes, olive oil, salt and the onion mixture. Knead for 3 minutes, then divide the mixture into about twenty-four balls, using your hands. Slightly flatten each ball.

Wash the cos lettuce, and break it up into leaves. Place three *köftes* in each lettuce leaf.

Cut the lemon into 6 slices. Place on a platter with the *köftes* for guests to help themselves.

KISIR
BULGUR, MINT AND CUCUMBER SALAD

This salad is associated with southeastern Anatolia, but it has spread all round the country, with regional variations. In my mother's restaurant in Bodrum I learned to include pickles and pickle juice to add saltiness and contrast to the sweetness of the molasses. The trick here is to use just the right amount of boiling water—too little and the grain will be crunchy, too much and it will be mush. The Turkish name is strange—the word *kısır* literally means 'infertile', which is hardly the case here.

SERVES 8

200 g (7 oz) fine bulgur
60 ml (2 fl oz/¼ cup) extra virgin olive oil
1 tablespoon tomato paste
   (to make your own, see page 24)
1 teaspoon capsicum (pepper) paste
   (see page 32)
3 large tomatoes
1 long green chilli
2 pickled cucumbers or gherkins
10 flat-leaf (Italian) parsley stalks,
   leaves picked
10 mint leaves
5 spring onions (scallions)
2 tablespoons gherkin juice
1 teaspoon chilli flakes
1 teaspoon ground white pepper
juice of 1 lemon
1 teaspoon pomegranate molasses
   (to make your own, see page 24)

Bring 125 ml (4 fl oz/½ cup) of water to the boil water over high heat. Place the bulgur in a large bowl and pour the boiling water over. Leave to rest for 15 minutes. Stir the olive oil, tomato paste and capsicum paste into the bulgur.

Score a shallow cross in the base of each tomato, then transfer to a heatproof bowl and cover with boiling water. Leave for 30 seconds, then plunge into cold water and peel the skin away from the cross. Cut the tomatoes in half and scoop out the seeds with a teaspoon. Finely chop the flesh.

Slice the chilli and remove the stalk and the seeds. Finely chop. Finely chop the cucumbers, parsley leaves, mint leaves and spring onions. Add all the chopped ingredients to the bulgur and mix well.

Finally, add the gherkin juice, chilli flakes, pepper, lemon juice and pomegranate molasses. Stir and serve the *kısır* in the bowl for people to help themselves.

TOPİK
ARMENIAN CHICKPEA DOMES

SERVES 6

CHICKPEA SHELLS
400 g (14 oz/2 cups) dried chickpeas
3 potatoes
½ tablespoon ground cinnamon
1 teaspoon salt
½ teaspoon freshly ground black pepper
1 teaspoon sugar
100 g (3½ oz) tahini

FILLING
10 onions
100 ml (3½ fl oz) olive oil
30 g (1 oz) currants
30 g (1 oz) pine nuts
1 teaspoon ground cinnamon
½ teaspoon salt
½ teaspoon freshly ground black pepper
½ teaspoon ground allspice
½ teaspoon sugar
250 g (9 oz) tahini

½ tablespoon cinnamon, to serve
juice of 1 lemon, to serve

A day ahead, start on the chickpea shells. Bring a large saucepan of water to a rapid boil. Add the chickpeas and blanch for 1 minute. Transfer the chickpeas to a bowl, cover with fresh water and leave to soak overnight.

The next day, start making the filling. Finely slice the onions. Heat the olive oil in a frying pan over medium heat. Add the onion and cook for 10 minutes, until translucent and slightly caramelised. Reduce the heat and gently simmer for 2 hours with the lid partly closed, stirring occasionally.

Strain and rinse the chickpeas, and then rub in a rough cloth to remove as much skin as possible. Place the skinned chickpeas in a large saucepan, cover with plenty of water (at least three times the volume of chickpeas) and boil for 1 hour, without the lid. Remove the pan from the heat and leave to cool. Once the chickpeas are cool enough to handle, remove any more skin, using your fingers, and then set aside.

Cut the potatoes in half, place in a large saucepan, cover with salted water and bring to the boil. Cook for 15 minutes, or until the potatoes are tender, then drain well. Leave to cool and then remove the skin.

Place the potatoes, chickpeas, cinnamon, salt, pepper and sugar in a food processor and blend to make a thick paste. Transfer to a mixing bowl, add the tahini and combine. Knead the mixture together for 2 minutes to make a smooth paste. Cover the bowl with plastic wrap and leave to rest for 10 minutes.

Meanwhile, resume making the filling. Place the currants in a bowl, cover with warm water, and leave to soak for 15 minutes. Toast the pine nuts in a frying pan over medium heat for 3 minutes, shaking often. Remove the simmered onion from the heat. Strain the currants, then add to the onion, along with the pine nuts, cinnamon, salt, pepper, allspice and sugar. Stir in the tahini.

Cut twelve 30 cm (12 in) squares of plastic wrap.

To make the *topik*, put 4 tablespoons of the chickpea mash in the middle of a square of plastic wrap. Flatten the mash into a round about 15 cm (6 in) across, pushing outwards so the centre is thicker than the edge. Put 2 tablespoons of the onion mixture in the middle of the mash. Lift one corner of the plastic wrap and fold the mash over the filling. Bring the other three corners up to meet the first corner and fold the other edges over. Pull the four corners of plastic wrap together and form the mixture into a ball. Twist the corners of plastic into a strand. Tie a knot in the strand just above the ball. Repeat to make twelve balls. Place the parcels on a tray and refrigerate overnight to set.

When you are ready to serve, snip off the top of the plastic wrapping (below the knot) and take the balls out of the plastic wrap. Sprinkle a little cinnamon on top of each, and a few drops of lemon juice, then serve.

Topik is a vegetarian dish originally consumed during Lent by the Armenian community, who are Orthodox Christians. Now it's one of the most treasured delicacies to go with a bottle of *rakı* in Armenian *meyhanes*.

As a child I fell in love with *topik* when our Armenian neighbours invited me to stay for supper while I was playing with their kids. I rediscovered it as a teenager in a *meyhane* called Madam Despina,

which was opened in 1946 in the multicultural suburb of Kurtuluş by a Greek lady whose signature dish happened to be Armenian. She's been immortalised in a nostalgic folk song, which goes: 'Set the table, Madam Despina. Are we tipsy again? Did you just run out of *topik*? We love you anyway.'

Madam Despina died in 2006, but she's still a hot *topik* in Istanbul.

The Aegean village of Türkbükü, where geese, normally confined to fresh water, have been breeding in the salt water since they were left at the beach by Somer's stepfather in 1995.

If you wander through the Istanbul suburb called Beyoğlu, you'll soon encounter men carrying circular aluminium trays full of mussels stuffed with spiced rice. Give the first man you see a lira and you'll get three or four mussels and a slice of lemon on a paper plate. You'll then become addicted, and feel compelled to go to the street called Nevizade where, with any luck, you'll find a *meyhane* that will serve you mussel *dolmas* sitting down.

When I came to Sydney, I met an Armenian lady named Bercük Anne, who made mussel *dolma* far superior to any I'd found in the streets of Istanbul. Her recipe had a lot of onions, spices and herbs, and very little rice.

So here's how you can make the true Armenian mussel *dolma* better than any you'll find in the streets of Istanbul.

MİDYE DOLMA
STREET HAWKER'S STUFFED MUSSELS

**SERVES ABOUT 4
(5 MUSSELS PER PERSON)**

20 black mussels
2 tablespoons tomato paste
   (to make your own, see page 24)
2 teaspoons capsicum (pepper) paste
   (see page 32)
2 tablespoons olive oil
4 lemons, cut into wedges, to serve

STUFFING
5 onions
100 ml (3½ fl oz) vegetable oil, for frying
30 g (1 oz) currants
30 g (1 oz) pine nuts
115 g (4 oz/½ cup) short-grain rice
2 tomatoes
2 teaspoons freshly ground black pepper
2 teaspoons ground pimento
1 teaspoon ground cinnamon
5 flat-leaf (Italian) parsley stalks
3 dill stalks

First, prepare the stuffing. Finely chop the onions. Heat the vegetable oil in a frying pan over medium heat. Add the onion and cook for 5 minutes. Reduce the heat and simmer, covered, for 20 minutes, stirring occasionally.

Meanwhile, place the currants in a bowl, cover with warm water, and leave to soak for 15 minutes. Toast the pine nuts in a frying pan over medium heat for 3 minutes, shaking often. Set aside.

Wash the rice under cold running water and then add to the simmering onion. Increase the heat to medium. Grate the tomatoes over the rice. Strain the currants and add to the pan. Add the pine nuts, pepper, pimento and cinnamon, and stir. Simmer the mixture for 5 minutes, then remove from the heat and leave to cool.

Pick the parsley leaves, discard the stalks and finely chop the leaves. Finely chop the dill. Mix the parsley and dill into the stuffing mixture, then set aside.

Now, open the mussels. If you've bought the mussels in a vacuum bag, open the bag over a bowl to catch any liquid inside. Scrub the shells clean. Using a blunt knife, carefully force the point of the knife into the gap at the pointy end of each mussel, and slice through the meat so the shell opens with half the meat attached to each half shell—once you cut through the thick, round connecting muscle at the bottom of the mussel, it will be easy to open. Pour the juice into a bowl. Snip off the beards and, using your finger, remove any grit at the base. Spread the half-shells to tear the muscle of the mussel, but leave the two halves connected. Put 2 teaspoons of the stuffing into the middle of each mussel and push the half-shells together again.

Place a bread and butter plate, face down, in the bottom of a saucepan about 25 cm (10 in) wide.

Place the mussels in the pan, with the tips pointing outwards towards the edge of the pan, with the shells slightly overlapping (to prevent them opening). Build a tight spiral of shells in the centre of the pan; there should be only one layer of mussels. Strain the mussel juice through a sieve lined with a double layer of muslin (cheesecloth) three times, to remove any grit.

Mix 250 ml (9 fl oz/1 cup) of the mussel juice in a small bowl with the tomato paste and capsicum paste. Pour the mixture over the mussels. Splash on the olive oil. Place another bread and butter plate over the mussels, then put the lid on the pan. Place the pan over medium heat and bring to the boil, then reduce the heat and simmer for 15 minutes.

Remove the mussels from the heat and leave to cool to room temperature. (You can also keep them in the fridge overnight.) Serve the *midye dolma* on a big platter with lemon wedges for guests to help themselves. The best way to eat them is with your hands, using the top shell to scoop the mixture out of the bottom shell.

SOMON PASTIRMA
SALMON PASTIRMA AND BABY ZUCCHINI

SERVES 6

CURED SALMON
500 g (1 lb 2 oz) sashimi-grade
    salmon fillet
1 kg (2 lb 4 oz) rock salt
440 g (15½ oz/2 cups) caster
    (superfine) sugar
15 garlic cloves
3 tablespoons ground fenugreek
3 teaspoons ground cumin
2 tablespoons sweet paprika
1 tablespoon hot paprika
1 teaspoon ground coriander
1 teaspoon sea salt

ZUCCHINI AND DILL TOPPING
500 g (1 lb 2 oz) small zucchini
    (courgettes)
60 ml (2 fl oz/¼ cup) extra virgin olive oil
juice of 1 lemon
4 tablespoons dried *yoğurt* cheese
    (or crumbly feta)
2 dill stalks, picked and chopped

Start by preparing the salmon. Place the salmon (which should already be skinned and filleted) on a board and remove any small bones, blood lines and white pieces of fat.

Spread a thin, lightweight tea towel over a cake rack (or steamer tray or large colander). Sit the rack on top of a baking tray or large pan. You will use this for the drying process.

Mix the rock salt and caster sugar together in a bowl. Spread half the mixture onto the towel-covered rack, about 1 cm (½ in) thick. Put the salmon fillet in the middle of the rack and cover it thoroughly with the rest of the rock salt mixture. Fold the tea towel over the top of the salt.

Place a flat-bottomed tray over the salmon, with a 3 kg (6 lb 12 oz) weight on top (using anything from a bag of potatoes to the *Oxford Dictionary*), to flatten out the salmon as it dries. Place the baking tray in the fridge and rest for 2 days.

Take the salmon out of the fridge, wash the salt and sugar off and plunge in iced water. Rest the salmon (in the water) in the fridge for 1 day.

Remove the salmon from the water and pat dry. Put the salmon on a rack with a drip tray underneath and refrigerate for 24 hours. Turn the salmon over and return to the fridge for one more day.

Mix the garlic, spices and sea salt together in a blender, to make a thick paste. If the mixture seems dry, drizzle about ½ teaspoon of water into the paste.

Remove the salmon from the fridge and coat it with the paste, making sure every part is completely covered. Put the salmon on the cake rack with the tray underneath, but this time without the tea towel, and return to the fridge for at least another 48 hours.

When you are ready to serve, prepare the topping. Finely slice the zucchini lengthways. Place in a bowl and toss with the olive oil, lemon juice and *yoğurt* cheese. Finely chop the dill and then add to the zucchini mixture.

Thinly slice the *somon pastırma*, diagonally, to make at least 24 slices, and serve with the topping.

This is an example of the new Turkish cooking. When you say *pastırma* to traditional Turks, they think beef. But the word simply means 'pressed', so there's nothing to prevent you from wrapping the wonderful spice paste around any form of protein.

Since the process involves leaving the protein to dry for at least a week, you need to be careful if you're using seafood. For me, the fish that works best is salmon—it can absorb the flavours of the paste while retaining its own.

Unlike beef *pastırma*, somon *pastırma* is kept in the fridge during the drying process, which means the coating will stay moist and crumble away when you're slicing the salmon. This is a good thing—it's the salmon you want to eat, not the wrapper.

Because somon *pastırma* has a strong taste, I decided to accompany it with the simple freshness of raw zucchini.

VOTKALI LEVREK
VODKA AND MUSTARD-CURED BREAM

This is another of my mum's specialities, perfected in her restaurant in Bodrum, where the visitors love their vodka cocktails and the favourite fish is *levrek* (normally translated as 'sea bass'). At my restaurant, we use sea bream. I like using vodka as a curing alcohol because it has a neutral taste, which does not interfere with the hints of ginger, bay leaves and dill in the *votkalı levrek*.

SERVES 4

20 whole black peppercorns
1 tablespoon sea salt
3 fresh or dried bay leaves
2 thin slices fresh ginger
1 tablespoon mild French mustard
50 ml (1¾ fl oz) vodka
100 ml (3½ fl oz) lemon juice
4 fillets deep sea bream
   (or another firm white-fleshed fish,
   such as snapper or cod)
50 ml (1¾ fl oz) olive oil
3 dill stalks, finely chopped, for
   decoration

In a bowl large enough to hold the bream fillets, mix together the peppercorns, salt, bay leaves, ginger, mustard, vodka and lemon juice, to make a marinade.

Place the bream fillets on a board and remove any small bones and blood lines. Thinly slice each bream fillet into five 'leaves'. Place them in the bowl and cover with the marinade. Cover the bowl with plastic wrap, then leave in the fridge for at least 6 hours—ideally, overnight.

To serve, remove the fish from the bowl and place five 'leaves' of bream on each plate. Drizzle with the olive oil, sprinkle on a little dill and serve.

AYVALI KEREVİZ
BRAISED CELERIAC WITH QUINCE AND ORANGE

It is thought that the Greek island of Samos, very close to the Turkish mainland, is where the ugly celeriac first grew. On that island, fossil remains of celeriac have been found in a grove sacred to the goddess Hera, created in seventh century BC. We're entitled to speculate that the warriors on both sides of the Trojan War were eating it. Homer writes in *The Iliad* that the horses of Achilles' soldiers were eating what we assume were wild celeriac leaves.

In Turkey, celeriac is better known than celery (which tends to appear mostly as sticks in bloody marys). It's often cooked with sour apples, but I agree with the Ottoman cooks in preferring to use quince if it's in season.

SERVES 4

½ lemon
1 celeriac (up to 500 g/1 lb 2 oz)
1 quince
1 onion
1 carrot
125 ml (4 fl oz/½ cup) olive oil
2 oranges
1 teaspoon sugar
2 teaspoons salt

Put 500 ml (17 fl oz/2 cups) of water in a bowl. Squeeze in the juice from the lemon, and then add the lemon. Peel the celeriac and chop into pieces, roughly 2 cm (¾ in) square. Add the celeriac to the bowl. Cut the quince in half, remove the pit and thinly slice the flesh. Add the slices to the bowl and set aside.

Finely chop the onion. Finely chop the carrot. Heat the olive oil in a frying pan over medium heat. Add the onion and cook for 4 minutes, until soft. Add the carrot and cook for 2 minutes.

Drain the quince slices and celeriac cubes, pat dry with paper towel, and then add to the pan. Fry for 4 minutes, until the mixture starts to change colour and softens a little.

Cut the oranges in half. Finely grate the zest of one orange half into the mixture. Squeeze the juice from both oranges into a cup and add enough warm water to fill the cup. Pour the orange mixture into the pan and add the sugar and salt. Bring to the boil, then simmer, covered, for 15 minutes.

Check the softness of the celeriac: if it's still hard, simmer for another 10 minutes. Turn off the heat and rest, covered, for 15 minutes.

Divide the *ayvalı kereviz* among four serving plates. Serve at room temperature.

In Turkish villages, the way most families eat is by sharing dishes placed in the middle of the table.

ÇERKEZ TAVUĞU
CIRCASSIAN CHICKEN

Circassia is a mountainous region in southern Russia, where walnut trees grow in abundance. In the nineteenth century, many Circassians were driven out of Russia and took refuge in parts of the Ottoman Empire, where they proceeded to introduce new cooking techniques. Turks, who thought chicken came on skewers, now learned they could eat it cold, smothered in a walnutty paste.

Coriander is one of my pet hates, and I don't use it in my restaurant, but I've included it here to honour the Circassians, who brought it to Turkey.

SERVES 6

2 flat-leaf (Italian) parsley stalks
2 coriander (cilantro) stalks
1 onion, quartered
1 carrot, quartered
1 tablespoon salt
1 tablespoon black peppercorns
1 whole chicken, about 1.2 kg (2 lb 10 oz)
3 slices day-old sandwich bread
200 g (7 oz) walnuts
1 garlic clove
2 tablespoons sweet paprika
60 ml (2 fl oz/¼ cup) walnut oil
pide bread, to serve (to make your own, see page 45)

Pick the leaves off the parsley and coriander, and set aside. Put the parsley and coriander stalks in a saucepan. Add the onion, carrot, salt, peppercorns, chicken and about 3 litres (105 fl oz/12 cups) of water. Place the pan over high heat and bring to the boil, then reduce the heat and simmer, partly covered, for 1½ hours. Remove any scum that forms on the surface.

Take the chicken out of the pan, place on a rack and leave to cool to room temperature. Leave the cooking liquid in the pan and set aside.

Remove the skin from the chicken and pick the meat off the bones. Place the skin and bones back in the cooking liquid and bring to the boil over high heat. Continue to boil vigorously for 1½ hours, uncovered, so the liquid reduces to half its original volume.

Strain the bones, skin and vegetables out of the chicken stock, and discard. Shred the chicken meat and spread the pieces on a deep serving platter. Pour on 2 tablespoons of stock, cover with plastic wrap and place the platter in the fridge.

Discard the crusts from the bread. Dunk the bread into the stock for a few seconds, then squeeze out any excess liquid. Blend the bread, walnuts, garlic and 1 tablespoon of the paprika in a food processor. Gradually add some stock, tablespoons at a time, to make a smooth paste.

Remove the serving platter from the fridge. Put the chicken in a bowl, stir one-third of the paste through the chicken pieces, then spread them across the platter again.

Chop the reserved parsley and coriander leaves and mix them with the remaining paste, then pour this mixture over the chicken.

Mix the walnut oil and the remaining paprika together, and drizzle over the chicken.

Serve the *çerkez tavuğu* platter cold, with pide bread, for people to help themselves.

YAPRAK SARMA
SOUR CHERRY-STUFFED VINE LEAVES

SERVES 4

100 g (3½ oz/½ cup) sour cherries
   (dried, frozen or tinned), pitted
½ lemon
30 vine leaves
150 ml (5 fl oz) olive oil
2 tablespoons pine nuts
4 onions
185 g (6½ oz/1 cup) short-grain rice
1 tomato
½ teaspoon ground cinnamon
½ teaspoon ground allspice
½ teaspoon freshly ground black pepper
1 teaspoon salt
½ teaspoon sugar
5 mint stalks
2 dill stalks

If you are using dried sour cherries, soak them in warm water for 1 hour. If frozen, thaw for 30 minutes. If tinned, rinse to remove the syrup. Halve the sour cherries, then set aside.

Zest the lemon half, and squeeze the juice. Set the lemon zest, lemon juice and the squeezed lemon half aside.

If you are using fresh vine leaves, place them in a bowl, cover with boiling water, add 1 tablespoon of salt, and leave to soak for 10 minutes. If they are in brine, wash to remove the salt. Set aside.

Heat the olive oil in a frying pan over medium heat. Add the pine nuts and fry for 2 minutes. Finely slice the onions, add to the pan and cook for 5 minutes, until soft. Wash the rice under cold running water and then add to the onion mixture. Grate the tomato into the rice, sauté for 2 minutes and then reduce the heat to a simmer.

Stir in the cherries, lemon zest, cinnamon, allspice, pepper, salt and sugar. Add 50 ml (1¾ fl oz) of water and simmer for 5 minutes. Remove from the heat; the rice should be softened, but still slightly crunchy. Finely chop the mint and dill, add the lemon juice and combine with the rice mixture.

Pat the vine leaves dry with paper towel. Snip off any stems and, if the spine in the centre of the leaf is woody, soften it by crushing it with the back of a knife. Put aside the five least attractive-looking leaves.

Next, stuff the vine leaves. Put a leaf on a board, shiny side down. Put a strip of rice mixture in the middle of the vine leaf, fold over the base of the leaf, then fold over each long side and roll into a çigar shape, about 6 cm (2½ in) long. Repeat to make about 25 stuffed vine leaves.

Place a bread and butter plate face side down in the bottom of a saucepan. Spread the five reserved vine leaves over the back of the plate. Arrange the stuffed leaves in a tightly packed spiral shape on top of the plate. Thinly slice the reserved lemon half and scatter over the vine leaves. Put another bread and butter plate on top.

Add 250 ml (9 fl oz/1 cup) of warm water to the pan and bring to the boil over medium heat. Reduce the heat and simmer, partly covered, for 30 minutes.

Remove from the heat, leave to cool and then serve, or keep in the fridge for up to 3 days.

The traditional cold vegetarian *dolma* stuffing involves spiced rice with currants and pine nuts. In recent years, Turkish chefs have started replacing the currants with sour cherries, which contribute great colour as well as flavour. They may think they are doing something new, but actually a sour cherry-stuffing recipe appears in the first published Turkish cookbook, *Melceu't-Tabbahin* (The Cook's Shelter) from 1844. Of course, those adventurous Ottomans thought of it first.

This recipe was inspired by my friend Batur, whose *yaprak sarma* is a signature dish at his scholarly Ottoman restaurant Asitane (see page 244).

Artichokes are common in the Greek-influenced western part of Turkey; the easterners have barely heard of them. But the artichoke fields that once fed the Ottoman palace have in recent years been turned into shopping centres. Now artichokes are grown way out of town.

If you're in Istanbul in early spring, make sure you try a type of artichoke called *bayrampaşa*, which is the name of the suburb where they used to grow.

They are sold already cleaned by street sellers, soaking in lemon water to retain their colour. They have a wider heart than most artichokes, and lend themselves to stuffing with broad beans. Once summer comes around, their texture becomes too woody for eating.

Artichokes became a staple on meze tables because Turkish drinkers believe these vegetables have liver-cleansing properties.

BAKLALI ENGİNAR

BAKLALI ENGİNAR
BRAISED ARTICHOKES
WITH BROAD BEANS

SERVES 6

6 globe artichokes
½ lemon
1 teaspoon salt
10 spring onions (scallions)
175 g (6 oz/1 cup) fresh broad beans
125 ml (4 fl oz/½ cup) olive oil
1 teaspoon salt
2 teaspoons sugar
2 dill stalks, leaves only

Clean the artichokes, discard the stalk and remove the leaves until you reach the heart. Put the hearts in a large bowl and cover with water. Cut the lemon half into two quarters and squeeze the juice into the water. Add the two squeezed lemon quarters and the salt, and set aside.

Wash the spring onions, remove the roots and tough outer leaves, and then slice into 3 cm (1¼ in) pieces. Make a slit in each broad bean skin, place them in a saucepan, then cover with water. Bring to the boil and allow to boil for 5 minutes. Strain the beans and leave to cool, then double peel.

Place the spring onions in a saucepan. Add the broad beans and the drained artichoke hearts. Add the olive oil, salt, sugar and 375 ml (13 fl oz/1½ cups) of water, then bring to the boil over high heat. Reduce the heat and simmer for 15 minutes, covered, until the broad beans are soft.

Lift the lid and scoop 2 tablespoons of the spring onion and broad bean mixture over the top of each artichoke heart. Simmer, covered, for another 15 minutes.

Remove the lid and place 2 dill leaves on each artichoke. Cover again, turn off the heat, and leave to rest for 15 minutes.

Carefully lift each artichoke with its bean and onion topping out of the pan and place on a serving platter for people to help themselves.

ÇİÇEK SARMA
AEGEAN STUFFED ZUCCHINI FLOWERS

SERVES 4

5 spring onions (scallions)
5 flat-leaf (Italian) parsley stalks
5 dill stalks
5 mint stalks
220 g (7 oz/1 cup) short-grain rice
100 ml (3½ fl oz) olive oil
1 teaspoon salt
½ teaspoon ground white pepper
½ teaspoon sugar
1 tomato
16 zucchini (courgette) flowers
    (preferably male)
½ onion
½ lemon

Wash the spring onions, then remove the roots and tough outer leaves. Finely chop. Pick the leaves from the parsley, dill and mint and finely chop. Set aside the stalks.

Wash the rice under cold running water, drain and place in a bowl. Add the chopped spring onion and herb leaves. Add half the olive oil, and all the salt, pepper and sugar, then mix together with the rice. Grate the tomato into the mixture.

Remove any stalk from each zucchini flower, gently fold back the petals and fill with a tablespoon of the stuffing. Fold the largest petal over to cover the mixture, then fold over the remaining petals.

Put a 20 cm (8 in) plate face down in the bottom of a large saucepan, about 25 cm (10 in) wide. Scatter the reserved parsley, dill and mint stalks over the plate. Place the half onion in the middle of the plate. Surround it with the zucchini flowers, stem side facing up, flowers down.

Add the remaining olive oil and 50 ml (1¾ fl oz) of warm water. Bring to the boil, then cover and simmer for 20 minutes; check after 15 minutes and add another 50 ml (1¾ fl oz) of water if the pan seems to be drying out.

Turn off the heat and squeeze the lemon half over the flowers. Rest, covered, for 15 minutes. Serve warm.

You don't say no to my friend Musa Dağdeviren, the custodian of Turkish traditional values in cooking. So when he told me to meet him outside his Istanbul restaurant at 5 am, I stayed up all night to be on time. We jumped in his pickup truck and drove for an hour to his farm in the country. The sun was just coming up. He wanted to show me the perfect moment to pick zucchini flowers for stuffing—the moment they open to the sun. He'd brought his own rice stuffing so we filled the flowers, steamed them and ate them that morning.

Two years later I saw a documentary about Middle Eastern cooking hosted by the London chef Yotam Ottolenghi, in which he enjoyed the same experience.

You might not be able to pick your flowers at sunrise, but you can come close to the experience if you choose male zucchini flowers (the ones with no zucchini attached), which taste better because they have not had to expend any energy producing fruit.

This recipe is not Musa's stuffing—it's a simpler version they use on the Aegean coast.

If you find this dish in a *meyhane*, you'll know the chef is from the Black Sea. Pickling is an ancient tradition all over Anatolia, a way of preparing vegetables at the end of summer to feed the family over the harsh winter months, but the Black Sea is the only area where they pickle vegetables and then pan-fry them. In addition to green beans (usually the flat kind), they fry pickled cabbage and silverbeet roots. But green beans are the best.

TURŞU KAVURMA
FRIED GREEN BEAN PICKLES

SERVES 4

1 kg (2 lb 4 oz) green beans
2 red chillies
4 garlic cloves
160 g (5½ oz/½ cup) rock salt
50 ml (1¾ fl oz) white vinegar
4 dried chickpeas
1 onion
60 ml (2 fl oz/¼ cup) vegetable oil
1 tablespoon capsicum (pepper)
    paste (see page 32)

Wash the green beans and cut off the ends. Bring 500 ml (17 fl oz/2 cups) of water to the boil in a saucepan, add the beans and simmer for 4 minutes.

Strain the beans and then plunge into iced water for 2 minutes. Strain the refreshed beans and then arrange them, upright, in a 2 litre (70 fl oz/8 cup) preserving jar.

Cut a slice along each chilli, leaving the seeds and the stalks intact, then push the chillies between the beans. Peel two of the garlic cloves and place them, whole, in the jar as well.

Dissolve the rock salt in 500 ml (17 fl oz/2 cups) of water. Add the vinegar to the brine, then pour the mixture into the jar. Put the chickpeas on top of the beans. Seal the jar tightly and store for 1 week at room temperature

Remove the chickpeas from the jar, scoop off any froth on top of the water, and then store for 1 more week (or a few days longer if the weather is cold).

A day before you want to serve the fried pickles, take out about 250 g (9 oz/2 cups) of the beans, and rest them in water overnight.

Pat the soaked beans dry and cut into 5 cm (2 in) lengths. Finely slice the onion and crush the remaining garlic. Heat the vegetable oil in a frying pan over medium heat. Add the onion and fry for 3 minutes, until soft. Add the garlic and capsicum paste, and fry for 2 more minutes, stirring regularly.

Add the beans and stir them through. Simmer, covered, for 5 minutes. Serve the *turşu kavurma* warm on a platter, for people to help themselves.

NOTE
You can keep the remaining *turşu kavurma* in a jar for up to 3 months at room temperature, and enjoy them as a side dish whenever you feel like pickles.

THE BROTHERS OF ORFOZ

An evening walk along the waterfront in the west-coast town of Bodrum is likely to be at first a charming experience and then a depressing one. Beneath the fifteenth-century Castle of Saint Peter, you stroll along a pebbly beach lined with candle-lit tables put out by the local eateries. The gentle waves are lapping just short of the table legs. It's idyllic until the waiters start beckoning and shouting: 'Check out our menu. We got schnitzel, we got pizza, we got Greek salad, we got waffles, we got kebabs.'

Well, an optimist would say at least 20 per cent of their repertoire is Turkish. Bodrum, once the site of one of the seven wonders of the ancient world (the Mausoleum of Halicarnassus), is now a tourist haven that could be anywhere in the Mediterranean. But to get back to Anatolia, you need only round the corner just past the beach, behind the museum of Turkey's favourite singer, Pasha of Bodrum, Zeki Muren, and look for a sign that says 'Orfoz'. There you'll find what might be the best seafood meze bar in the country.

Orfoz is run by the Bozçağa brothers—Çağri is the cook and Çağlar is the host (and also a cook). Their parents were bakers, but they'd both gone off and studied chemical engineering at university before they realised their real passion was experimenting with food. So they opened Orfoz in 2003.

When I remark that the bistros along the waterfront do not seem very Turkish, Çağlar says: 'Well, you could say that in Orfoz we are not doing Turkish cuisine either—we are just doing *our* cuisine. We cook local seafood in the best way we can think of.'

There's no written menu. In the great tradition of *meyhanes*, Çağlar just keeps bringing dishes and asking what we'd like.

But afterwards he's happy to write down, in a mixture of Turkish and English, what he gave us. Here's what he wrote down after our meal:

- *Keçirpeynir*—goat cheese with own local cold-pressed olive oil
- *Sardalya sasimi*—fish, sashimi, sardines
- Smoked eel
- Sea snails with wine sauce *patlangoz*
- Fish soup from grouper fish, fresh leaves of celery
- Mixed salad
- Fresh clams and local oysters
- Oysters with parmesan cheese
- Mussels in casserole (wine, parsley, garlic, olive oil)
- Rice with seafoods cinnamon
- Eggplant in oven (garlic, pepper, olive oil)
- Grilled octopus
- Baby calamari with onion and garlic
- Shrimps in olive oil
- Mother's cookie and cream caramel
- Seasonal fruits

Çağlar insists that Orfoz is just a meze bar with a large wine list. Anywhere else in the world, it would be called a great restaurant.

Çağlar (left) and Çağrı Bozçağa preparing *kidonya,* one of their unique shellfish mezes.

Local scampi served in Orfoz in
Bodrum, on the Aegean coast.

Many Turks would have trouble recognising this dish as part of their cuisine. *Kadayıf* pastry is mostly used for desserts (in a sugar and cheese confection called *künefe*) and jumbo prawns are not a common ingredient, being pretty much confined to the area around Mersin on the Mediterranean coast. But I still claim this recipe for my culture because it was a gift from my Aunty Meral, who suggested the idea of wrapping prawns in pastry when I first opened my restaurant in Sydney in 2007. It went down a treat.

Kadayıf pastry isn't easy to make at home, so buy it ready-made. In Turkey it's created in an elaborate process whereby thin streams of batter are drizzled onto a spinning hot plate, so they dry instantly and form bunches. Its full name is *tel kadayıf*, or 'string dough'. It is similar to Italian vermicelli, so you could use vermicelli or fresh angel hair pasta instead. You'd soften the pasta in boiling water for a minute, drain it, add the ghee and orange, and bunch it into ribbons about 1 cm (½ in) wide, to wrap around the prawns.

KADAYIF KARİDES
CRUNCHY PRAWNS

SERVES 4

8 fresh king prawns
1 tablespoon ghee (to make your own,
  see page 18)
juice of ½ orange
1 teaspoon orange zest
100 g (3½ oz) *kadayıf* pastry
  (or vermicelli or fresh angel hair pasta)
2 teaspoons ground sumac, for
  decoration
pomegranate seeds, for decoration

MUHAMMARA SAUCE
2 tablespoons olive oil
2 red bullhorn peppers
  (or 1 red capsicum/pepper)
2 garlic cloves, lightly roasted
50 g (1¾ oz) walnuts
1 teaspoon *isot* pepper (or chilli flakes)
1 teaspoon ground cumin
pinch of salt
1 tablespoon capsicum (pepper) paste
  (see page 32)
1 tablespoon lemon juice
1 tablespoon pomegranate molasses
  (to make your own, see page 24)
10 pomegranate seeds

First make the *muhammara* sauce. Rub half the olive oil on the bullhorn peppers and roast over an open gas flame, using tongs to rotate the skin and evenly char. (If you prefer a milder garlic taste to raw garlic, you can repeat with the garlic cloves.) Transfer the peppers to a bowl, cover the bowl with plastic wrap, and leave to sweat for 15 minutes. Peel the skin from the peppers and remove the stalk and seeds. Roughly chop.

Put the chopped peppers, garlic, walnuts, *isot*, cumin, salt, capsicum paste, lemon juice, pomegranate molasses and the remaining olive oil in a blender. Pulse for 15 seconds to make a coarse paste. Stir in the pomegranate seeds.

Preheat the oven to 180°C (350°F).

Remove the heads from the prawns. The best way to do this is to straighten the body with one hand and twist the head 90 degrees with the other hand, gently pulling the head off so that the black thread along the spine comes away. Peel off the skin but leave the tail on.

Put the ghee in a frying pan over low heat and warm it slightly (so you can still put a finger in it). Add the orange juice and zest. Place the *kadayıf* in a mixing bowl and gently loosen the pastry, slowly adding the ghee mixture and smearing it through with your fingers so it's evenly spread. When the dough is softened, pull it apart into ribbons about 1 cm (½ in) wide.

Wrap a *kadayıf* ribbon tightly around each prawn, starting at the tail and pressing the strands of dough into the prawn flesh. Keep the wrapping in a neat single layer to ensure even cooking. Place the prawns in a baking tray and cook for about 5 minutes, or until the pastry is golden brown. If your oven cooks unevenly, turn the tray round once during cooking.

Spread a heaped tablespoon of the *muhammara* sauce on four plates. Sit two prawns on top of the sauce, tails up. Sprinkle over a little sumac and a few more pomegranate seeds and serve.

MİDYE TAVA
BOSPHORUS-STYLE MUSSELS WITH TARAMA

If you wanted a glass of beer and a plate of fried food to soak up the alcohol, you'd go to a *birane* rather than a *meyhane*. The dish you're most likely to find there is deep-fried mussels, where beer appears in the batter as well as in a glass.

The tradition is to serve the mussels with a *tarator* (dipping sauce) made with stale bread, walnuts and garlic. Our refined version includes the roe of grey mullet, which makes it a *tarama* (what the Greeks call a *tarama salata*).

In Turkey, *tarama* is always light beige, because that's the colour of the roe. I was surprised to find in Australia that *tarama salata* is pink—and then I learned that it is often artificially coloured. I do not recommend that you buy commercial *tarama salata* to serve with this dish. If you can't find the grey mullet roe, make a simple *tarator* by replacing the roe with 100 g (3½ oz) of walnuts.

SERVES 4

16 blue mussels, scrubbed
60 g (2 oz/½ cup) chickpea flour (besan)
100 ml (3½ fl oz) lager beer
1 egg, separated
75 g (2½ oz/½ cup) plain (all-purpose) flour
1 teaspoon salt flakes
1 teaspoon freshly ground black pepper
vegetable oil, for shallow-frying

TARAMA SAUCE
2 thick slices white bread
100 g (3½ oz) mullet roe
1 garlic clove, roughly chopped
juice of 2 lemons
250 ml (9 fl oz/1 cup) olive oil
250 ml (9 fl oz/1 cup) vegetable oil

First, make the *tarama* sauce. Remove the crusts from the bread and discard. Roughly chop the bread, place in a mixing bowl and add about 125 ml (4 fl oz/½ cup) of water, to just cover. Leave to soak for 1 minute, then remove the bread and squeeze out the water. Transfer to a food processor, add the roe, garlic and half the lemon juice, and pulse to make a paste. Mix the two oils together and gradually drizzle them into the mixture as it's processing. After you've added about 100 ml (3½ fl oz) of the oils, loosen the mixture with 2 tablespoons of ice-cold water. Keep adding oil and iced water in similar amounts to completely emulsify, and finish by adding the remaining lemon juice. Set aside.

Sniff each mussel and if it has a strong smell, discard it. Place the mussels in a bowl and cover with boiling water. When they start to open (after about 5 minutes), scoop them out of the water. Using a knife with a point but a blunt edge, force open any shells that are not open enough, and then pull all the mussels out of their shells. Snip off the beards and place the mussels on paper towel to drain.

Using eight 20 cm (8 in) long bamboo skewers, put two mussels, lengthways, on each skewer. Sift the chickpea flour into a wide bowl, pour in the beer and egg yolk and mix well. Whisk the egg white until soft peaks form, then fold it into the flour mixture.

Sift the plain flour in a separate bowl and mix in the salt and pepper.

Pour the vegetable oil into a frying pan, about 2 cm (¾ in) deep, and heat over medium heat. Add a drop of water to the oil: if it sizzles, the oil is ready. Toss the mussel skewers through the flour, shake off any excess flour, then dip in the batter. Fry four skewers at a time in the hot oil, using tongs to turn after 1 minute, then cook for 1 minute more until golden brown. Place the cooked skewers on paper towel to absorb the excess oil.

Spread 2 tablespoons of *tarama* sauce onto one side of four plates. Place two skewers (four mussels) next to the sauce and serve.

SÜBYE KOKOREÇ
SAUTÉED SQUID WITH GREEN CHILLIES

Kokoreç is my favourite street food, made with lamb intestines, but you may be relieved to hear there are no lambs or intestines in this dish. I've used the word in the Turkish name because the squid has a similar texture to the intestines, and the spicing is the same. We use green chillies as a colour contrast to the red bullhorn peppers. I prefer squid to calamari in a dish like this because of its softer texture. Calamari is better stuffed, as you'll see on page 228.

SERVES 4

3 garlic cloves
2 green chillies
2 red bullhorn peppers
   (or 1 red capsicum/pepper)
3 spring onions (scallions)
4 oregano stalks
1 tomato
500 g (1 lb 2 oz) squid, cleaned
2 tablespoons olive oil
1 tablespoon capsicum (pepper) paste
   (see page 32)
1 teaspoon sea salt
1 teaspoon freshly ground black pepper
1 teaspoon ground cumin
1 tablespoon dried thyme
pita bread (to make your own,
   see page 45) or baby cos lettuce,
   to serve

Finely slice the garlic. Slice the chillies and bullhorn peppers, and remove the seeds and stalks. Wash the spring onions, then remove the roots and tough outer leaves. Finely chop. Pick the leaves from the oregano and finely chop. Finely chop the tomato.

Finely chop the squid, including the head and tentacles.

Heat the olive oil in a wok over high heat. Add the garlic, chilli, sliced peppers and spring onion. Fry for 3 minutes, then add the squid, capsicum paste, salt, black pepper, cumin and thyme. Fry for 5 minutes, stirring constantly. Add the oregano and tomato, stir, and then remove from the heat.

Serve hot, in open pita bread or in baby cos lettuce, on a large platter for people to help themselves.

KÖMÜRDE AHTAPOT
MEDITERRANEAN GRILLED OCTOPUS

SERVES 4

1 kg (2 lb 4 oz) octopus, cleaned
250 ml (9 fl oz/1 cup) red wine
1 teaspoon dried oregano
1 garlic clove
185 ml (6 fl oz/¾ cup) olive oil
1 tablespoon dark soy sauce
4 spring onions (scallions)
juice of 1 lemon
3 flat-leaf (Italian) parsley stalks,
    leaves only, finely chopped
1 small bunch of fresh cranberries
    (optional)

Put the octopus in a bowl with the red wine and oregano, and leave to marinate for 2 hours.

If you're using a charcoal grill, light it 1 hour before you're ready to cook. Burn the charcoal for at least 45 minutes and when the flames have died down, and the coals are glowing with a covering of white ash, the barbecue is ready. (If you're using a gas barbecue, turn it on to medium–high about 5 minutes before you're ready to cook.) If you are using the oven, preheat to 200°C (400°F).

Remove the octopus from the marinade, place it on a board and stretch it out into a tube shape. Tightly wrap the octopus tube in three layers of foil. Discard the marinade.

Place the foil-wrapped octopus on the grill and cook for 2 hours, turning every 30 minutes (or cook in the oven for 1½ hours).

Crush the garlic and mix together in a bowl with 125 ml (4 fl oz/½ cup) of the olive oil and the soy sauce.

Remove the octopus from the heat, unwrap from the foil and brush with the oil and soy mixture. Brush the spring onions with the same mixture. If you're using a charcoal barbecue, put the octopus and spring onions over the coals for 2 minutes on each side. Or sear the octopus and spring onions in a frying pan over high heat for 2 minutes each side until the octopus skin darkens.

Cut the octopus and divide it among four plates. Or place the octopus, whole, on a serving plate for people to help themselves as part of a meze platter. Decorate with the spring onions and drizzle with the lemon juice and the remaining olive oil. Top with the parsley and serve. If it's the season for fresh cranberries, you can also decorate the plate with a few of them.

Octopus is one of the most common ingredients on any Aegean seaside meze table. At 3 pm in the coastal towns you'll see kitchen workers emerge from the restaurants and throw handfuls of octopus against the rocks beside the sea, to tenderise them ahead of the 6 pm rush. My mum used to automate the process by putting them in an old top-loading washing machine with some rocks and churning them for an hour (without washing powder!). Luckily, in fish markets now you can buy them already tenderised.

I love cooking octopus whole with its tentacles on. My good friend İvgen, from Evgenia *meyhane* in Bodrum, gave me a version of this recipe, which has the octopus boiling with mulberry-tree branches before it's char-grilled. She says it makes the octopus melt in your mouth.

For convenience, ecology and flavour, I've instead substituted oregano—so no mulberry trees were harmed in the making of this dish. I can't say the same for the octopus.

Chestnuts are a favourite Turkish street food in winter, sold from wood-fired braziers by hawkers who probably sell ice cream in the summer.

Bursa, a town near Istanbul, is famous for its chestnuts (and *Iskender kebap*). It is in the foothills of Mount Uludağ, which has forests full of chestnut trees.

In this meze, I've paired the chestnuts with leeks, another winter ingredient. It involves a fair bit of folding, as you're required to turn a tube into a triangle. Don't get hung up on a perfect fold. Anything vaguely resembling a three-sided parcel will do, as long as you eat it quickly.

PIRASA SARMA
LEEKS STUFFED WITH CHICKEN AND CHESTNUTS

SERVES 4

9 chestnuts
3 large leeks
220 g (8 oz/1 cup) short-grain rice
1 French shallot (eschalot)
3 garlic cloves
50 ml (1¾ fl oz) olive oil
300 g (10½ oz) minced (ground) chicken
1 tomato
1 tablespoon tomato paste
 (to make your own, see page 24)
1 tablespoon capsicum (pepper) paste
 (see page 32)
2 teaspoons freshly ground black pepper
1 teaspoon ground allspice
1 teaspoon ground cumin
2 teaspoons salt
50 g (1¾ oz) craisins (dried cranberries)
5 flat-leaf (Italian) parsley sprigs,
 chopped
5 dill sprigs, chopped

CAPSICUM SAUCE
1 tablespoon butter
1 tablespoon capsicum (pepper) paste
 (see page 32)
1 tablespoon pomegranate molasses
 (to make your own, see page 24)
1 teaspoon salt

You can use frozen or tinned chestnuts, as long as they are skinned. If using fresh chestnuts, cut a cross in the flat base, place in a saucepan of boiling water and boil for 10 minutes. Remove from the pan and leave to cool, then peel the skin off. Roughly chop the chestnuts.

Remove the roots and green tops from the leeks, then rinse to remove any dirt. Slice down one side of each leek and peel off the outer two layers. Wash these thoroughly, flatten them out and place them across the bottom of a saucepan.

Peel off another four layers of each leek and place in a separate saucepan. Reserve the remaining white centres. Add 750 ml (26 fl oz/3 cups) of salted water to the second pan, bring to boil and then simmer for 5 minutes, until the leek sheets are translucent and soft. Transfer to a bowl of iced water for 2 minutes to refresh. These twelve pieces are the leek skins you are going to stuff.

Wash the rice under cold running water. Finely chop the cores of the leeks and finely chop the shallot. Finely crush the garlic. Heat the olive oil in a frying pan over medium heat. Add the chestnut pieces and shallot. Fry for 1 minute, then add the chopped leek, garlic and the chicken mince and fry for 2 minutes more. Add the rice, then grate in the tomato. Fry for 2 minutes, then add the tomato paste, capsicum paste, spices and dried cranberries, and stir to combine. Add 125 ml (4 fl oz/½ cup) of boiling water and simmer for 5 minutes, covered. Turn off the heat. Stir in the chopped parsley and dill, close the lid, and leave to rest for 15 minutes.

Pick up one sheet of leek skin and put a heaped tablespoon of the rice mixture onto one side. Fold the edges over to make a tight triangular parcel. Repeat to stuff the remaining leek skins.

Put the parcels into the first leek-skin covered pan, folded sides down, on top of the spread skins. Pack them in tightly. Add 250 ml (9 fl oz/1 cup) of warm water and put a small bread and butter plate on top to hold the parcels down. Put the lid on and simmer for 30 minutes over low heat.

Meanwhile, make the capsicum sauce. Melt the butter in a frying pan over low heat. Add the capsicum paste, pomegranate molasses and salt, and stir to combine. Simmer for 5 minutes.

Remove the parcels from the pan. Place three parcels on each plate. Drizzle the capsicum sauce over the top and serve.

ÖRDEK GÖZLEME
DUCK AND SOUR CHERRY GÖZLEME

SERVES 6

4 onions
2 carrots
9 garlic cloves
1 kg (2 lb 4 oz) duck legs
4 dried bay leaves
1 tablespoon salt
1 tablespoon black peppercorns
½ bunch flat-leaf (Italian) parsley
½ bunch mint
200 g (7 oz) haloumi
125 ml (4 fl oz/½ cup) olive oil
80 g (2¾ oz) blanched almonds
2 tablespoons capsicum (pepper) paste
    (see page 32)
200 g (7 oz/1 cup) sour cherries, pitted
juice of ½ lemon
1 sheet *yufka* (see page 27), 60 cm (24 in)
    wide; or 12 sheets of filo pastry, about
    30 x 40 cm (12 x 16 in)
1 egg
4 tablespoons butter

Cut two of the onions into quarters, quarter the carrots, squash five of the garlic cloves, and place them all in a large saucepan. Add the duck legs, bay leaves, salt and peppercorns, cover with water and bring to the boil over medium heat. Reduce the heat and simmer for 1½ hours, until the duck legs are fully cooked.

Meanwhile, chop the remaining onions and crush the remaining garlic. Pick the leaves from the parsley and mint, and finely chop. Coarsely grate the haloumi.

Remove the duck legs from the cooking liquid. Leave to cool slightly, then pull the meat off the bones. Shred the duck meat, and discard the bones and cooking liquid.

Heat the olive oil in a frying pan over medium heat. Add the almonds and toast for 2 minutes, shaking the pan constantly to evenly brown. Add the chopped onion and cook for 5 minutes, until translucent. Add the garlic, capsicum paste and the duck meat. Cook for a further 3 minutes. Remove the pan from the heat and leave to cool.

Halve the sour cherries, then stir them into the duck mixture. Add the lemon juice, and the parsley, mint and haloumi. Stir to combine.

Cut the *yufka* into six wedges. (Or if you're using filo, overlap two sheets to make a square, painting a little melted butter where they overlap to help them stick together.)

Divide the duck mixture into six portions. Put one portion in the middle of each wedge of *yufka* (or each square of filo). Whisk the egg.

Fold the three points of the *yufka* wedges over the filling to make a triangular parcel, or fold the four corners of the filo over the filling to make a square parcel. Paint some beaten egg onto the last layer to stick the parcels together.

Heat 1 tablespoon of the butter in a frying pan over high heat. Add one *gözleme* and fry for 3 minutes on the multi-layered side of the parcel, then flip over and cook the other side for 1 minute. Place on paper towel and repeat with the remaining *gözleme* and butter. Serve hot on a platter for people to help themselves.

The stuffed pancakes known as *gözleme* are hard to find in Istanbul—even though they are well known outside Turkey. They are associated with the Yörük people who live in mountainous regions. *Yörük* means 'walker' or 'nomad', but the Yörüks are not gypsies. They walked into Anatolia around 800 years ago and set up agricultural communities. Nowadays, Yörük women with scarves round their heads arrive in small towns with their tents made of horsehair and fry *gözleme* stuffed with spinach and cheese, potatoes or minced lamb.

I decided to make the concept upmarket by including duck, which nobody would do in Turkey. Strictly speaking, this dish is not a meze (they don't serve *gözleme* in *meyhanes*), but in my restaurant I serve it as part of my meze selection.

İçli köfte literally means 'a meatball with something inside'. The word *içli* is also poetic language for 'deeply felt', and I've seen this translated on Turkish tourist menus as 'sentimental meatballs'.

Tarsus is a historic city in south-central Turkey, in the middle of the wheat and cotton belt. It was where Cleopatra met Mark Antony. Biblical scholars know it as the home of Saul who became Saint Paul.

No doubt he ate these dumplings, which are known as *kibbeh* on the Arab peninsula.

Tarsus these days has many citizens of Arab descent, who moved to the area in the nineteenth century and introduced this dish, using the wheat of the area. Their version is different from the standard form because it is boiled instead of fried, making it healthier.

İÇLİ KÖFTE
TARSUS LAMB AND BEEF DUMPLINGS

SERVES 6

LAMB FILLING

4 onions
4 garlic cloves
80 ml (2½ fl oz/⅓ cup) vegetable oil
500 g (1 lb 2 oz) minced (ground) lamb
2 tablespoons capsicum (pepper) paste
  (see page 32)
2 teaspoons salt
2 teaspoons freshly ground black pepper
1 tablespoon chilli flakes
1 teaspoon ground cinnamon
1 teaspoon ground allspice
150 g (5½ oz) walnuts

BULGUR SHELLS

500 g (1 lb 2 oz) fine bulgur
200 g (7 oz) lean ground (minced) beef
1 tablespoon cornflour (cornstarch)
1 teaspoon salt
2 teaspoons capsicum (pepper) paste
  (see page 32)
50 g (1¾ oz) butter
1 egg
80 ml (2½ fl oz/⅓ cup) vegetable oil

YOĞURT AND TAHINI TOPPING

200 g (7 oz) plain *yoğurt*
1 tablespoon tahini
pinch of sumac

First make the filling. Finely chop the onions and crush the garlic. Heat the vegetable oil in a frying pan over medium heat. Add the onion and cook for 5 minutes until translucent, then add the garlic and fry for 2 minutes more. Add the lamb mince and fry for 5 minutes, stirring frequently. Add the capsicum paste, salt, pepper, chilli flakes, cinnamon and allspice, and fry for a further 3 minutes. Remove the pan from the heat and leave to cool.

Put the walnuts in a blender and coarsely chop. Transfer the filling mixture into a bowl, add the walnuts and mix together, then refrigerate for 2 hours.

Now start making the bulgur shells. Put the bulgur in a heatproof bowl and cover with 750 ml (26 fl oz/3 cups) of boiling water. Leave to soak for 30 minutes, then drain. Mix the beef mince, cornflour, salt, capsicum paste and butter into the bulgur. Break the egg into the mixture and knead for 10 minutes, to make a smooth paste.

Mix 125 ml (4 fl oz/½ cup) of water with the vegetable oil. Wet your palm with the oily water, and place a ping-pong-ball-sized lump of the beef mixture in your palm. Press it into a pattie the size of your palm. Partly close your fist to turn the pattie into a cup, and put a heaped tablespoon of the lamb filling in the middle. Fold the wrapping around the mixture to make a ball. Transfer the ball onto a tray. Repeat to make twelve balls, then refrigerate for 2 hours.

When you are ready to serve, bring about 3 litres (105 fl oz/12 cups) of water to the boil in a saucepan over high heat. Carefully add the dumplings, six at a time, and cook for 5 minutes, until the skin is firm and crusty. Remove each batch of dumplings from the pan with a slotted spoon and place on paper towel.

Meanwhile, make the topping by mixing the *yoğurt* and tahini together in a small bowl.

Place the *icli köfte* on a serving plate. Spoon a tablespoon of the *yoğurt* and tahini topping over each dumpling, decorate with a pinch of sumac, and serve.

KURU DOLMA
STUFFED DRIED EGGPLANT

SERVES 4

1 packet dried eggplants (aubergines),
    about 20 pieces (or 10 fresh eggplant)
3 red capsicums (peppers)
1 onion
1 tablespoon tomato paste
    (to make your own, see page 24)
1 tablespoon capsicum (pepper) paste
    (see page 32)
2 tablespoons olive oil
juice of ½ lemon

LAMB AND BULGUR STUFFING
1 green capsicum (pepper)
1 red capsicum (pepper)
10 mint leaves, finely chopped
10 flat-leaf (Italian) parsley leaves
1 garlic clove
175 g (6 oz/1 cup) fine bulgur
150 g (5½ oz) ground (minced) lamb
100 g (3½ oz/½ cup) chickpeas, boiled
1 tablespoon pomegranate molasses
    (to make your own, see page 24)
1 tablespoon capsicum (pepper) paste
    (see page 32)
1 teaspoon ground cumin
1 teaspoon salt
1 teaspoon ground white pepper
50 ml (1¾ fl oz) olive oil
1 tomato

YOĞURT SAUCE
125 g (4½ oz/½ cup) plain *yoğurt*
2 tablespoons tahini
2 teaspoons ground sumac

Start by making the stuffing. Remove the stalks and seeds from the green and red capsicums and finely chop the flesh. Finely chop the mint and parsley leaves. Crush the garlic to a paste.

Put the bulgur in a bowl, cover with 125 ml (4 fl oz/½ cup) of water and leave to soak for 20 minutes. Stir in the chopped capsicum, mint, parsley and garlic. Add the lamb mince, chickpeas, pomegranate molasses, capsicum paste, cumin, salt, white pepper and olive oil. Halve the tomato and grate it into the mixture, discarding the skin. Mix together well, then set aside.

Put the dried eggplants in a bowl, cover with warm water and leave to hydrate for 6 minutes. Remove from the bowl and pat dry with paper towel. Stuff each of them with 1–2 tablespoons of the lamb mixture, until three-quarters full.

Cut the 3 red capsicums in half and remove the stalks and seeds. Cut the halves into pieces to fit inside the top of the eggplants. Push the capsicum lids on top of the stuffing, shiny side up. These will stop the stuffing from falling out when the eggplant swells during cooking. Peel the onion, but leave it whole.

Using a deep 25 cm (10 in) wide pot, place a 20 cm (8 in) wide dinner plate upside down at the bottom of the pan. Sit the eggplants, capsicum-lids upwards, around the inside of the pot, with the onion in the centre to create a tight fit.

To make the cooking liquid, mix the tomato paste, capsicum paste and olive oil in 500 ml (17 fl oz/2 cups) of water. Pour the liquid over the eggplants and add the lemon juice. Bring to the boil over high heat, then reduce to a simmer and cook, covered, for 45 minutes.

Meanwhile, to make the sauce, mix the *yoğurt*, tahini and sumac together in a small bowl.

Spoon 2 tablespoons of the cooking liquid onto four plates. Add five *kuru dolma* to each plate, distribute the sauce on top and serve.

You see the dried shells of baby eggplants hanging in markets all over eastern Turkey, and you can safely assume they came from a village called Oğuzeli, near Gaziantep, which specialises in emptying and drying eggplants, zucchini and capsicums at the end of summer, ready to be stuffed during winter.

Of course, the stuffing in this recipe can also be used with fresh baby eggplants. Just slice off the top, hollow out the core (leaving thickish walls) and fill it with the stuffing. You can use the scooped out flesh to make the eggplant salad on page 160.

I used to joke that the word *paçanga* (pronounced 'pachanga') sounds like a Spanish dance, and when we were researching this book, I got two shocks. First, it is the name of a type of music popular in Cuba since the late 1950s; and second, there are scholars who claim the dish was brought to Anatolia by Jews escaping the Spanish Inquisition in the

sixteenth century. I hope that's true, because then this dish would represent a blend of three communities that contributed greatly to Turkish cuisine—the Armenians, with their pastırma-making skills; the Bulgarians, with their dairy farming; and the Spanish Jews, with their sophisticated technique (and the name).

PAÇANGA
PASTIRMA BÖREKS

MAKES 8

1 sheet *yufka* (see page 27), or 4 sheets
 of filo pastry
1 tomato
65 g (2½ oz/½ cup) shredded aged *kaşar*
 (or aged mozzarella)
2 green chillies, about 10 cm (4 in) long
8 pieces beef *pastırma* (or another cold
 cut of meat, including corned beef)
3 eggs
1 teaspoon salt
250 ml (9 fl oz/1 cup) vegetable oil
60 g (2 oz/1 cup) breadcrumbs

Cut the *yufka* into eight wedges. Halve the tomato and thinly slice. Grate the cheese. Remove the stalks from the chillies, but leave in the seeds. Finely slice.

Cut the *pastırma* or cold meat into strips about 3 cm (1¼ in) wide and 10 cm (4 in) long. Place a strip across each segment of *yufka*, about 5 cm (2 in) from the bottom. On top of the strip, put 4 slices of tomato, 2 tablespoons of cheese, and 1 teaspoon of chilli pieces. Whisk the eggs and the salt together in a bowl. Fold the *yufka* base over the strip of filling, then fold in the sides (about 3 cm/1¼ in flap). Tightly fold up the parcel, but before you finish the rolling, brush the top triangle of pastry with a little of the egg mixture to make the roll stick. Set aside the eight parcels.

Heat the vegetable oil in a deep frying pan over medium heat. Add a drop of water to the oil: if it sizzles, the oil is ready. Dunk the *böreks* into the egg mixture, two at a time, then roll in the breadcrumbs. Pan-fry the rolls for 2 minutes on each side, until golden. Place on paper towel to absorb the excess oil and then repeat with the remaining *börek*.

Serve on a platter for people to help themselves.

YAPRAK CİĞER
THRACE-COOKED VEAL LIVER

SERVES 4

LIVER
1 veal liver, about 200 g (7 oz)
250 ml (9 fl oz/1 cup) milk
75 g (2½ oz/½ cup) plain (all-purpose)
    flour
50 g (1¾ oz) unsalted butter
1 teaspoon salt
3 dried whole red chillies
1 teaspoon freshly ground black pepper
1 teaspoon dried thyme
1 teaspoon hot paprika
1 teaspoon *isot* (or chilli flakes)
1 teaspoon ground cumin

SUMAC SALAD
½ red onion
1 tablespoon ground sumac
3 flat-leaf (Italian) parsley stalks,
    chopped

Peel the thin skin off the liver. With a very sharp knife, slice the liver into about eight 'leaves', about 5 mm (¼ in) thick. Place the liver strips in a bowl, cover with the milk and leave to rest for 1 hour. Pat the liver strips dry with paper towel.

Sift the flour into a bowl. Roll the liver in the flour to coat well. Shake off any excess flour.

Heat the butter in a frying pan over medium heat until it begins to sizzle. Add the liver and cook for 2 minutes on each side, until the corners are crisp. Sprinkle on the salt and chillies and sauté quickly, then remove the pan from the heat.

Mix the pepper, thyme and spices together in a large bowl. Toss the cooked slices of liver into the mixed spices.

To prepare the salad, thinly slice the red onion, place in a bowl and add the sumac and chopped parsley. Knead the onion mixture for 1 minute to mix the parsley with the juice of the onion.

Place the liver slices on a large plate, add a dollop of salad on top, and serve.

Thrace is a region that overlaps Greece, Bulgaria and Turkey. In the Turkish part, the town of Edirne (named after the Roman emperor Hadrian) is known for two things: olive oil wrestling, and the livers of the cattle that grow in the neighbourhood. The liver is sliced very long and thin so that it looks like 'leaves' (*yaprak*), and is always pan-fried.

One thing I learned from an Edirne liver master was to rest the liver in milk to drain away the excess blood and soften the taste. I've had customers who have never enjoyed liver turn into converts when they try this dish.

When I put testicles on the menu many people thought I was trying to create a sensation, but I was actually making a point about sustainability. When I was growing up, Turkey was going through economically tough times, and it was important not to waste anything. The butchers would reserve offal for the families that had young children, as a source of protein. I grew up eating liver, kidneys, brains and testicles, and anyone looking at my height today would say that they must have been a great source of nutrition. Nowadays, when the food elite talks about sustainable eating, I like to ask: 'How did we go from fillet steak to fried crickets without using the rest of the animal first?'

KOÇ YUMURTASI
RAM'S EGGS

SERVES 4

4 ram's testicles
1 slice day-old white sandwich bread
50 ml (1¾ fl oz) milk
80 g (2¾ oz/½ cup) blanched almonds
1 garlic clove, peeled
juice of ½ lemon
1 tablespoon white vinegar
2 teaspoons sea salt
1 tablespoon extra virgin olive oil
2 tablespoons butter
1 teaspoon ground cumin
1 teaspoon isot (or chilli flakes)
2 teaspoons ground sumac, to decorate

It's likely you will have bought the testicles frozen. Let them thaw for 15 minutes. Chop off the top and bottom. Remove the translucent skin and the white membrane, then cut the soft meat in half lengthways. Set aside.

Put the bread in bowl, cover with the milk and leave to soak for 5 minutes. Discard the crusts and squeeze the bread to remove excess liquid.

Put the almonds, garlic, lemon juice, vinegar, salt and the bread in a food processor and purée, slowly adding the olive oil. If it's too thick, add 2 teaspoons of water.

Melt the butter in a frying pan over low heat. Add the half testicles, cut side down, and sauté for 2 minutes. Turn, sprinkle on the cumin, isot and some extra salt, and fry for 1 minute more. Remove from the pan and rest on paper towel.

Spread 1 tablespoon of the almond and garlic sauce on one side of each plate, with pieces of testicle on the other side. Sprinkle with the sumac and serve.

DINNER

TRADITIONS & INNOVATIONS

DINNER

For most Turks, dinner is the most important meal of the day, particularly during the thirty nights of Ramadan (spelt *Ramazan* in Turkish). That's the month when adult muslims are expected to refrain from eating, drinking, smoking or having sex from dawn to sunset.

When the drums and cannons signal that the sun has set, the faithful sit down to a feast called *iftar*, which begins with easily digested foods such as dates and olives, then moves on to lavish lamb and eggplant stews, and concludes with cinnamon-flavoured rice puddings and baklava.

Paradoxically, although Ramadan is the month for fasting, Turks tend to put on weight then, because they have a gourmet party every night—either at home or in *lokantas* and *restorans* that set up trestle tables in the street to provide instant gratification to the desperate fasters.

The other 335 nights of the year, Turks have the leisure to contemplate the way their dining scene is changing, and the rise of what is being labelled 'the new Anatolian cuisine'.

The classic European image of a 'restaurant', serving starters, main courses and desserts from a written menu, with matching wines, is not part of the Turkish tradition. Until the twenty-first century, our approach to meals outside the home mostly involved going to eateries that specialised in one type of cooking (just *kebaps*, say, or just *köfte*, or just grilled fish, or just pide), and sharing dishes delivered to the middle of the table in no particular order, apart from the broad principle of 'cold first, then hot'.

There was no tradition of hero-worshipping chefs. Eateries were chosen for the friendliness of the host or the celebrities that might be seen there. Chefs saw their job as perfecting the standard recipes of their predecessors, not creating their own works of art.

If people wanted to show off, they would look for restaurants purporting to offer Italian, French, Japanese or whatever was that year's international fad. They saw no reason to spend big money on anything described as Turkish.

Then a bunch of radicals came along and applied to Anatolian food a concept known in English-speaking societies as 'fine dining', or in French-speaking societies as *nouvelle cuisine*.

Mehmet Gürs was the first of the fine dining pioneers, and became internationally known. With a Turkish father and

a Finnish mother, and eight years' kitchen training in the United States, he was bound to come up with something unusual when he opened his first restaurant, Downtown, in 1995 (which had evolved by 2006 into the very posh Mikla on top of the Marmara Pera Hotel). Here's how Mehmet summarises his philosophy:

The Anatolian kitchen is not restricted to the Turkish or the Ottoman kitchen. All products of different ethnic origins and religions of Anatolia, the birthplace of cultures during a very long span of time before and after the Ottoman Empire, constitute the kitchen of this region. Wine born in this region is an indispensable part of the New Anatolian kitchen. Diversity of ingredients and revitalisation of endangered and almost extinct rich resources is as important as the methods used ... Respect the elders and listen to them, yet do not be crushed by them and do not be afraid to turn age-old ideas upside down.

Other pioneers include Şemsa Denizsel, who moved from advertising to cooking and now runs a culinary centre in Ayvalık, on the Aegean coast; US-trained Didem Şenol, who runs the mostly vegetarian Gram restaurant in Istanbul; Maksut Aşkar, whose restaurant neolokal, in the Salt art museum near Galata Tower, has a worldwide reputation for innovation; and Civan Er, who studied international relations in London before opening Yeni, which means 'new'. I've detailed how to find these places at the end of this book.

Thanks to chefs like them, it's possible for visitors to Istanbul to enjoy sophisticated Turkish dinners that use contemporary methods, but respect the produce and have regional authenticity. That's an approach I share. But in addition, I've had to develop my style in a land thousands of miles from Turkey. I've found those adaptations exciting, and I hope the fun I've had comes across in this chapter.

Mehmet Gürs prepares for dinner at Mikla, one of Istanbul's most innovative restaurants.

The almond, now grown along the Aegean and Mediterranean coasts, is another delicacy that was cultivated first in Anatolia, and was one of only two nuts to be mentioned in the holiest Christian, Jewish and Muslim texts—the other being the pistachio.

I first had the cold version of this sixteenth-century Ottoman dish in Şemsa Denizsel's famous Kantin restaurant in the posh Istanbul suburb of Nişantaşi. She was inspired by Spanish cuisine in deciding to include grapes. I like the addition of unripened green almonds (picked in late spring before the outer skin becomes tough and inedible) because they give a sour balance to this mellow soup.

BADEM ÇORBASI
COLD ALMOND AND GRAPE SOUP

SERVES 4

50 ml (1¾ fl oz) almond milk
1 slice thick sandwich bread
2 garlic cloves, unpeeled
160 g (5½ oz) blanched almonds
1 teaspoon sea salt
125 m (4 fl oz/½ cup) olive oil
60 ml (2 fl oz/¼ cup) white wine
   or sherry vinegar

TOPPING

3 garlic cloves
2 teaspoons lemon juice
pinch of sugar
80 ml (2½ fl oz/⅓ cup) olive oil
2 green almonds (optional)
180 g (6 oz/1 cup) green
   seedless grapes

Put the almond milk in a saucepan with 50 ml (1¾ fl oz) of water. Bring to the boil and then turn off the heat. Cut the crusts from the bread and discard. Soak the bread in the boiled almond milk for 2 minutes. Squeeze the excess milk out of the bread and set the milk aside to cool.

Dry-fry the unpeeled garlic cloves in a frying pan over medium heat for 4 minutes, shaking the pan constantly to evenly brown them. Remove from the heat and leave to cool slightly. Peel away the skin and any burnt spots.

Place the blanched almonds, soaked bread, toasted garlic and salt in a food processor, and blend to make a fine paste. Slowly mix in the olive oil, then the almond-milk water, and then 200 ml (7 fl oz) of cold water. Pour the soup into a large bowl and stir in the vinegar. Chill in the fridge for 30 minutes.

Next, make the topping. Finely slice the garlic lengthways into about eighteen thin pieces. Drizzle with the lemon juice and sprinkle with sugar.

Heat the olive oil in a frying pan over high heat. Add a drop of water to the oil: if it sizzles, the oil is ready. Add the garlic to the pan and fry for 3 minutes, until golden brown. Scoop the garlic chips out with a slotted spoon and place on paper towel to drain the excess oil.

Quarter the green almonds. Cut the grapes in half. Ladle the soup into four bowls, then decorate with the halved grapes, green almond pieces and garlic chips. Serve chilled.

KIRLANGIÇ ÇORBASI
SCORPIONFISH SOUP

When I was growing up, this delicacy made with the ugliest fish I'd ever seen was a speciality of my father. He is a devoted sailor and amateur fisherman, and we spent our summers in the seaside village of Bayramoğlu, an hour from Istanbul. He'd go out on the water all day in his small boat, and come back with a catch that always included scorpionfish. They are bony and hard to clean, so there's no point trying to turn them into fillets. Best to cook them before you remove the flesh.

Like many Turkish soups, this is enriched at the end with a *terbiye*—a word that translates as 'teaching good manners'. The basic ingredients of a *terbiye* are egg and lemon, sometimes with *yoğurt* or flour added. Old-school chefs would call this 'binding' the soup, but we prefer to say we're polishing it to perfection.

SERVES 4

1 scorpionfish, about 1.5 kg (3 lb 5 oz)
    (or any rockfish)
1 garlic clove, peeled
1 onion, quartered
1 potato
1 carrot
¼ celeriac
1 celery stalk
½ bunch dill
½ bunch flat-leaf (Italian) parsley
125 ml (4 fl oz/½ cup) dry white wine
1 egg yolk
100 ml (3½ fl oz) olive oil
juice of 1 lemon
1 teaspoon salt
1 teaspoon freshly ground black pepper

Clean the fish, removing the guts and gills. Place on a board and chop into three pieces.

Put 1.5 litres (52 fl oz/6 cups) of salted water in a saucepan. Add the fish, whole garlic clove and onion quarters, and bring to the boil over high heat. Continue to boil for 20 minutes, uncovered. Turn off the heat, remove the fish from the pan and rest for 20 minutes. Remove the flesh from the bones and set the flesh aside.

Return the fish bones and head to the pan, bring back to the boil, and then continue to boil over high heat for 15 minutes.

Peel the potato, carrot and celeriac and roughly chop. Remove the leaves from the celery and reserve. Chop the celery stalk.

Strain the hot fish liquid into another pot and discard the bones, garlic and onion. Add the vegetables and bring back to the boil, then reduce the heat and simmer for 20 minutes.

Pick and chop the reserved celery leaves, dill and parsley, add to the original pan with the fish and mix together. Add the wine and boil vigorously for 2 minutes to let the alcohol evaporate. Add 250 ml (9 fl oz/1 cup) of the soup and bring to the boil over high heat. Boil for 5 minutes.

Put 250 ml (9 fl oz/1 cup) of the soup in a bowl with the egg yolk and whisk to combine. Return the mixture to the pan and simmer for 5 minutes, stirring frequently.

Mix the olive oil, lemon juice, salt and pepper in a bowl. Divide the fish among four bowls. Ladle the soup over each lump of fish. Drizzle a little of the lemony oil over each bowl and serve.

KELLE PAÇA
SHEEP'S HEAD SOUP

This is a dish to help you sober up at 4 am, and in Istanbul is likely to be found in an offal specialist that is closed during daylight hours. These places, in the more colourful suburbs, catch customers who stagger out of a *meyhane* in a confused condition after midnight and look after them until the breakfast cafés start opening around 6 am. I first encountered *kelle paça* when I was seventeen at an eatery called Apik in the abattoir district Dolapdere. It's filled with Romany musicians, prostitutes, and characters you'd not want to meet in a dark alley. In my merry condition I found the scene intriguing, and happily agreed with the Turkish conviction that the soup's gelatine and protein helps you sober up.

Clearly, this recipe depends on you being able to source a whole sheep's head. If you can't, leave out the head and make the soup with lamb knuckles and brains.

SERVES 4

1 sheep's head, skin off, top of skull
    removed
1 teaspoon white vinegar
2 teaspoons salt
1 egg
1 tablespoon plain (all-purpose) flour
pinch of freshly ground black pepper
125 ml (4 fl oz/½ cup) vegetable oil,
    for frying

STOCK
2 lamb knuckles
1 onion, peeled and halved
1 tablespoon salt
3 tablespoons plain (all-purpose) flour
2 tablespoons lemon juice
1 egg

GARLIC SAUCE
2 garlic cloves
juice of 1 lemon
70 ml (2¼ fl oz) red wine vinegar

Remove the brain from the sheep's head and wash it under running water. Remove the outer membrane. Put the brain in a saucepan and cover with water. Add the vinegar and half the salt, and bring to the boil over high heat. Reduce the heat to medium and boil for 5 minutes. Strain off the water and put the brain in a bowl. Cover with cold water, then transfer to the fridge to cool.

To make the stock, put the sheep's head, minus the brain, in a saucepan with the lamb knuckles. Add the onion halves and enough water to cover. Add the salt. Boil for 1½ hours over medium heat, partly covered with the lid. Skim any scum off the surface.

Remove the sheep's head from the pan and remove the tongue. Return the head to the pan and set aside the tongue. Cook for another 20 minutes. Remove the head and knuckles from the pan and leave to cool on paper towel. Strip all the meat off the head. Take the meat from the knuckles and discard the fat. Set aside in a bowl.

Peel the outer layer from the tongue and remove any connective tissue from the base. Thinly slice the tongue.

Strain the stock into another saucepan to remove the onion and any floating scum. Put the stock and all the meat back in the original pan and place over low heat. When the soup is warm (not boiling), scoop out 250 ml (9 fl oz/1 cup) of the liquid and mix in a bowl with the flour, lemon juice and egg. Whisk together, then add to the soup. Increase the heat to medium and bring to the boil, then reduce to a simmer.

Remove the brain from the fridge, strain off the water, and slice into four pieces. Mix the egg, flour, pepper, remaining 1 teaspoon of salt, and 1 tablespoon of water in a bowl, then coat the pieces of brain in the mixture.

Heat the vegetable oil in a frying pan over medium heat. Add a drop of water; if it sizzles, the oil is ready. Fry the brain pieces for 2 minutes on each side until golden. Using a slotted spoon, scoop four heaped spoons of meat out of the soup, into each bowl. Put one piece of brain on each mound of meat, then ladle the soup around it.

To make the sauce, crush the garlic and mix together with the lemon juice and red wine vinegar. Drizzle a little of the sauce over each bowl and serve.

EFENDY SALATA
FIG AND HAZELNUT SALAD

SERVES 4

140 g (5 oz/1 cup) hazelnuts
6 fresh figs
150 g (5½ oz) wild (or baby) rocket
　(arugula)
70 g (2½ oz/½ cup) crumbly goat's feta

MUSTARD DRESSING
2 tablespoons olive oil
1 tablespoon seed mustard
1 tablespoon grape molasses
1 tablespoon red wine vinegar
2 teaspoons lemon juice

Preheat the oven to 180°C (350°F).

Spread the hazelnuts on a baking tray and roast for 5 minutes. Remove from the oven and leave to cool, then rub the skins off. Crush the hazelnuts or roughly grind them in a food processor.

Mix all the mustard dressing ingredients in a bowl.

Remove the stalks from the figs and slice each fig into six pieces, lengthways. Toss the rocket and hazelnuts in a salad bowl with the dressing. Crumble the feta and sprinkle it over the salad. Top the salad with the fig slices and serve.

I like to think the simple ingredients in this salad represent the diversity of my country—hazelnuts are favourites of the Black Sea region, rocket is a specialty of the Aegean coast, the best feta comes from Marmara in the northwest, and the best figs are from the Mediterranean Sea region. This has been the house salad ever since I opened my Sydney restaurant in 2007. It was one of my team's first creations, and I must confess it has one non-Turkish ingredient—mustard, with the seeds left in.

If it's winter and figs are out of season, you could soak dried figs in warm water for 15 minutes. The figs won't be quite as luscious as the fresh version, but the salad will still be delicious.

This dish commemorates the pivotal historical event shared by Australia and Turkey, and combines ingredients from these two great cultures. Gallipoli, in northwest Turkey, is a popular scuba-diving area, and a major source of scallops. It is best known to Australians as the site of an attempt in 1915 to secure territory in Turkey, which had joined the First World War on Germany's side.

Australia's major public holiday each year is 25 April, which was when the Australian and New Zealand troops (called ANZACs) took part in the ill-fated Allied assault on the Turkish peninsula. They were repelled by the Turks under General Mustafa Kemal Atatürk, who went on to create the Turkish republic out of the ruins of the Ottoman Empire.

When I came to live in Sydney, I was curious to see how kangaroo meat would respond to the drying and preserving process we call *pastırma*. It turns out that kangaroo works even better than beef, because it's almost fat-free. If you can't find roo, try venison.

KANGURMALI TARAK
LIME-MARINATED SCALLOPS WITH KANGAROO PASTIRMA

SERVES 4

500 g (1 lb 2 oz) kangaroo fillets
1 kg (2 lb 4 oz) rock salt
500 g (1 lb 2 oz) caster (superfine) sugar
15 garlic cloves
3 tablespoons ground fenugreek
3 tablespoons ground cumin
1 teaspoon ground fennel
2 tablespoons sweet paprika
1 tablespoon hot paprika
1½ teaspoons salt
8 tarragon leaves
4 mint leaves
juice of 1 lime
1 teaspoon ground white pepper
1 teaspoon grape molasses
1 tablespoon olive oil
1 teaspoon *rakı*
12 sea scallops (or 6 large scallops)

Place the kangaroo fillets on a board and, using a sharp knife, remove any sinews. Using a cake rack (or steamer tray or a large colander), cover the rack with muslin (cheesecloth) or a tea towel. Place the rack on a baking tray or in a large pan. You will use this for the drying process.

Mix the rock salt and caster sugar in a bowl. Spread half the rock salt mixture onto the muslin-covered tray, about 1 cm (½ in) thick. Put the kangaroo fillets in the middle of the rack and thoroughly cover with the rest of the rock salt mixture. Fold the cloth over the top of the salt.

Place a flat-bottomed tray over the fillets, with a 3 kg (6 lb 12 oz) weight on top (using anything from a case of beer to wine bottles), to flatten out the meat as it dries. Place the baking tray in a cool spot for 2 days, checking occasionally that the accumulated water does not reach the meat.

Unwrap the meat and wash off the salt. Place the meat in a bowl, cover with water and leave to rest for 24 hours.

Remove the meat from the water and pat dry with paper towel. Put the meat on a rack with a drip tray underneath and refrigerate for 24 hours. Turn the fillets over and return to the fridge for one more day.

Now, make the spice paste. In a blender, mix the garlic, fenugreek, cumin, fennel, sweet and hot paprika and 1 teaspoon of the salt into a paste. If the mixture seems dry, drizzle in about ½ teaspoon of water.

Remove the kangaroo from the fridge and coat with the paste, making sure every part is completely covered. Put the fillet on the cake rack with the tray underneath, but without the cloth, and return to the fridge for at least another 5 days.

A few hours before serving, finely chop the tarragon and mint leaves, and place in a small bowl. Add the lime juice and mix in the white pepper, grape molasses, olive oil, *rakı* and the remaining ½ teaspoon of salt. Slice the scallops into rounds about 1 cm (½ in) thick, and rest them in the marinade for 2 hours.

Slice through the kangaroo fillet, diagonally, as thinly as possible (about 1–2 mm); use a slicer if you have one. Divide the scallop slices among four plates, top each with a slice of kangaroo and serve.

KALAMAR DOLMA
STUFFED BABY CALAMARI

SERVES 4

1 kg (2 lb 4 oz) small calamari, each
    about 6–8 cm (2½–3¼ in), cleaned
1 tablespoon white vinegar
100 g (3½ oz) prawns, peeled
100 g (3½ oz) firm white-flesh fish
    (such as ling, blue eye trevalla,
    mahi mahi)
1 garlic clove
60 ml (2 fl oz/¼ cup) olive oil
100 g (3½ oz) rice
½ teaspoon salt
1 teaspoon sugar
1 tablespoon ground turmeric
50 g (1¾ oz) butter
50 g (1¾ oz) grated *kaşar* (or mozzarella)
10 tarragon leaves, chopped
10 mint leaves, chopped

CREAM SAUCE
50 g (1¾ oz) butter
2 garlic cloves
1 tablespoon soy sauce
150 ml (5 fl oz) pouring (whipping) cream

We recommend you buy the calamari cleaned, but if you prefer to use whole calamari, remove the tentacles, the cartilage in the middle, and the skin, and thoroughly wash the bodies (you can use the tentacles, chopped, as part of the stuffing).

Put 1 litre (35 fl oz/4 cups) of water and the vinegar in a saucepan over high heat and bring to the boil. Add the calamari tubes, reduce the heat to medium and cook for 25 minutes. Scoop the tubes out of the water and place on a board to cool. Reserve the cooking liquid.

Peel and clean the prawns, then finely chop. Check there are no bones in the fish fillets, then finely chop.

Finely slice the garlic. Heat the olive oil in a frying pan over medium heat. Add the garlic and cook for 1 minute. Wash the rice under cold running water, then add to the pan. Stir for 1 minute to coat the rice with the oil. Add the chopped fish, prawns and the salt and sugar. Stir for 1 minute to combine.

Put 250 ml (9 fl oz/1 cup) of the reserved cooking liquid in a small bowl and stir in the turmeric. Add the turmeric liquid to the rice mixture and cook, covered, for 5 minutes. Remove from the heat and leave to rest, with the lid on, until the mixture cools to room temperature.

Finely chop one of the calamari tubes (and the tentacles, if you've kept them), and add to the rice. Stir in the butter, cheese, tarragon and mint.

Use a teaspoon to stuff the rice into the remaining calamari tubes (about 2–3 teaspoons per tube). Tightly pack the calamari tubes into a saucepan, with the wide open ends facing upwards. If the calamari seem too loosely packed and are at risk of falling over, put a large (washed) potato in the middle and pack the calamari around it. Pour 250 ml (9 fl oz/1 cup) of the cooking liquid into the pan, so that the liquid comes about two-thirds of the way up the tubes. The tops should be at least 2 cm (¾ in) clear of the liquid. Cover with a lid and simmer for 20 minutes over low heat.

Meanwhile, make the cream sauce. Melt the butter in a saucepan over low heat. Halve the garlic cloves and add them to the pan. Increase the heat to medium and cook for 3 minutes. Add the soy sauce and reduce the heat to a simmer. Add the cream and simmer, uncovered, for 5 minutes, stirring regularly until the mixture starts to bubble. Remove from the heat, and remove the garlic halves.

Put 2 tablespoons of the sauce onto each serving plate. Divide the calamari tubes among the plates, sitting them on top of the sauce, and serve.

As you've gathered by now, we Turks will stuff anything. We love baby calamari because, when cleaned, they form little pouches—just waiting to be filled. To make life more challenging, I decided to fill the pouches with an elaborate stuffing, using other seafood that would either eat or be eaten by calamari.

You may be surprised to see soy sauce among the ingredients here, and yes, it's not typically Turkish. I first encountered this mixture of cream and soy in the *meyhane* of my friend Ivgen, in Bodrum, and mistook it for a form of tahini. It turned out Ivgen had successfully brought together the two ends of the spice route.

Outside and inside one of the massive mosques built in Istanbul with the wealth of the Ottoman Empire.

The traditional recipe involves stuffing and wrapping *hamsi*, the most prized fish of the Black Sea region. Similar to a European anchovy, they are impossible to find outside of the Black Sea. You could instead make this dish with sardines, or small red mullet, although I prefer garfish because it is milder in taste and can absorb some of the saltiness of the vine leaves. Because they're cooked on the barbecue or grill, the vine leaves will char a little. That just adds flavour.

ASMADA ZARGANA
CHAR-GRILLED GARFISH IN VINE LEAVES

SERVES 4

15 fresh or preserved vine leaves
10 flat-leaf (Italian) parsley leaves
10 mint leaves
2 garlic cloves, peeled
2 tablespoons pine nuts
juice of ½ lemon
12 garfish (about 1 kg/2 lb 4 oz),
    butterflied, heads and tails on
2 tablespoons olive oil
2 lemons, cut into 8 wedges each,
    to serve

If you're using a charcoal grill, light it 1 hour before you're ready to cook. Burn the charcoal for at least 45 minutes, and when the flames have died down and the coals are glowing with a covering of white ash, the barbecue is ready. If you're using a gas barbecue, turn it on to medium heat about 5 minutes before you're ready to cook. Or use a frying pan.

If the vine leaves are fresh, place them in a bowl, cover with boiling salted water and soak for 10 minutes. If they are in brine, wash thoroughly to remove most of the salt.

Using a mortar and pestle, crush together the parsley leaves, mint leaves, garlic, pine nuts and lemon juice. Open out each fish and place a tablespoon of the mixture inside, then close the two halves of the fish.

Spread the vine leaves out flat on a board, shiny side down. Roll each garfish in a vine leaf. If the vine leaves are small, add half of another vine leaf.

Drizzle the vine leaves with the olive oil and cook on the grill, close to the heat, for 2 minutes on each side, until the vine leaves are charred. (If you don't have a barbecue, heat the olive oil in a heavy-based frying pan over high heat. Add a drop of water to the oil; if it sizzles, the oil is ready. Place the wrapped fish in the pan and cook for 4 minutes on each side.)

Serve the *asmada zargana* with the lemon wedges. You should eat the vine leaves.

SARDINE BIRDS

SERVES 4

1 tablespoon roasted hazelnuts
30 wild rocket (arugula) leaves
2 onions
290 ml (10 fl oz) olive oil
2 tablespoons rice
2 teaspoons salt
½ teaspoon sugar
1 teaspoon freshly ground black pepper
zest of 1 lemon
18 sardines, butterflied, tails on
4 tablespoons maize flour
2 eggs

Finely chop the roasted hazelnuts. Finely chop the wild rocket. Finely slice the onions.

Heat 2 tablespoons of the olive oil in a saucepan over medium heat. Add the onion and cook for 5 minutes, until soft and translucent. Wash the rice under cold running water, then add to the pan and stir for 1 minute. Add 250 ml (9 fl oz/1 cup) of hot water and the salt. Bring to the boil and then simmer, covered, for 15 minutes.

Stir in the hazelnuts, sugar, pepper and lemon zest. Remove from the heat and leave to rest, covered, for 15 minutes.

Slice six of the sardines into two fillets each, so you have twelve 'lids' to go on the 'birds'. Toss all the sardines (halves and whole), in the maize flour.

Now stuff the birds. Holding a butterflied sardine in your hand, place a little less than 1 tablespoon of the rice mixture between the halves, and push them gently together. Repeat with the other eleven butterflied sardines. Put a half-sardine lid on each stuffed sardine, to make a triangle shape. Squeeze the pieces together.

Whisk the eggs in a bowl. Heat the remaining olive oil in a frying pan over high heat. Add a drop of water to the oil: if it sizzles, the oil is ready. Dip the 'birds' into the egg and carefully place in the hot oil. Fry for 2 minutes on each side, until golden. Place on paper towel to absorb the excess oil.

Serve three *hamsi kuşu* per person.

This is very much a hands-on recipe, requiring you to squeeze three egg-coated fish fillets into the shape of a bird (or what must have looked like a bird to the Black Sea chef who named this dish centuries ago). There's a song about this dish, by local folk singer Volkan Konak, which goes: 'I wish I was a *hamsi* bird, so I could fly up into the branches, and the mothers-in-law wouldn't eat me.'

Similar to a European anchovy, the strongly flavoured *hamsi* is the staple protein of the Black Sea region. In the season (autumn and winter) you find them everywhere in Istanbul, and you can buy them in the fish markets for as little as 2 lira a kilo.

Being so plentiful, *hamsi* feature in hundreds of Turkish recipes—in simple dishes such as pan-fried *hamsi*, some more complex recipes like this one, and some totally weird, like the cornbread in our breakfast chapter (see page 49), or '*hamsi* jam' (which everyone mentions but nobody admits to having eaten). Outside Turkey, the best substitute for *hamsi* is sardines.

Partly out of laziness, partly out of convenience, Turkish restaurants outside Turkey have made swordfish on skewers a clichéd dish, but they're not doing their country any favours. Charcoal works best with an oily fish that doesn't dry out as easily as swordfish, so inevitably most swordfish skewers turn out dry and overcooked.

Putting something on a skewer doesn't make it Turkish. What does is the right application of techniques and flavourings to a fresh ingredient. Sole, like most fish fillets, is much more suitable for pan-frying, and rolling the fillets before skewering means you can achieve a crispy outside and a juicy inside.

DİL ŞİŞ
SKEWERED SOLE WITH BRAISED FENNEL

SERVES 4

16 sole fillets (or other flat fish)
4 spring onions
125 ml (4 fl oz/½ cup) olive oil
8 bay leaves
1 red onion
1 lemon
12 bay leaves
1 small fennel bulb
zest of 1 orange, plus the juice of
    2 oranges
2 teaspoons salt
1 teaspoon sugar
1 teaspoon plain (all-purpose) flour
2 tablespoons butter
1 teaspoon ground white pepper

Ask your fishmonger to slice four fillets each from four soles. Lay the fillets on a board. Slice the spring onions into 4 cm (1½ in) tubes. Heat 1 tablespoon of the olive oil in a frying pan over medium heat. Add the spring onion and cook for 2 minutes, shaking the pan constantly. Remove from the heat.

Put a spring onion piece across the bottom of each fillet and roll the fillet around it. Now make the skewers. Cut the red onion in half, crossways. Reserve one half, then cut the remaining half into eight pieces. Cut the lemon in half, then slice one half into three rounds about 1 cm (½ in) wide, then slice each round into quarters. Reserve the remaining lemon half for the sauce.

Each skewer will contain four rolls of fish, three small pieces of lemon, three bay leaves, and two pieces of onion that will form brackets at either end of the skewer. Push one piece of onion onto the skewer. Add one roll of fish, then one bay leaf, one piece of lemon, then fish again, bay leaf again, lemon, fish, bay leaf, lemon, fish, and finally the other onion bracket. Make three more skewers the same way.

Remove the outer layer from the fennel and slice the remaining bulb into four rounds, lengthways. If the fennel came with the green fronds attached, keep them for decoration. Finely slice the remaining onion half and any remaining pieces not used for the skewers.

Heat 2 tablespoons of the olive oil in a frying pan over medium heat. Add the remaining onion and fry for 1 minute. Add the fennel pieces and fry for 1 minute, then stir in the orange zest, salt and sugar. Mix the flour into the orange juice. Reduce the heat to a simmer. Add the orange juice mixture and enough water to cover the fennel. Close the lid and simmer for 15 minutes. Check the fennel; if it isn't soft by now, simmer for another 10 minutes.

In a separate large (30 cm/12 in) frying pan, heat all but 2 tablespoons of the remaining olive oil with the butter over medium heat. Add a drop of water to the oil: if it sizzles, the oil is ready. Add the skewers and cook for 4 minutes on each side, until golden brown.

Place a quarter of the fennel mixture on each serving plate. Place a skewer on top. Juice the remaining half lemon, and combine the juice with the remaining olive oil and the white pepper, then drizzle a little over each skewer. Decorate with fennel tips (if you have them) and serve.

USKUMRU DOLMASI
'FORGET-ME-NOT' MACKEREL WITH BARBERRIES

SERVES 4

4 blue mackerel, whole
150 g (5½ oz/1 cup) plain (all-purpose)
    flour
3 eggs
200 g (7 oz/1 cup) fine polenta
300 ml (10½ fl oz) olive oil

BARBERRY STUFFING

50 g (1¾ oz) dried barberries
    (or currants)
1 large onion
200 ml (7 fl oz) olive oil
100 g (3½ oz) pine nuts
1 teaspoon ground cinnamon
1 teaspoon ground allspice
3 teaspoons salt
20 flat-leaf (Italian) parsley leaves,
    finely chopped, plus extra to garnish

POMEGRANATE DRESSING
(OPTIONAL)

1 tablespoon pomegranate molasses
    (to make your own, see page 24)
1 tablespoon olive oil
20 pomegranate seeds
10 parsley leaves, finely chopped

Clean the blue mackerel by removing the gills and the organs without a knife. You need to push your fingers into the throat of the fish and hook them under the gills. Pull gently so the gills and the attached organs come out. Use scissors to cut off the fins, being careful not to tear the skin. Wash thoroughly.

Gently massage the fish on each side for 5 minutes to soften the flesh until you can feel the spine. Gently break the tail, turning it 90 degrees, up then down, without puncturing the skin. Push the points of a pair of scissors through the gill hole and use them to sever the head from the spine. You can now remove the spine from inside the fish. Cover the fish with a dry cloth so you can hold it with one hand. With the other hand, reach through the gill hole and, with your thumb and forefinger, gently pull out the spinal bones. Scrape off any meat that's attached to the spine and place in a bowl. Using a cocktail spoon, remove all the flesh from inside the fish and add to the bowl.

To make the stuffing, put the barberries in a bowl, cover with water and leave to soak for 15 minutes. Finely chop the onion. Meanwhile, heat the olive oil in a large frying pan over medium heat. Add a drop of water to the oil; if it sizzles, the oil is ready. Sauté the pine nuts for 2 minutes, then add the onion and fry for 3 minutes. Add the fish meat, spices, salt, parsley and barberries and fry for another 2 minutes, stirring constantly. Remove from the heat and leave to cool for 5 minutes.

Stuff a quarter of the mixture into each fish, using a long-handled cocktail spoon. Pack the stuffing in tightly, and use your fingers to mould it into a fish shape.

Sift the flour into a bowl. Lightly whisk the eggs in a separate bowl. Put the polenta in a third bowl. Heat the olive oil in a frying pan over medium heat. Add a drop of water to the oil: if it sizzles, the oil is ready. Coat each fish with the flour, dip in the egg, then thoroughly coat with the polenta. Carefully place the stuffed fish in the pan, two at a time, and cook for 8 minutes each, giving them a quarter turn every 2 minutes, until the skin is golden brown and crisp. Drain on paper towel.

If using the dressing, mix the pomegranate molasses, olive oil, pomegranate seeds and parsley together in a small jug.

Serve the *uskumru dolmasi* hot, splashed with a little olive oil and parsley and, if you like, the pomegranate dressing.

In this dish you are required to reach down the throat of a fish and pull out its insides, including the bones, in order to make it empty enough to satisfy the Turkish compulsion to stuff everything they see.

Uskumru dolmasi is one of the oldest surviving Ottoman seafood recipes, mentioned in seventeenth century palace documents, and nicknamed *unutma beni* ('don't forget me') because *meyhanes* in past centuries would send plates of stuffed mackerel to the homes of their regular customers on the last night of the fasting month of Ramadan, to remind them of what they'd been missing. It was the earliest form of advertising by letterbox drop, but we doubt if anybody rejected it as junk mail.

This late-summer dish combines two much-loved ingredients. There's the pretty pink sweet-tasting fish called *barbunya* by Turks and Greeks, *triglia* by Italians, and red mullet or goatfish by the unpoetic English. And there's the 'green bullet' called *bamya* by the Turks and Arabs, ladies fingers' by Malaysians, okra by the English and gumbo by the people of Louisiana.

Okra are edible seed pods that originated in Africa. They had become a fad food by the fifteenth century in the Ottoman Empire, when the sultan in Istanbul organised palace war games between teams named 'the cabbages' and 'the okras'.

Okra is very good for you, but has a reputation for being slimy. Here's the solution to the slime: use very small pods. If you can't find small okra, choose medium-sized ones, no longer than 10 cm (4 in) or they'll have a woody texture, and soak for 30 minutes in 1 litre (35 fl oz/4 cups) of water with 100 ml (3½ fl oz) of vinegar and 2 tablespoons of salt. Rinse them well, peel off the skin, and remove the woody stalks.

BAMYALI BARBUNYA
PAN-FRIED RED MULLET WITH OKRA

SERVES 4

2 French shallots (eschalots)
2 garlic cloves
1 carrot
300 g (10½ oz) okra
1 green tomato or 2 tablespoons
    unripened grapes
1 red capsicum (pepper)
80 ml (2½ fl oz/⅓ cup) olive oil
125 ml (4 fl oz/½ cup) verjus
juice of ½ lemon
½ teaspoon sugar
1 teaspoon ground white pepper
2 teaspoons salt
16 small red mullet
75 g (2½ oz/½ cup) plain (all-purpose)
    flour
1 teaspoon freshly ground black pepper
250 ml (9 fl oz/1 cup) vegetable oil
1 lemon

Finely slice the French shallots and garlic. Roughly chop the carrot. Cut the stalks off the okra. Quarter the green tomato. Remove the stalk and seeds from the red capsicum and roughly chop.

Heat the olive oil in a saucepan over medium heat. Add the shallot and carrot and fry for 3 minutes. Add the garlic and cook for 2 more minutes. Add the okra, tomato and capsicum, and fry for 1 minute. Add the verjus, lemon juice, sugar, white pepper and half the salt, and bring to the boil. Add 250 ml (9 fl oz/1 cup) of warm water, reduce the heat and simmer, covered, for 10 minutes.

Clean and scale the red mullet. Sift the flour into a bowl and mix in the black pepper and the remaining salt. Coat each fish in the flour, shaking off the excess flour.

Heat the vegetable oil in a frying pan over medium heat. Add a drop of water to the oil: if it sizzles, the oil is ready. Carefully add the mullet, four at a time, and fry for 2 minutes on each side, until the skin is golden brown and crisp. Transfer to paper towel to remove the excess oil.

Cut the top and bottom off the lemon and slice into 8 rounds. Place the lemon rounds in the frying pan and cook for 1 minute on each side, until starting to caramelise.

Spread the okra mixture on one half of each plate, and place the mullet on the other half. Decorate with the fried lemon rounds and serve.

MERCAN BUĞULAMA
WHOLE SNAPPER IN CELERIAC MILK

SERVES 4

1 celeriac
500 ml (17 fl oz/2 cups) milk
1 white onion
4 caperberries
1 snapper, about 1 kg (2 lb 4 oz), cleaned
4 celery stalks, leaves picked (use the
    stalks to make bloody marys!)
2 tarragon stalks, leaves picked
2 tablespoons thickened (whipping)
    cream
250 ml (9 fl oz/1 cup) dry white wine
juice of 1 lemon
½ bunch chives
3 silverbeet (Swiss chard) leaves

Peel the celeriac and cut it into rounds about 1 cm (½ in) thick. Place the celeriac rounds in a bowl, add the milk and leave to rest overnight in the fridge.

The next day, remove the celeriac from the bowl and pat dry with paper towel. Reserve the milk.

Preheat the oven to 180°C (350°F).

Slice the onion. Chop the stalks off the caperberries and slice the berries in half.

Clean and scale the fish, if necessary. Place the snapper on a board and slice through the belly to open a pocket for the stuffing. Stuff the fish with the onion, caperberries, celery leaves and tarragon leaves.

Place the celeriac rounds on the bottom of a baking tray. Place the snapper on top. Mix the reserved soaking milk with the cream and white wine, then pour over the fish. Sprinkle the fish with the lemon juice and lay the chives on top. Cover with the silverbeet leaves, then cover the baking tray tightly with foil. Bake for 40 minutes.

Serve the *mercan buğulama* on a serving platter, pouring any remaining juice over the fish, for people to help themselves.

One day when I was a kid, my father came home very late saying my stepmother was in hospital with food poisoning, because 'she ate *yoğurt* and fish together'. That started my fascination with combining seafood and dairy.

It's a common myth in Turkey that milk and fish don't mix, but if it were true, there'd be nobody left alive in the west coast town of İzmir (formerly known as Smyrna and very close to Troy). All along the promenade there, restaurants compete to offer the best version of *sütlü balık* (literally 'fish in milk').

Normally it's done with fillets, but I always prefer to use whole fish if I can. I've included celeriac here, because it adds a great flavour to the milk.

THE OTTOMAN EXPERIMENT

Batur Durmay happily admits that his restaurant, Asitane, is an indulgence. 'We didn't open this place to make a lot of money', he says. 'I just have to be sure I get it right.' Getting it right means ensuring the dishes on his menu are what you could have eaten had you been invited to a banquet with the sultan at the Topkapı Palace around 1700.

Asitane was set up by Batur's family in 1991 so they'd have an interesting place to take clients in their primary business, which was making steel moulds for heavy industry. Batur, the most obsessive foodie in a family of gourmets, was tasked with unearthing recipes that displayed the opulence and diversity of one of the greatest empires in history.

He soon encountered a problem. Before the year 1844 (when the first cookbook in the Turkish language was published), the Ottoman kitchen workers did not write down recipes. But they were meticulous record keepers, giving names to every dish served at banquets and noting the ingredients purchased for the pantry. Batur found a particularly helpful document from 1539 listing the 100 dishes served at a circumcision ceremony for the sons of Süleyman the Magnificent.

He hired scholars to dig further into the palace records, and chefs to theorise on how the ingredients must have been combined and served, and ultimately came up with more than 300 dishes that he is confident would be recognisable to a time traveller from the seventeenth century.

Modern Turks have an ambiguous relationship with the Ottoman Empire. They are proud that for 500 years, their ancestors were the fairly humane rulers of a collection of countries now called Albania, Bulgaria, Egypt, Greece, Hungary, Iran, Iraq, Israel, Jordan, Lebanon, Macedonia, Romania, Saudi Arabia, Syria and Tunisia. They are annoyed that after 200 years of decline, the Ottoman caliphs had become so decadent by the early twentieth century that they dragged Turkey into the First World War on the wrong side, and ended up losing what was left of this great empire.

Whether they admire or disapprove, they are fascinated by the lavish lifestyle the Ottomans created for themselves, especially since the success in 2011 of a TV melodrama called *Muhteşem Yüzyıl* (Magnificent Century), about the life of Sultan Süleyman the Magnificent. Batur was a food consultant for the series.

The Istanbul eating scene is now enjoying an Ottoman revival. Batur estimates there are 200 restaurants that claim to serve the food of the emperors. Many of them think that all they have to do is cook meats with dried fruits, or serve spiced rice in several colours, or give fancy names to standard *kebaps*.

Some places have sent spies to Asitane, to steal Batur's recipes. But Batur is fighting back. Occasionally he includes a dish on his menu that contains typically Ottoman ingredients but has no background in any scholarship. He invents a name that sounds as if it might have been used in the sixteenth century, and then waits to see how long it takes for that name to appear on the menus of his competitors. Then he has a little word to them about laziness and plagiarism.

Fortunately, he now has plenty of customers who recognise the work his researchers and cooks have put into ensuring authenticity. Asitane has become so popular that he finds himself seriously at risk of financial success.

Batur Durmay recreates dishes served to the seventeenth-century sultans at Asitane restaurant, in Istanbul's historic Fatih district.

My family used to keep quails in cages on the balcony of our apartment in Istanbul because my father believed eating their eggs would help my stepsister's asthma.

Quails are thought to have originated in China, but they were cultivated for food by the Egyptian pharaohs, and became popular in Anatolia during the Seljuk period (in the eleventh and twelfth centuries). We don't know how the Seljuks cooked them, because they weren't big on written records, but a few hundred years later, this recipe was created by the Ottomans, which explains the carob glaze. Before the arrival of chocolate from the Americas in the seventeenth century, carob was the sultans' favourite sweetener.

Nowadays, grape and pomegranate molasses have become more fashionable than carob molasses, but I think the thick caramel flavour contrasts beautifully with the smoky freekeh, which I've used in the stuffing instead of the Ottomans' rice.

FİRİKLİ BILDIRCIN
SUPER FREEKEH QUAILS

SERVES 4

8 quails
4 tablespoons butter

FREEKEH STUFFING
50 g (1¾ oz) green lentils
1 onion
2 tablespoons olive oil
250 g (9 oz) freekeh
1 teaspoon chilli flakes
1 tablespoon capsicum (pepper) paste
 (see page 32)
500 ml (17 fl oz/2 cups) chicken stock
1 tablespoon butter
pinch of salt
pinch of freshly ground black pepper

COATING
80 ml (2½ fl oz/⅓ cup) vegetable oil
4 tablespoons carob molasses
1 teaspoon hot paprika
5 sage leaves

To make the stuffing, soak the lentils overnight, or simmer them in a pan of boiling water for 30 minutes, and then drain.

Finely chop the onion. Heat the olive oil in a frying pan over medium heat. Add the onion and fry for 5 minutes, until soft. Add the freekeh and the lentils and fry for a further 3 minutes, stirring regularly. Add the chilli flakes, capsicum paste, chicken stock and butter. Stir thoroughly and bring to the boil, then add the salt and pepper. Cover and simmer for 15 minutes. Remove from the heat and leave to rest, covered, for 15 minutes.

Wash the quails. Sizzle 1 tablespoon of the butter in a frying pan over medium heat. Add the quails, two at a time, and cook for 2 minutes on each side, until the skin crisps up. Add a new tablespoon of butter for each two quails. Leave to rest on paper towel.

Preheat the oven to 180°C (350°F).

Using a tablespoon, stuff each quail with the freekeh and lentil mixture.

Now make the coating. Mix the vegetable oil, carob molasses and paprika together in a bowl. Finely chop the sage leaves, add to the carob mixture and combine. Brush the quails thoroughly in the coating, retaining a little of the molasses mixture to serve.

Pour 250 ml (9 fl oz/1 cup) of water into a baking tray. Sit the quails in the water. Bake for 25 minutes, until golden brown. After 10 minutes of baking, spoon some of the liquid from the tray over the quails to keep them moist.

Serve two quails per person, with a tablespoon of the molasses mixture drizzled over each plate.

KAVUN DOLMASI
STUFFED MELON WITH CHICKEN AND CASHEWS

SERVES 4

50 g (1¾ oz) craisins (dried cranberries)
2 onions
10 parsley stalks
10 mint stalks
50 ml (1¾ fl oz) vegetable oil
75 g (2½ oz) almonds
75 g (2½ oz) cashews
300 g (10½ oz) minced (ground) chicken
1 teaspoon freshly ground black pepper
½ teaspoon ground allspice
½ teaspoon ground cinnamon
1½ teaspoons salt
1 Galia melon, rockmelon or honeydew
   (about 1 kg/2 lb 4 oz)
2 tablespoons butter
50 ml (1¾ fl oz) olive oil

Put the cranberries in a bowl, cover with warm water and leave to soak for 15 minutes. Finely chop the onions. Pick and chop the mint and parsley leaves.

Heat the vegetable oil in a frying pan over medium heat, add the onion and cook for 4 minutes. Add the almonds and cashews, and fry for 1 minute. Add the chicken mince and fry for 5 minutes, stirring regularly until the chicken is evenly golden brown. Add the spices and 1 teaspoon of the salt. Drain the cranberries, add to the pan and stir. Remove the pan from the heat.

Preheat the oven to 180°C (350°F).

Slice the cap off the melon, about 2 cm (¾ in) below the top. Scoop out and discard all the seeds. Mix the butter with a pinch of salt and rub it inside the cavity. Push in the stuffing mixture. Place the cap back on, secured with two toothpicks. Rub the olive oil all over the outside of the melon.

Place on a baking tray and bake for 35 minutes.

Remove the cap and serve the whole melon at the table. Scoop out four servings, or slice into quarters.

Melon has been one of the staples of Anatolian cuisine since Roman times, and was probably first cultivated near what is now eastern Turkey. The Ottoman palace chefs apparently liked the theatre of being able to lift the lid and expose the filling. They adopted the Persian fascination for mixing meat and fruit, and mostly used lamb mince in the stuffing, but I think that's too heavy for the delicate fruit, so I changed it to chicken.

I like to use Galia melon (developed in Israel in the 1970s) because it's almost perfectly round, but if you can't find it, go for rockmelon, and choose the smallest one you can find.

This is a kind of chicken and rice pie, which originated in Siirt, a city in southeastern Turkey. In the classical version the cooks simply mixed the chicken into the spiced rice and wrapped pastry around it, but I find the end result quite dry.

It makes for a spectacular presentation if you upend the pie and cut away to unveil layers of different ingredients inside—caramelised onions on top, which keep the other layers moist, then a layer of shredded chicken, and under that the spiced rice.

PERDELİ PİLAV
VEILED RICE

SERVES 4

125 ml (4 fl oz/½ cup) olive oil
10 brown onions
440 g (15½ oz/2 cups) medium-grain rice
1½ tablespoons butter
100 g (3½ oz) flaked almonds
1 tablespoon ground cinnamon
2 teaspoons ground allspice
2 teaspoons freshly ground black pepper

CHICKEN STOCK
2 onions, halved
2 carrots, halved
1 small chicken (less than 1.8 kg/4 lb)
1 tablespoon salt
5 saffron threads

PASTRY
450 g (1 lb/3 cups) plain (all-purpose)
    flour, plus extra for dusting
250 g (9 oz) butter
3 eggs
½ teaspoon baking powder
1 teaspoon salt
2 tablespoons vegetable oil, for greasing
5 blanched almonds, halved

First, get the onion confit started for the filling. Heat the olive oil in a saucepan over low heat. Finely slice the onions, add to the pan and fry, covered, for 10 minutes. Move the lid so it's partly open and gently simmer for 1½ hours, stirring occasionally. The confit onion should reduce to half the size of the uncooked onions.

Meanwhile, make the chicken stock. Place the onion and carrot halves in a large saucepan with the chicken. Add the salt, cover with water and boil, partly covered, for 30 minutes over medium–low heat. Turn off the heat. Transfer the chicken to a board and leave until cool enough to handle, then strip off the skin and meat. Shred the meat into thin strands and set aside. Put 375 ml (13 fl oz/1½ cups) of the warm chicken stock in a bowl, add the saffron and set aside to soak. Put the chicken skin and bones back in the pan and simmer, without the lid, so the stock reduces.

Now, make the pastry 'veil'. Sift the flour into a mixing bowl. Make a well in the middle. Melt the butter in a frying pan over medium heat (or microwave for 30 seconds). Whisk the eggs in a bowl. Whisk the butter into the eggs, then whisk in the baking powder and salt. Fold the egg mixture into the flour and knead for 5 minutes. Sprinkle some flour on your work surface and roll the dough into a ball. Return the dough to the bowl, cover with a damp cloth and rest in a warm place for at least 30 minutes.

Meanwhile, cook the rice. Rinse the rice under cold running water. Melt the butter in a medium saucepan over medium heat. Stir in the flaked almonds and fry for 2 minutes. Add the rice and toss it in the butter for 1 minute, to coat. Remove the saffron threads from the bowl of chicken stock and discard them, then mix the cinnamon, allspice and pepper into the saffron liquid. Add the liquid to the rice and stir. Add 500 ml (17 fl oz/2 cups) of the simmering chicken stock. Bring the rice to a boil, then reduce the heat and simmer, covered, for 15 minutes. Remove from the heat and leave to rest, covered, for 15 minutes.

Preheat the oven to 180°C (350°F). Place the rested dough on a floured work surface. Roll into a round sheet about 60 cm (24 in) wide. Paint half the vegetable oil inside a 25 cm (10 in) cake tin to grease it well. Place the half almonds around the bottom of the cake tin in any pattern you like. Line the tin with the pastry sheet so the sides of the sheet come up and overlap the rim of the tin. There should be about 12 cm (4½ in) of pastry hanging over the edge (this will be folded over the rice).

Remove the onion confit from the heat. Scoop out the onion confit with a slotted spoon and spread it over the pastry in the tin. Add a layer of chicken meat, then spoon in the rice, to about 1 cm (½ in) below the rim. Fold the pastry over the rice. If it doesn't completely cover the rice, squeeze the pastry out with your fingers so it stretches across. Brush on the remaining vegetable oil. Bake the 'pie' for 20 minutes, until golden. Lift the cake tin out of the oven and turn the pie out onto a baking tray. Put the baking tray in the oven and bake the pie for another 10 minutes.

Serve the whole pie at the table, slicing it into eight wedges (two per diner).

ÖRDEK SARMA
DUCK AND SILVERBEET PARCELS

SERVES 4

4 duck legs
1.5 litres (52 fl oz/6 cups) chicken stock
200 g (7 oz/1 cup) freekeh
2 tablespoons dried barberries
    (or cranberries)
1 red capsicum (pepper)
1 onion
1 garlic clove
2 tablespoons butter
2 tablespoons olive oil
4 tablespoons flaked almonds
125 ml (4 fl oz/½ cup) dry sherry
½ teaspoon ground cinnamon
1 teaspoon ground pimento
1 teaspoon salt
1 teaspoon freshly ground black pepper
2 teaspoons capsicum (pepper) paste
    (see page 32)
2 teaspoons tomato paste (to make
    your own, see page 24)
10 silverbeet (Swiss chard) leaves

PAPRIKA SAUCE
2 garlic cloves
1 tablespoon olive oil
1 tablespoon smoked paprika
250 g (9 oz/1 cup) plain *yoğurt*

Put the duck legs and chicken stock in a large saucepan. Bring to the boil over medium heat, then reduce the heat and simmer, covered, for 1 hour.

Remove the duck legs from the pan and place on a board to cool slightly. When cool enough to handle, remove the meat. Put the skin, sinews and bones back in the pan and simmer, with the lid off, for another 5 minutes. Remove from the heat.

Put the freekeh in a bowl and cover with 375 ml (13 fl oz/1½ cups) of warm strained chicken stock. Leave to rest for 30 minutes. Meanwhile, put the barberries in a bowl, cover with warm water and leave to soak for 15 minutes. Halve the capsicum, remove the stalk and seeds, and finely chop. Finely chop the onion and the garlic.

Melt the butter in a frying pan over medium heat. Add the olive oil. Add the onion and flaked almonds and cook for 2 minutes. Add the garlic and fry for 1 minute. Add the duck pieces and fry for 2 minutes. Add the sherry, cinnamon, pimento, salt and pepper. Increase the heat to high for 3 minutes to cook out the alcohol.

Put the capsicum and tomato pastes in a bowl, add 125 ml (4 fl oz/½ cup) of the warm chicken stock and stir to combine. Add the mixture to the duck and stir. Add the capsicum and the strained freekeh to the duck mixture, and stir. Bring to the boil, then turn off the heat. Strain the barberries and stir them into the duck mixture. Leave to cool, covered, for 10 minutes.

Wash the silverbeet leaves under cold running water. Put them in a bowl and cover with boiling water. Leave for 2 minutes, then plunge the leaves in iced water for 1 minute to refresh. Remove the stalks. If the leaves are large, cut them in half; you should have at least ten leaf pieces. Put the two largest leaves aside, to line the bottom of the cooking pot. Place 3 tablespoons of the duck mixture across one of the other leaves, about 4 cm (1½ in) from the bottom. Fold in the edges around the stuffing and tightly roll the leaf up. Repeat to make eight parcels.

Cover the bottom of a saucepan with the two reserved leaves. Place the eight parcels on the leaves. Pour in the chicken stock to almost cover the parcels, then weigh the parcels down with a plate. Bring the liquid to the boil, then reduce the heat and simmer, covered, for 20 minutes.

Meanwhile, make the paprika sauce. Crush the garlic. Heat the olive oil in a frying pan over medium heat. Add the crushed garlic and paprika and fry for 3 minutes, stirring constantly. Remove from the heat and leave to cool. Transfer to a bowl and mix in the *yoğurt*.

Place a quarter of the *yoğurt* sauce on each serving plate. Scoop the parcels out of the stock with a slotted spoon, adding two parcels to each plate, and serve.

When I first came to Sydney I found duck was a popular meat with Australians, and so I started serving this dish in winter. It is a modern variation of a Black Sea recipe, where silverbeet is usually wrapped around lamb mince and rice. There they would never use duck (which is a meat cooked at home by the wives of hunters), or freekeh (which is from the southeast).

My justification for the change is that spit-roasted duck was served in Istanbul at the circumcision ceremony for the son of Sultan Mehmet II, in 1457. That's the rule: when challenged, quote the Ottomans.

ELBASAN TAVA
GOAT AND DATES IN BAKED YOĞURT

Along with cubed and deep-fried spiced liver, this goat stew is one of two famous Albanian dishes that influenced the cuisine of Anatolia. It is named after the city of Elbasan, which means 'crushing fist', presumably because Mehmet II built a huge fortress there to keep the Albanians under control in the fifteenth century.

Strangely, you'd have a hard time finding either this dish or the fried liver in modern Albania, where waiters are inclined to say 'They do that in Turkey—we don't do it anymore'. It's their loss.

If you can't find goat, use lamb.

SERVES 4

835 g (1 lb 13 oz) plain *yoğurt*
3 French shallots (eschalots)
3 garlic cloves
500 g (1 lb 2 oz) goat (shoulder meat)
1 tablespoon butter
1 tablespoon black peppercorns
1 teaspoon salt
10 basil leaves
1 bay leaf
12 dates, pitted
500 ml (17 fl oz/2 cups) beef stock
3 egg yolks
450 g (1 lb/3 cups) plain (all-purpose) flour
1 tablespoon sweet paprika
mixed cress salad, to serve (optional)

Place the *yoğurt* on a sheet of muslin (cheesecloth) and tie up the corners. Hang the muslin over a pot overnight to allow the *yoğurt* to thicken.

Quarter the French shallots. Finely chop the garlic. Remove any fat from the goat shoulder and cut the meat into 3 cm (1¼ in) cubes. Melt the butter in a frying pan over high heat. Add the meat and fry for 2 minutes, turning to evenly brown. Add the shallot and fry for 2 minutes. Add the garlic, peppercorns, salt, basil and bay leaf and fry for 2 minutes.

Add 250 ml (9 fl oz/1 cup) of water to the pan. Bring to the boil, then reduce the heat and simmer, covered, for 45 minutes; the liquid should reduce and thicken. Pour the goat stew into a casserole dish. Sprinkle the dates over the stew.

Preheat the oven to 180°C (350°F). Gently warm the stock in a saucepan to about 35°C (95°F).

Put the egg yolks in a bowl; sift in the flour and whisk. Put the yoghurt in a large saucepan, add the flour mixture, then stir in the warm beef stock.

Gently warm the *yoğurt* mixture over low heat, constantly whisking, but remove it from the heat as soon as you see bubbles forming (you do not want it to boil).

Pour the *yoğurt* mixture over the goat stew and add the paprika. Place the casserole dish in the oven and bake for 40 minutes.

Serve the stew in the casserole dish at the table with a mixed cress salad, for people to help themselves.

EFENDY BEĞENDY
BRAISED BEEF CHEEKS AND EGGPLANT PURÉE

There are as many folk stories about the origin of Turkish dishes as there are combinations of lamb and eggplant. The story I like about this dish is that it was served to the French empress Eugenie when she passed through Istanbul on her way to the opening ceremony of the Suez Canal in 1869. Eugenie's personal chef got together with the sultan's chef and added béchamel sauce to the original palace recipe. It then was named Hünkar Beğendi ('The sultan liked it')—probably because all possible combinations of the words for lamb and eggplant had been used up.

I solved the lamb-repetition problem by using beef cheeks (rare in Turkish cuisine), and I've lightened the mash by not using flour. There are no sultans in Turkey anymore, so I've changed the Turkish title to 'the gentleman liked it', making this dish more democratic—if not gender-neutral.

SERVES 4

4 beef cheeks, about 180 g (6 oz) each
1 onion
1 green bullhorn pepper (or ½ green capsicum/pepper)
1 garlic clove
3 tomatoes
100 ml (3½ fl oz) olive oil
50 g (1¾ oz) cumin seeds
200 g (7 oz) tomato paste (to make your own, see page 24)
1 litre (35 fl oz/4 cups) beef stock
1 teaspoon salt
1 teaspoon freshly ground black pepper
250 ml (9 fl oz/1 cup) dry red wine
200 g (7 oz) green olives, pitted

EGGPLANT PURÉE
4 globe eggplants (aubergines)
juice of 2 lemons
120 g (4 oz) butter
300 ml (10½ fl oz) pouring (whipping) cream
1 teaspoon freshly grated nutmeg
200 g (7 oz) grated kaşar (or provolone)
½ teaspoon ground white pepper
1 teaspoon salt

Place the beef cheeks on a board and trim off any sinew or fat. Finely slice the onion. Remove the stalk and seeds from the bullhorn pepper and roughly chop. Roughly chop the garlic and tomatoes.

Heat the olive oil in a large flameproof casserole dish over medium heat. Add the onion and cumin seeds and brown for 4 minutes. Add the chopped bullhorn pepper and garlic, and fry for 2 minutes. Add the tomatoes and tomato paste and stir to combine. Add the beef stock, salt, pepper and red wine.

Add the beef cheeks, reduce the heat to low and simmer, covered, for 5 hours.

While the beef cheeks are stewing, prepare the the eggplant purée. Pierce the eggplants with a fork and char the skins by placing the eggplant directly onto a gas flame. Using tongs, move the eggplant around to evenly blacken the skin, then remove from the flame.

Once the eggplants are cool enough to handle, scoop out the flesh into a large bowl. Discard the skin. Add 1 litre (35 fl oz/4 cups) of water and the lemon juice. Leave to soak for 2 minutes, then remove the eggplant, pat dry with paper towel and place in a colander to drain for about 10 minutes. Finely chop.

Near serving time, melt 100 g (3½ oz) of the butter in a frying pan over low heat. Add the eggplant pieces and whisk together to make a mash. Add the cream, nutmeg and grated kaşar. Add the white pepper and salt. Simmer for 5 minutes, stirring regularly.

Meanwhile, add the olives to the casserole dish and continue to stew for 5 minutes. Remove from the heat. Pour 250 ml (9 fl oz/1 cup) of the beef-cheek cooking liquid into a saucepan with the remaining butter and boil over medium heat for 5 minutes to reduce.

To serve, divide the eggplant purée among four plates, and place one beef cheek on each plate. Drizzle a little of the reduced sauce over each cheek, and serve.

Yes, I admit it: Turkish people are obsessed with lamb, which we eat nose-to-tail. Every suburb and every village boasts a wide choice of lamb butcheries, some specialising in prime cuts and mince, and others in offal. This recipe is the pinnacle of the lamb cook's art.

The fashionable modern cooking style called *sous vide*, which involves cooking in a sealed bag, echoes an old Ottoman technique. We've been using pastry to seal the flavour in meat and vegetables for centuries—as evidenced by the title of this dish, which literally translates as 'enclosed lamb'.

In this case, the lamb is sealed and cooked for so long the meat falls off the bone. I've been inspired by the Australian meat pie, and made an edible dough.

KUZU KAPAMA
LAMB SHOULDER PIE

SERVES 4

1 lamb shoulder, about 1.5 kg (3 lb 5 oz),
    bone in, shank removed
2 carrots
1 onion
2 garlic cloves
1 celeriac, peeled
5 small potatoes
2 cardamom pods
1 cinnamon stick
2 bay leaves
1 star anise
125 ml (4 fl oz/½ cup) olive oil
250 ml (9 fl oz/1 cup) dry red wine
1 litre (35 fl oz/4 cups) beef stock

SPICE RUB
2 garlic cloves
1 tablespoon sea salt
1 tablespoon sweet paprika
½ tablespoon ground cinnamon
½ tablespoon freshly ground black
    pepper
½ tablespoon lemon pepper
1 teaspoon ground aniseed
125 ml (4 fl oz/½ cup) olive oil

POMEGRANATE GLAZE
125 ml (4 fl oz/½ cup) olive oil
1 tablespoon pomegranate molasses
    (to make your own, see page 24)

PASTRY
½ teaspoon dried yeast
1 teaspoon sugar
300 g (10½ oz/2 cups) plain (all-purpose)
    flour, plus extra for dusting
2 thyme sprigs, leaves picked
    and finely chopped
1 garlic clove, crushed
1 teaspoon salt
zest of 1 lemon
50 g (1¾ oz) butter
1 egg white
1 tablespoon plain *yoğurt*

Trim any large pieces of fat from the outside of the lamb shoulder. To make the spice rub, crush the garlic, and mix in a bowl with the salt, spices and olive oil. Rub the mixture over the lamb, including in the cavities. Rest the lamb for 20 minutes.

To make the glaze, heat the olive oil and the pomegranate molasses in a wide frying pan for 2 minutes over high heat. Place the lamb in the glaze and fry for 2 minutes on each side, caramelising the glaze onto the meat.

Preheat the oven to 140°C (275°F).

Roughly chop the carrots, onion, garlic, celeriac and potatoes. Place in a large ovenproof pot (one with a lid), with the cardamom pods, cinnamon stick, bay leaves and star anise. Pour in the olive oil, red wine and beef stock to cover the lamb. Cover with the lid and bake for 4½ hours, until the meat is very tender. Remove the lamb from the oven and cool to room temperature.

Meanwhile, make the pastry. Mix the yeast and the sugar in 375 ml (13 fl oz/ 1½ cups) of lukewarm water and set aside for 5 minutes; it should start to form bubbles. Sift the flour into a mixing bowl, make a well in the middle and pour in the yeast mixture. Knead the dough for 5 minutes, or until the dough is as soft as an earlobe. Mix the thyme, crushed garlic, salt, lemon zest and butter together, and then add to the dough. Knead for a further 5 minutes. Sprinkle some flour on your work surface and roll the dough into a ball. Return the dough to the bowl, cover with a damp cloth and leave to rest for at least 1 hour. The dough should double in size.

Transfer the lamb and vegetables to a casserole dish. Increase the oven temperature to 200°C (400°F).

Roll the dough into a sheet big enough to cover the casserole dish, with an overhang of about 4 cm (1½ in) on all sides. Beat the egg white, then paint it around the rim and outside edge of the dish. Drape the pastry sheet over the dish, and use the egg white to stick the overhang to the sides. Mix the *yoğurt* with ½ tablespoon of water, then paint the *yoğurt* mixture over the dough.

Put the pie in the oven and bake for 15 minutes, or until the pastry is golden brown.

Slice the pie crust into four segments and put one on each plate. Scoop out a generous portion of the filling to put on top of the pastry, and serve.

LAMB SHOULDER PIE
For recipe, see page 257.

KEŞKÜL
PALACE PUDDING

SERVES 4

40 g (1½ oz) blanched almonds
40 g (1½ oz) pistachios
250 ml (9 fl oz/1 cup) milk
250 ml (9 fl oz/1 cup) pouring (whipping)
   cream
100 g (3½ oz) sugar
25 g (1 oz) cornflour (cornstarch)
pashmak (Persian fairy floss) and
   pomegranate seeds, to decorate
   (optional)

Put the almonds in a food processor and pulse finely. Pulse the pistachios separately.

Put the milk and cream in a saucepan and mix. Heat over medium heat, then add the sugar. Cook for 2 minutes, then whisk in the finely ground almonds. Continue to whisk for 2 minutes, then scoop out 125 ml (4 fl oz/½ cup) of the mixture into a bowl. Whisk the cornflour into the bowl, and then slowly add it to the cooking mixture, whisking constantly.

Continue to whisk, and bring to the boil. Add the ground pistachios, reduce the heat and simmer for 3 minutes, whisking. When the mixture starts to thicken, remove the pan from the heat and leave to cool to room temperature.

Divide the *keşkül* mixture among four bowls or cups. Refrigerate for 3 hours to set.

Remove from the fridge, decorate with *pashmak* and pomegranate seeds, if you like, and serve.

This gluten-free summer favourite is one of the oldest Ottoman recipes, derived from a dish called *Keşkül-ü Fukara* ('begging bowl'), which was generously served to the populace by the sultans to celebrate war victories, religious holidays and other significant occasions.

The word *keşkül* refers to a bowl made out of a coconut half-shell, which the dervish monks would wear around their necks in the hope people might throw in donations (which would have been difficult if they were whirling dervishes). Nowadays, the poor don't need to go to the palace—they can find versions of *keşkül* in pudding shops across Istanbul.

There are several traditional variations—some using only almonds, some using coconut flakes. I like crushed pistachios to give a bright green colour and a crunchy texture.

You could have eaten this dish 2000 years ago in Anatolia. The world's first cherry and quince growing happened there. Writings from 72 BC discuss how the military leader Lucullus brought a cultivated cherry to Rome from a part of the empire called Pontus in northeastern Anatolia. The Romans at the time were happy to combine it with their quinces stewed in honey.

The Ottoman chefs made a habit of stewing fruits with sugar syrup and combining them with *kaymak* (clotted cream). The secret here is to cook very slowly and include the quince skins and cores while simmering, to enhance the pink colouring the Ottomans loved.

AYVA TATLISI
POACHED QUINCES WITH SOUR CHERRIES AND CLOTTED CREAM

SERVES 4

100 g (3½ oz/½ cup) frozen sour cherries; you'll need 24 cherries
juice of 1 lemon
4 quinces
1 cinnamon stick
5 cloves
660 g (1 lb 7 oz/3 cups) sugar, approximately
16 walnut kernels
125 g (4½ oz/½ cup) *kaymak* (or thick/ double cream)
finely ground pistachios, for sprinkling (optional)

Take the cherries out of the freezer about 1 hour before you want to serve the dish.

Put the lemon juice and 1 litre (35 fl oz/4 cups) of water in a bowl.

Working with one quince at a time, peel the skin off, and reserve the skin. Halve the peeled quince, lengthways, and remove and reserve the hard core. As soon as you finish with each one, add the quince halves to the bowl of lemon water to stop them turning brown.

Lay the quince skins, shiny side down, in the bottom of a wide saucepan. Place the cinnamon stick, cloves and quince cores on top. Put the quince halves, cut side up, on top of the spices. Put 3 tablespoons of the sugar on each quince half. Pour 500 ml (17 fl oz/2 cups) of water into the pan around the quince halves, being careful not to cover the quinces or wash the sugar off.

Put the lid on the pan and simmer for 1 hour, until the quince is pink and soft.

Mix another 115 g (4 oz/½ cup) of the sugar with the sour cherries. Place three cherries in each quince half, put the lid back on and simmer for 30 minutes.

Remove the pan from the heat and leave to cool for 30 minutes—with the lid off if the quince is soft, lid on if the quince is still slightly firm.

Place the quince halves on a serving platter. Put two walnuts on top of each.

Add a dollop of *kaymak* on top of each quince. Drizzle about 1 tablespoon of the cooking liquid over the top, sprinkle with ground pistachios if you like, and serve.

KÜNEFE

BUFFALO MOZZARELLA AND PISTACHIO PASTRY

SERVES 4

SYRUP
440 g (15½ oz/2 cups) sugar
1 tablespoon lemon juice

PASTRY
300 g (10½ oz) fresh buffalo mozzarella
  (or unsalted mozzarella)
500 g (1 lb 2 oz) *kadayıf* pastry
200 g (7 oz/1 cup) ghee (to make your
  own, see page 18)
125 ml (4 fl oz/½ cup) grape molasses
70 g (2½ oz/½ cup) finely ground
  pistachios

First make the syrup, so it has time to cool. Put the sugar and 500 ml (17 fl oz/2 cups) of cold water in a saucepan and bring to the boil over medium heat. Reduce the heat and simmer for 8 minutes. Add the lemon juice and simmer for 1 minute more. Remove from the heat and leave to cool to room temperature.

Roughly chop the mozzarella. Roughly cut the *kadayıf* pastry into chunks. Put the pastry in a bowl with half the ghee and mix with your hands until completely combined. Divide the buttered pastry into two balls.

Brush the grape molasses and a little ghee onto the base of a frying pan (or divide among smaller frying pans to make individual *künefe*). Spread half the pastry over the pan, pressing it down with the (clean) base of another pan. Spread the mozzarella evenly over the pastry, and spread the other half of the pastry over the mozzarella. Press down again on the second layer of pastry.

Place the pan over medium heat. After about 6 minutes, as the bottom is turning golden brown, turn the *künefe* out onto a plate, and then put it back into the pan with the uncooked side down. Cook the second side for a further 4 minutes.

Turn off the heat and slice the *künefe* into four segments. Pour the cold syrup over the segments.

Divide the *künefe* among each serving plate, sprinkle with pistachios and serve.

There is constant debate about the ownership of this dish between the neighbouring cities Antakya, Adana and Mersin. I prefer to eat the Antakya version (bigger and cheesier), but I will not take sides in the origin argument, because all three cities have many citizens of Syrian ancestry and there are versions of this dish all over the Arab world. So the Turkish ownership debate may be academic.

There are cheeses made in those towns specifically to go inside *künefe*. The challenge in making the dish outside Turkey is to find a fresh cheese, low in salt, that oozes when heated. I like to use buffalo mozzarella.

More than half the world's dried figs and dried
apricots come from Turkey, so of course we have
to stuff them. Turkey is the fourth-biggest producer
of walnuts in the world, and the number-eight
almond producer. So of course they'd be the best
nuts for the stuffing.

İNCİR & KAYISI DOLMASI
WALNUT-STUFFED FIGS AND ALMOND-STUFFED APRICOTS

SERVES 4

500 ml (17 fl oz/2 cups) milk
1 cinnamon stick
4 cloves
8 dried figs
60 g (2 oz/½ cup) walnuts
1 tablespoon vegetable oil
2 tablespoons grape molasses
2 tablespoons sugar
8 dried apricots
1 tablespoon almond meal
1 teaspoon icing (confectioners') sugar
2 tablespoons pouring (whipping) cream
2 tablespoons pistachios

Heat the milk, cinnamon stick and cloves in a saucepan over medium heat and bring to the boil. Remove from the heat. Remove the stalks from the dried figs, then soak the figs in the warm milk for 30 minutes.

Preheat the oven to 180°C (350°F).

Roughly chop the walnuts. Remove the figs from the milk with a slotted spoon and place on a board. Open the figs with a teaspoon and stuff 1 teaspoon of the chopped walnuts inside. Mix the oil and grape molasses together in a bowl, then brush over the figs.

Place the figs on a baking tray and bake for 10 minutes, until soft. Remove from the oven and leave to cool.

Meanwhile, put the sugar and 250 ml (9 fl oz/1 cup) of water in a saucepan and bring to the boil. Add the dried apricots, reduce the heat and simmer, covered, for 15 minutes. Remove from the heat and leave to cool. Remove the apricots from the syrup and leave to drain on paper towel.

Mix the almond meal, icing sugar and cream together in a bowl. Make a pocket in each apricot with a teaspoon and stuff 1 heaped teaspoon of the cream and almond mixture inside. Use the teaspoon to smooth the exposed stuffing.

Finely chop the pistachios, then roll the cream side of each apricot in the pistachio pieces.

Serve two figs and two apricots per person.

SEMOLINA HELVA WITH RASPBERRY ICED YOĞURT

SERVES 4

ICED YOĞURT

6 eggs
220 g (8 oz/1 cup) sugar
500 ml (17 fl oz/2 cups) thickened
   (whipping) cream
2 tablespoons plain *yoğurt*
1 punnet (200 g/7 oz) raspberries

HELVA

200 g (7 oz) butter
2 tablespoons pine nuts
285 g (10 oz/1½ cups) fine semolina
250 ml (9 fl oz/1 cup) milk
220 g (8 oz/1 cup) sugar

First, make the iced *yoğurt*. Separate the eggs. You are going to use all six yolks, and three of the whites. Blend the egg yolks and the sugar together in a bowl. Using an electric mixer, whip the cream until thick, then fold in the egg yolk mixture. Whisk three egg whites until peaks form, then gently fold into the yolk mixture. Fold in the *yoğurt*. Finally, fold in the raspberries, reserving a few to serve.

Use plastic wrap to line four cups (which you can half-fill if you'd like dome shapes), a rectangular tray (if you want to slice the iced *yoğurt* to serve), or any container you prefer, making sure the wrap overhangs the sides. Using a wooden spoon, push the cream mixture into the moulds, then place in the freezer overnight.

About 30 minutes before you'd like to serve the dessert, make the *helva*. Melt the butter in a frying pan over medium heat. Add the pine nuts and cook for 3 minutes, tossing constantly to evenly brown. Add the semolina and brown for 10 minutes, stirring constantly.

In a separate pan, mix the milk, sugar and 250 ml (9 fl oz/1 cup) of water, and bring to the boil over low heat. Immediately pour the boiling mixture over the semolina and continue to stir for about 10 minutes, until all the liquid is absorbed.

To serve, put one iced *yoğurt* dome (or a thick slice) on each plate and surround it with warm *helva*. Decorate with the reserved raspberries and serve quickly, so the iced *yoğurt* does not melt.

This is not a deconstruction of a traditional dish, but a sensible reconstruction of a bastardised one. Some fashionable restaurants in Istanbul are now serving ice cream (either vanilla or *sahlep*) covered with a dome of warm semolina *helva*. Some of them even name it 'Sultan's helva' to add vintage credibility. I don't get it. For me, a good semolina *helva* should be warm and crumbly, so you can't make a dome out of it. And a good ice cream should be firm and cold, not half melted.

I've made the assumption that most home cooks don't have an ice cream machine, so I've explained here how to make what the Italians call a semifreddo, using raspberries and *yoğurt*.

Güllaç is thought to be the original form of baklava, which was turned into a more elaborate dish by the chefs in the palaces of the Ottoman sultans. For eleven months of the year in Turkey, it is almost impossible to find sheets of *güllaç*—a fine dried pastry made of cornflour (cornstarch). That's because it's an ingredient associated with the banquet served after sunset during the fasting month of Ramadan.

I used to serve *güllaç* in my restaurant for one month of the year, until Owen, a Chinese chef who had worked with me since it opened, showed me a rice paper round that is readily available at Asian grocers. It's smaller than the traditional *güllaç* sheets, but with milk, rosewater and nuts makes a dessert that to me, tastes even better than the cornflour version. It's also appropriate that a Chinese person was responsible for my improved recipe. The first recorded mention of *güllaç* was in a fourteenth-century Chinese text called *Yinshan Zhenyao*, written by a doctor of Turkish origin in the court of the Yuan dynasty.

GÜLLAÇ
RAMADAN RICE-PAPER BAKLAVA

SERVES 4

75 g (2½ oz/½ cup) hazelnuts
75 g (2½ oz/½ cup) pistachios
500 ml (17 fl oz/2 cups) milk
115 g (4 oz/½ cup) sugar
½ teaspoon rosewater
12 rice paper sheets, about 20 cm
   (8 in) wide
24 pomegranate seeds, for sprinkling

Using a grinder or a food processor, coarsely crush the hazelnuts. Finely crush the pistachios.

Put the milk and sugar in a saucepan over low heat and gently heat for 5 minutes to combine, being careful not to let the mixture boil. Remove from the heat and stir in the rosewater.

Put 2 tablespoons of the milk mixture in a deep round serving dish (one with a lid). Layer the rice papers in the dish, one at a time, shiny side up, spreading 2 tablespoons of the warm milk mixture over each sheet as you go. After the first three layers, sprinkle on half the hazelnuts. After three more layers, sprinkle on half the pistachios. After three more layers, sprinkle on the remaining hazelnuts and, three layers after that, sprinkle on the remaining pistachios.

Sprinkle the pomegranate seeds over the top. Put the lid on the dish, then chill in the fridge for 1 hour.

Slice the milky baklava into quarters and serve chilled.

TÜRK İŞİ
TURKISH MESS (SMASHED PAVLOVA)

Australians and New Zealanders are usually good friends, except for one serious argument: which nation invented the dessert called pavlova? Named after a Russian ballerina, it consists of a baked meringue topped with whipped cream and pieces of fruit (usually strawberries).

I decided to resolve the international argument by smashing up the pavlova, adding a few Ottoman ingredients and calling it 'Turkish Mess'—a name inspired by the English boys' school Eton, which claims credit for a mixture of strawberries, cream and meringue that they call 'Eton Mess'. By making this final dessert in our book (and using whatever berries are in season), you will help to bring about harmony between four nations—or possibly provoke a world war.

SERVES 4

CHARCOAL MERINGUES
4 eggs, separated
pinch of salt
220 g (8 oz/1 cup) sugar
10 g (¼ oz) activated charcoal powder

MESS CREAM
250 ml (9 fl oz/1 cup) milk
2 heaped tablespoons cornflour
   (cornstarch)
75 g (2½ oz/⅓ cup) sugar
2 teaspoons mastic liqueur
100 ml (3½ fl oz) pouring (whipping)
   cream

BERRY SAUCE
125 g (4½ oz) raspberries
125 g (4½ oz) strawberries
150 g (5½ oz) sugar

TOPPINGS
200 g (7 oz) mixed strawberries,
   raspberries and blueberries
1–2 tablespoons ground pistachios,
   for sprinkling
2 teaspoons dried rose petals
   (or fresh organic edible rose petals),
   for sprinkling

Preheat the oven to 120°C (250°F). Line a baking tray with baking paper, and grease the paper.

For the meringues, bring the egg whites to room temperature. (You can use the leftover egg yolks to make pasta, in the proportion of 100 g/3½ oz of flour for each yolk, plus a sprinkling of water.) Using a blender, whisk the egg whites and salt for about a minute, until soft peaks form. Gradually add the sugar and mix at the highest speed until the sugar dissolves. Gently stir the charcoal through the mixture. Spoon the mixture onto the prepared baking tray, in lumps about 2 cm (¾ inch) deep. Place in the oven and bake for 1½ hours. Turn off the oven and let the meringues cool while you make the mess cream and berry sauce.

For the mess cream, combine the milk, cornflour, sugar and mastic liqueur in a saucepan. Simmer over low heat for about 30 minutes, until the texture becomes thicker. Take the pan off the heat and whisk the mixture to cool it down. Next, stir in the cream and whisk for another 5 minutes, or until combined. Keep in the fridge until ready to use.

Meanwhile, put all the berry sauce ingredients in a saucepan and simmer over low heat for 15 minutes. Allow to cool, then purée the berry mixture using a blender or food processor. Keep in the fridge until ready to use.

To serve, put 2 heaped tablespoons of the mess cream in the centre of four serving plates. Break the meringues into chunky fragments and distribute them over the top of the mess creams. Drizzle with the berry sauce and serve garnished with the fresh berries, ground pistachios and dried rose petals.

The pebbly shoreline and
a big high tide at the end
of the day in Bodrum.

Bodrum's marina and the
Castle of Saint Peter, a former
Crusader fortress, at night.

SOMER SUGGESTS...

This is not a definitive list of the 'best' eating experiences in Istanbul, but a rough guide to the places I like to visit every time I return to my hometown. Bear in mind that Istanbul is divided by the Bosphorus strait, between what locals call 'the European side' and 'the Asian side'. I grew up on the Asian side (in the waterside suburb of Kadıköy). Most tourists stay on the European side, which is their loss.

FOR BREAKFAST

Van Kahvaltı Evi is the restaurant that started the big breakfast phenomenon in Istanbul. Arrive early and arrive hungry! I have not seen anyone yet who can clear the entire meal, but it is the best introduction to the Eastern Turkish way of starting the day.

Address: Defterdar Yokuşu 52/A, Cihangir, Beyoğlu
Phone: 0212 293 6437

Recel Turevleri is located just round the corner from the very busy Breakfast Road (Kahvalti sokagi) in Besiktas market. It is different from most breakfast cafes as Turev's mum still makes the jams in-house and the food is more varied than many on the main street.

Address: Sinanpasa Mahallesi, Sair Veysi Sok No. 31/1, Besiktas, Istanbul
Phone: 0212 227 4477
Website: recelturevleri.com

Kale Cafe opened in 1982 and started the trend of having breakfast on the Bosphorus—classics such as menemen or eggs with sucuk. Views are to die for.

Address: Yahya Kemal Cad No. 2, Rumelihisarı
Phone: 0212 265 6563
Website: kalecafe.com

FOR LUNCH

Çiya means not one but three restaurants under the command of Musa Dağdeviren, whose research and skill put regional Anatolian food on the world map long before any other chef in Turkey cared for it. The three Çiyas alone are enough reason to visit the bustling markets of Kadıköy, but I suggest you sample the many food wonders there, if you have any room left after Musa's menu.

Address: Caferağa Mh., Güneşli Bahce Sk No. 43, Kadıköy
Phone: 0216 330 3190
Website: ciya.com.tr

Pandeli is located on top of the incredible Spice Bazaar. It's a national culinary treasure, re-opened in 2018 thanks to the Ozalp family. In the era of new-age variations and modernisation, they kept the menu true to its original form that had lasted more than a century, hosting many historical figures and celebrities such as Mustafa Kemal (Atatürk), Queen Elizabeth II, King Juan Carlos of Spain, Robert De Niro and Audrey Hepburn.

Address: Rüstempaşa Mah. Balık Pazarı Kapısı Sokağı 1/2, Mısır Çarşısı İçi, Eminönü, Fatih | İstanbul
Phone: 0212 527 3909
Website: pandeli.com.tr

Hacı Abdullah is a traditional Ottoman/homestyle eatery, run for 120 years by the same family. Their olive oil braised vegetable dishes (*zeytinyağlılar*) are particularly good.

Address: Ağa Camii Atıf Yılmaz Cad No. 9/A, Beyoğlu
Phone: 0212 293 8561
Website: haciabdullah.com.tr

Sultanahmet Koftecisi Selim Usta is a cheap and delicious lunch pit-stop for kofte (meatballs), in the middle of the tourist hub called Sultanahmet, the oldest part of the city.

Address: No. 12 Divanyolu Street, Sultanahmet
Phone: 0212 520 0566
Website: sultanahmetk.ftesi.com

FOR KEBAPS

Çiya Kebap is one of Musa's three restaurants in Kadıköy, offering charcoal-grilled treats that change with the season and are authentic to their region of origin.

Address: Caferağa Mh., Güneşli Bahce Sk No. 43, Kadıköy
Phone: 0216 330 3190
Website: ciya.com.tr

Adana Ocakbasi is definitely not the choice for posh and stylish but it is a true gem in one of the few remaining multicultural suburbs in Istanbul. Food is cooked on a huge charcoal mangal in front of you, so just point out your choice and they'll cook it for you.

Address: Bozkurt Mahallesi No. 2, Baysungur Sk, 34375 Şişli
Phone: 0212 247 0143
Website: adanaocakbasi.com

Zübeyir caters for people who love to sit around the grill and receive whatever the chef passes over the counter.

Address: Şht. Muhtar Mh., 34435 Beyoğlu
Phone: 0212 293 3951

FOR SEAFOOD

Zipkin is a labour of love from an avid fisherman and you can choose fresh fish and mezes from the old school display counter. Great views and a true Bosphorus seafood restaurant style.

Address: Arnavutköy Mahallesi, Arnavutköy Yolu No. 60, Arnavutköy
Phone: 212 358 5158
Website: zipkin.com.tr

Bebek Balıkcısı is quite special for water views, simply preparing delicious local fish such as lufer, kalkan and levrek. Like anything in the affluent suburb of Bebek, it's expensive.

Address: Cevdet Paşa Caddesi No. 26, Bebek
Phone: 0212 263 34 47
Website: bebekbalikci.net

İsmet Baba, on the Asian side of the Bosphorus, has a less spectacular view but great atmosphere: wooden walls, fishnets, pictures of generations of owners and local customers who look older than the restaurant (founded in 1951).

Address: Carsi Caddesi İskelesi Yanı 1A, Usküdar, Kuzguncuk
Phone: 0216 341 33 75
Website: ismetbaba.com.tr

PUDDINGS AND PASTRIES

Ozkonak is one of the few pudding shops that still use real chicken breast in their tavukgogsu pudding. The chicken-free version, called kazandibi (bottom of the pan), is ideal for the less adventurous.

Address: Akarsu Caddesi 46/B, Cihangir
Phone: 0212 249 1307

Inci. If you don't know the French-Italian influence on Turkish patisserie tradition during the Orient-Express era especially on Istiklal street, Beyoglu, you'll be surprised that Inci has been one of the most famous pastry shops in Turkey since 1940s. This is the third location within the same street, but while the location may change, the profiteroles and the home made lemonade tradition continues to woo Turks and visitors.

Address: Şehit Muhtar Mahallesi, Mis Sk. 18/A, 34435 Beyoğlu
Phone: 0212 243 2412

Güllüoğlu Baklava Shop in Karakoy is justly famous as one of the most authentic baklava houses out of Gaziantep.

Address: Karakoy, Katlı Otopark Altı
Phone: 0212 293 0910
Website: gulluoglu.biz

MEZE TIME/MEYHANES

I am never against innovation, but nothing boils my blood more than new-age meyhanes where you pay a set price, have a set menu and unlimited raki and wine, then it turns into a dance club. It reduces the quality and undermines the meyhane tradition.

Imroz is the most interesting meyhane in a district where many meyhanes have second-rate food and gypsy musicians blowing trumpets in your ear.

Address: Nevizade Sok No. 24, Balıkpazarı/Beyoğlu
Phone: 0212 249 9073
Website: krependekiimroz.com

Sofyali 9 is my local when I visit Istanbul, because the food is consistent and it's away from the bustle of the main Beyoğlu district.

Address: Asmalımescit Cad. Sofyalı Sok No. 9, Beyoğlu
Phone: 0212 252 3810
Website: sofyali.com.tr/en

Koco is a typical Greek meyhane, with the surprise of a small church inside the building. It was a drinking place for my grandad and my dad. I had many *rakı*-filled nights there and probably my son will follow the family tradition when he is of age.

Address: Moda Caddesi No. 171, Kadık.y /Istanbul
Phone: 0216 336 07 95
Website: kocorestaurant.net

Despina was a rare breed of female meyhane owner, who opened her place in 1946. Madame Despina is dead now, but her place kicks on with live traditional Turkish music every night.

Address: Acıkyol Sokak No. 9, Kurtuluş
Phone: 0212 247 3357

Firuze ticks every box—incredible views, fresh and delicious mezes, prompt and knowledgeable service. Make sure to try the liver and the smallest kibbeh you can find anywhere in the world.

Address: Nejat Eczacıbaşı Binası Sadi Konuralp Caddesi No. 5,
   Şişhane, kat 6, 34433 Beyoğlu/İstanbul
Phone: 0212 238 5050
Website: firuze-iksv.business.site

WINE TASTING

Sensus Şarap & Peynir is a wine, cheese and olive oil shop in a basement under the Anemon Hotel near the Galata Tower. They claim to have 300 Turkish wines available for tasting, along with interesting snacks.

Address: Bereketzade Mah. Büyükhendek Cad. No. 5, Galata
Phone: 0212 245 5657

FOR DINNER

Mikla, created by Mehmet Gürs, is the only Turkish restaurant listed every year among the World's 50 Best Restaurants. It's on top of the Marmara Pera Hotel. Go just before sunset and have panoramic pre-dinner drinks at the rooftop bar.

Address: The Marmara Pera Hotel, Meşrutiyet Cad. Tepebaşı Beyoğlu
Phone: 0212 293 56 56
Website: miklarestaurant.com

Yeni Lokanta translates as 'new bistro', but its chef, Civan Er, ran the famous Changa restaurant before switching to a more relaxed style.

Address: İstiklal Caddesi Kumbaracı Yokuşu No. 66, Beyoğlu
Phone: 0212 292 25 50
Website: lokantayeni.com

Asitane is the best and most authentic of the Ottoman revival restaurants, located next door to Kariye museum.

Address: Derviş Ali Mh., Kariye Cami Sk No. 6, 34240 Edirnekapı
Phone: 0212 534 8414
Website: asitanerestaurant.com

Neolokal is the creation of Maksut Aşkar, who is brave enough to display his team in an open kitchen, creating light adventurous dishes with a focus on regionality and sustainability.

Address: SALT Galata Bankalar Caddesi No. 11, Karakoy
Phone: 0212 249 8930
Website: neolokal.com

STREET FOOD

The eating never stops in Istanbul. There are street sellers with queues around the block at 4 o'clock in the morning. But the best of late dining is in places called işkembeci—offal eateries that sell everything from tripe soup to whole roasted sheep's head.

There are iskembeci in every neighbourhood, generally open from dusk till dawn. The best is Apik in the suburb called Dolapdere. This is not a tourist destination, so you should go there with a cab, have your soup, and get out of there with a cab.

My favourite street hawker dish is *kokorech*, a kind of sausage made with sheep's intestines spiced with chilli flakes, oregano and cumin. Only buy the ones cooked over charcoal, never from a flat grill. Other stalls sell midye dolma—fresh mussels in their shells, stuffed with aromatic rice. It's safer for your stomach if you buy them from shops, not strolling street hawkers. And then of course there's *simit*, sourdough pretzels dipped in molasses and sesame, which cure the munchies at any time of the day.

And these are the top three foodie things to do that don't involve eating.

The Spice Market is overwhelmingly touristy, with hagglers and pushy storekeepers, but an oasis can be found at Area 51—Bilge's Ucuzcular shop. Bilge is the only female shop owner and speaks perfect English. She does not have higher prices for tourists and the quality of her spices are exceptional.

The Topkapı Palace kitchens are opened after a long renovation, giving a great sense of the food culture of the Ottoman Empire for 500 years.

Kadıköy Market is not your average shopping mall. It's crammed with specialist shops selling nuts, pickles, offal, oils and pastries.

ODD ACCOMMODATIONS

If you're rich and have an interest in twentieth century history, try the **Pera Palace** in Beyoglu, where the travellers on the Orient Express, including Agatha Christie, stayed in the 1920s. Is that Hercule Poirot taking *tisane* in the corner of the red lobby? Or you might prefer a former prison, **the Four Seasons** in Sultanahmet, or a former Ottoman Palace, **Ciragan Palas**, on the Bosphorus.

At more reasonable prices, with stylish designs, are the four House Hotels, in Bosphorus, Galatasaray, Nisantasi and Karakay (details at thehousehotel.com).

EATING IN GAZIANTEP

Metanet, near the central market, is a *lokanta* where you can eat fiery lamb soup *(beyran)* for breakfast, and where they do an excellent *lahmacun* (thin-crust pizza) closer to lunchtime.

Address: Kozluca Mahallesi, Kozluca Cad 11.

Phone: 0342 231 4666

Zekeriya Usta is where Mehmet Ozsimitci makes crisp *katmer* pancakes stuffed with pistachios and clotted cream. He closes at midday.

Address: Katmerci Zekeria Usta. Cukur Mahallesi, Korukcu Sk, B. Himli Gecidi 16/C-D. Gaziantep

Phone: 0342 230 0971

Website: katmercizekeriya.com

Ali Haydar makes liver *kebaps* for breakfast, just near the castle. He opens at 6 am, closes by 8 am.

Address: Yaprak Mh. Dere Kenan Sk, Tabakane Mevkii

Imam Cagdas does great k*ebaps* and legendary baklava near Gaziantep's central market.

Address: Uzun Carsi 49, Sahinbey

Phone: 0342 231 2678

Website: imamcagdas.com

IN BODRUM

Kismet in Bodrum is probably in the weirdest location, on a highway behind a wholesale cheese market. No views, no tourists. It's only open for lunch and most dishes sell out by 2 pm. So, what makes this unassuming restaurant the best vegetarian *lokanta* on the Aegean coast? It is their amazing produce, most gathered from the villagers around the town and some from their own garden. If you think Turkish cuisine is kebabs and breads, you should visit this vegetarian haven as a mind-opening variation.

Address: Çırkan Mahallesi Çelebi Kaptan Sokak No. 3/A, Konacık-Bodrum

Phone: 0252 319 0096

Website: kismetlokantasi.com

Miam in Turkbuku (the Cote d'Azur of Turkey) is open all year round – unlike the tourist traps that only open in 'the season'. It's a village favourite (and my mum's), specialising in local seafood.

Address: Menemene, A, Attaturk Cd. 51, 48400 Bodrum/Mugla

Phone: 0252 377 5612

Orfoz, just off the main beach, is where the Bozcaga brothers play endless variations on local seafood, in convenient meze portions.

Address: Kumbahce Mah. Cumhuriyet Cad. No. 177B

Phone: 0252 316 4285

Website: orfoz.net

Istanbul's Hagia Sophia and
surrounding mosques at dusk.

No longer grinding flour for pide bread, these eighteenth century windmills are scattered over the hills behind Bodrum, on the Aegean coast.

ACKNOWLEDGEMENTS

I want to offer my thanks to ...

David Dale, for taking a chance on me and on Turkish cuisine. And to Susan Williams and Millie Dale, for allowing me to borrow David for weeks at a time.

Janni Kyritsis, the Greek chef who introduced the Turkish chef to the Italophile author.

My children Deniz and Derin, for being the reason I do this, and their mother Aslı for giving me the best gifts of my life.

My mother Ülkü, who taught me to fly and my father Güngör who taught me to land. My two sisters, Begüm and Çiğdem, living so far away yet so close to my heart.

Ace photographer Bree Hutchins for endangering her life and her digestive system countless times to get the best possible shots.

The team at Murdoch Books: Sue Hines who had the vision to get this show on the road; editing whiz Emma Hutchinson; designers Hugh Ford and Sarah Odgers; stylist Michelle Noerianto; publisher Diana Hill; and Lou Johnson and Corinne Roberts, who supervised this new edition.

The loyal team at Efendy and Anason: my brother-in-crime Fatih Külle and the rest of the musketeers Utku Görmez and Mehmetcan Ermihan; Anason manager Burak Cebi, Efendy Manager Gizem Demen; our amazing kitchen team at both restaurants led by Burak Cakir, Ozge Donmezoglu, Inal Erdener, Ilkan Durukan and Burak Yildirim and all past and current staff contributing to the success of Efendy and Anason.

I have been cooking in Australia in my two restaurants for 15 years now but my popularity in Turkey is mainly due to Masterchef Turkiye and its visionary producer Uygar Ates and his amazing team at Bloom Medya, my Masterchef partners Hazer Amani and Mehmet Yalcinkaya, my agent and trusted friend in Turkey, Rengin Atik.

Musa and Zeynep Dağdeviren, who run three Çiya restaurants in Istanbul and produce the magazine *Yemek Ve Kültür* (Food and Culture). Their website is ciya.com.tr.

Greg Malouf, mentor and friend, who paved the way for my generation of chefs to professionalise Middle Eastern, Turkish and Greek cuisines in Australia.

For sharing their scholarship with us: Filiz Hösükoğlu (in Gaziantep); Aylin Öney Tan (Istanbul); Nilhan Aras (Istanbul); Tuba Şatana of istanbulfood.com.

For inspiring us with their specialties: Akife Malkoç (Istanbul); Melek Boz (Bodrum); İvgen Özön (Bodrum); Bercuk Anne (Sydney); Meral Ballı (Istanbul); Fouad Kassab (Sydney); Arman Uz (Kiama); Ömer Mutlugun (Malatya).

For opening their kitchens to us: Batur Durmay of Asitane; Ezgi Güven of Ayna of Cunda Island, Ayvalik; Mehmet Gürs of Mikla, Istanbul; Şemsa Denizsel of Kantin; Maksut Aşkar of neolokal; Civan Er of Yeni; Pando Şestakof of Pando's, Istanbul; Ali Haydar, the liver master of Gaziantep; Mehmet Özsimitci, the katmer master of Gaziantep; Mustafa Hasırcı, the beyran master of Metanet; Hatice Kalan of Yörem; Çağlar and Çağrı Bozçağa of Orfoz; the ladies of Sacide, Bodrum; the Bingöl family of Miam, Bodrum; Kanat Kıral of Bodrum Lokum.

For showing us their skills: Mehmet Tembel (in Oğuzeli); Aydın Kilitoğlu of Asri Bakery, Gaziantep; Telat, Burhan and Telat Jr Çağdaş of Imam Çağdaş, Gaziantep; Enis Güner of Sevilen wines.

For their hospitality: Timur Schindel of Anatolian Houses, Gaziantep; Kalamis Wyndham Grand Hotel in Istanbul; Lucio Galletto of Lucio's; Armando Percuoco of Buon Ricordo in Sydney.

These books informed and entertained us:

500 Years of Ottoman Cuisine, by Marianna Yerasimos (Boyut)
The Sultan's Istanbul on Five Kurush A Day, by Charles Fitzroy (Thames & Hudson)
World Food Turkey, Dani Valent (Lonely Planet)
Western Anatolia Wine Culture, by A. Nedim Atilla (Bilgi)
Osmanlı Mutfağı, by Tuğrul Şavkay (Şekerbank)
Kaz dağları'ndan bir lezzet öyküsü, by Erhan Şeker (AMK)
Osmanlı Mutfak Sözlüğü, by Priscilla Mary Işın (Kitap)
Tatlı-pasta Öğretimi, by Ekrem Muhittin Yeğen (Inkilap)

And above all, to the many peoples of many ethnicities, faiths and philosophies who enriched the food culture of Anatolia.

INDEX

VEGETARIAN DISHES

This abridged edition published in 2019 by Murdoch Books, an imprint of Allen & Unwin.
First published in 2015.

Murdoch Books Australia
83 Alexander Street
Crows Nest NSW 2065
Phone: +61 (0) 2 8425 0100
murdochbooks.com.au
info@murdochbooks.com.au

Murdoch Books UK
Ormond House
26–27 Boswell Street
London WC1N 3JZ
Phone: +44 (0) 20 8785 5995
murdochbooks.co.uk
info@murdochbooks.co.uk

For corporate orders & custom publishing, contact our business development
team at salesenquiries@murdochbooks.com.au.

Publisher: Diana Hill
Design Manager: Hugh Ford, Vivien Valk
Design: Sarah Odgers, Susanne Geppert
Photographer: Bree Hutchins
Stylist: Michelle Noerianto
Editor: Emma Hutchinson
Production Manager: Mary Bjelobrk

A cataloguing-in-publication entry is available from the catalogue of the National Library of Australia
at nla.gov.au. A catalogue record for this book is available from the British Library.

ISBN 978 1 76052 552 1 Australia
ISBN 978 1 91163 272 6 UK

Colour reproduction by Splitting Image Colour Studio Pty Ltd, Clayton, Victoria
Printed by C & C Offset Printing Co. Ltd., China
10 9 8 7 6 5 4 3